Low-fat for Life

Ordering Information

The fastest, easiest way to get your copy of *Low-fat for Life* is to order it directly from the Heuses. Call their toll-free order number **1-800-269-1630** anytime, 24 hours a day. They'll send one right out to you with a bill.

If you prefer, send a check or money order (figure amount below) to: **Micamar, P.O. Box 56, Barneveld, WI 53507**

Low-fat for Life	16.95
shipping*	+2.00
Total	$18.95
Wis. residents add sales tax	+0.93
Total	$19.88

* If ordering more than one book, shipping is $2.00 for the first and $1.00 for each additional book.

Low-fat for Life

An integrated program for making the change to a healthier, low-fat lifestyle

by Mike, Marilyn,
Greg and Jeff Heus

Micamar Publishing
Barneveld, Wisconsin

Low-fat for Life

An integrated program for making the change to a healthier, low-fat lifestyle

by Mike, Marilyn, Greg and Jeff Heus

Published by:
Micamar Publishing
P.O. Box 56
Barneveld, WI 53507

Copyright © 1994 by Michael J., Marilyn J., Gregory M. and
Jeffery J. Heus
First Printing 1994
Second Printing 1994 (with minor revisions)
Third Printing 1995 (with minor revisions)
Printed in the United States of America

Publisher's Cataloging in Publication

Low-fat for life: an integrated program for making the change to a
    healthier, low-fat lifestyle / by Mike Heus ...[et al.].
    p. cm.
    Includes bibliographical references and index.
    Preassigned LCCN: 93-91552.
    ISBN 0-937373-05-2

1. Low fat diet.   2. Nutrition.   3. Health.   I. Heus, Mike.

RM237.7.L68 1994   613.2'5
                                    QBI93-22375

Disclaimer

The purpose of this book is to educate, encourage and occasionally entertain. The authors and Micamar Publishing shall have neither liability nor responsibility to any person or entity with respect to any loss or damage caused or alleged to be caused directly or indirectly by the information it contains. Every effort has been made for completeness and accuracy, but typographical or content mistakes are possible. As with any health and fitness book you should consult your health professional before commencing a nutrition or exercise regimen.

Acknowledgements

Thanks to friends and family: Keri Johnson, Linda Heus, John and Nancy O'Neill, Ann Lynaugh, Allen and Judy Pincus, Nick DePaolo, Lorraine Davis and Mark Shaffer for all the proof-reading, recipe-testing and encouragement.

Thanks also to Joan Arnold, Carol Cullen, Jeannie Eloranta, Kathy Glover, Dorothy Handrick, Nancy Homes, Margaret Koeller, Ann Landmark and Donna Stevenson, the staff of our local library. Their support in this and other research/writing projects is appreciated.

Table of Contents

More Antioxidants to Fight Free Radicals
More Cauliflower for Indole Power

Bottom Line: Less fat means more carbohydrates
and that means more health-promoting
fiber, vitamins and minerals.

Bottom Line: The human body was designed to
thrive on a low-fat and high-
carbohydrate diet.

Bottom Line: High-fat eating clogs our blood vessels
with fat and cholesterol.

Bottom Line: Most of our cholesterol problems
come from high-fat eating.

Bottom Line: High-fat eating creates biochemical
conditions that pave the way for
cancer, heart disease, stroke, obesity,
diabetes, hypertension and other health
problems.

About the Book

Whether we're talking about the health of a single individual or that of our entire planet, it's now quite clear that America's high-fat habits have terrible costs.

Over the past few years our Surgeon General and a long list of other authorities and agencies have told us in no uncertain terms—cutting the fat is a national health priority.

Every day, countless books, articles, talk shows and news programs tell us if we want to take better care of ourselves and our environment, if we want to have more energy and vitality, if we want to get rid of excess body fat and avoid the devastating effects of major illness and disease—we've got to make the low-fat change.

The question of the hour is *how* to go about doing it.

Low-fat for Life shows a way. It's a program based on extensive research and personal experience. It's a program that simplifies a complex subject and translates it into practical guidelines for action.

This is a book written for ordinary people—individuals and families who want to get an important job done once and for all.

Teachers, counselors, social workers, health care workers, health and fitness instructors, personal trainers and other professionals will also find this book an accurate, comprehensive and "user-friendly" resource. It can be offered to a wide audience of readers.

Low-fat for Life cuts through promotional hype, technical jargon and impossible food labels with common sense bottom lines. It offers workable strategies for dealing with bad habits, heckling friends and other common obstacles. Its eating, exercise and meditation routines train healthy habits and its family-tested recipes (all under 20% fat) train healthy appetites.

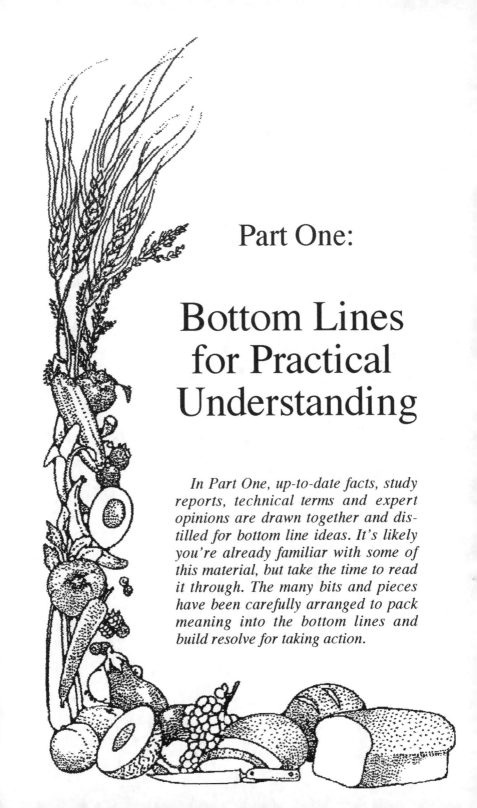

Part One:

Bottom Lines for Practical Understanding

In Part One, up-to-date facts, study reports, technical terms and expert opinions are drawn together and distilled for bottom line ideas. It's likely you're already familiar with some of this material, but take the time to read it through. The many bits and pieces have been carefully arranged to pack meaning into the bottom lines and build resolve for taking action.

1

What Can We Do to Look and Feel Better?

If you're concerned about your weight and appearance, the condition of your health—welcome to America.

Pushed and Pulled in All Directions

Advertising compels us to be fit and trim with pills, drinks, exercise equipment, videos and club memberships. At the same time, it arouses and feeds our habits of sugar and grease, alcohol, caffeine, nicotine and nearly anything else thought to jeopardize health or facilitate flab.

Every conceivable psychological ploy is used to induce our continued purchasing. Fast food ads invade our thinking with very slick images of wholesome American life. Aggressively they promote themselves as community centers where shared burgers mean shared friendship and love.

Family celebrations are pictured in the great outdoors with gleeful smiles, loving hugs, slow motion running and a bottle of soda in every hand. After work, conviviality is pictured in neighborhood taverns where rounds of laughter are lubricated with rounds of beer. Our most trusted celebrities make eating beef seem a rugged expression of personal freedom.

A Sane Alternative

What are the facts of the matter? Well, we don't need any more research to tell us the majority of Americans are either overweight or struggling to keep it under control. It's no secret that our eating habits have helped us achieve some of the highest rates of cancer and cardiovascular disease in the world.

We feel guilty about the way we eat, the way we look, the way we procrastinate. And that guilt has us cash-in-hand, ready to buy the newest, fastest, easiest way to do things right.

Our fears and fantasies translate into big bucks when it comes to product sales. It's therefore in the best interests of the marketplace to intensify our confusions and encourage our contradictory behaviors.

So round and round it goes. In a single TV commercial break, beer, junk food, antacid tablets, a diet support group and a public service announcement on the evils of drugs and alcohol are pasted together as if this craziness is a necessary part of modern life—it isn't!

A sane and enjoyable alternative does exist. Evidence has been accumulating over the last two decades. In the midst of all the hype, gimmicks and hustlers, a consistent message about health, fitness and nutrition has emerged. Study after study reports the benefits of *low-fat living*.

Bottom Line: We can make some healthy, low-fat changes.

2

So What's Wrong With the Way We Eat?

Though every school child has heard about the importance of eating from all of the "four basic food groups," we Americans have been overindulging in two (meat and dairy) and backsliding on the other two (vegetables/fruits and grains).

A Meat and Dairy Mindset

When we ask "What's for dinner?" we want to know what *meat* we'll be having. Whether hamburgers, pork chops or steak, the choice of meat defines the meal. Vegetables, fruits and grains are only there to compliment the choice of meat.

The average American has believed without question that a balanced diet should include a substantial piece of meat and a tall glass of milk every day. Why? These foods are high in protein and we have thought of protein as our road to health.

Where carbohydrates and fats fuel body activity, protein is its building material. It is the essential stuff of muscle and bone growth.

We could, of course, get ample protein from a diet of seeds, nuts, fruits, vegetables and grains supplemented with very small amounts from the meat and dairy food groups. Studies demonstrate a diet with only 10% of its protein coming from meat, milk and eggs still gives us 50% more protein than we need.[1]

Many other cultures thrive on this sort of diet. When they grow grain, they eat most of it themselves. The largest portion of the grain we grow is fed to animals we raise for meat and dairy protein.

We erroneously came to believe that domesticating animals is the best way to get high quality protein. It may seem a bit wasteful and expensive to get it this way, but what's a little extra cost when it comes to the health of our nation, right?

How wasteful and expensive? Well, it takes about 16 pounds of grain to get a pound of beef. That little eight ounce steak you had at the restaurant could have fed 40 people a bowl of cooked cereal.

Estimates are that the protein wasted in American eating habits would take care of 90% of the protein deficit for the entire world.[2]

In the past, high-protein foods were available only to the rich. Ordinary folks reserved them for special occasions.

You can see how poor countries would envy us for our commonplace luxuries, the way we routinely and matter-of-factly eat foods they identify with wealth and celebration.

We've been proud of the quantity and quality of foods we produce. We've viewed them as the important achievements of a wealthy, successful nation.

Believing a strong country must have strong people, we listened closely when our science told us animal protein would give us strong muscles and bones, healthy skin and organs. If that's what we needed, that's what we'd have— lots of animal protein, the best money could buy!

More Than Protein on the Plate

We were wrong. Our scientific picture was incomplete. For a long time we thought domesticating animals for protein was the cornerstone of our nation's health and strength. It's not and we've been getting more than protein on our plates.

About 25% of the calories in a lowly pot of pinto, navy or kidney beans are protein and 72% are carbohydrate. Only 3% are fat.

Compare this to our protein-rich, domesticated meats. How about a slice of ham? While 40% of its calories *are* protein, the other 60% of the calories are all *fat*.

Maybe you'd like to have a T-bone steak instead. Though 30% of its calories are protein, a whomping 70% are fat.

Want a glass of whole milk with your meal? Okay, that's 21% protein calories, 29% carbohydrate calories and 50% fat calories.

All our high quality, cultivated, concentrated, prepack- aged, convenient and tasty animal protein is giving us a lot of something else...

FAT!

And fat is making the price tag on our affluent diet much higher than we thought. We've been paying all sorts of hid- den costs in terms of our health. In fact, the way most of us eat almost guarantees degenerative diseases.

The High Costs of Excess Fat

For the average American roughly 40% of daily calories come from fat. This is way too much. For many of us this kind of eating leads to excess body fat. And even if you're one of those fortunate characters who seems to stay thin no matter what you eat, don't assume you're *fit*.

If your diet is high-fat, the quality of your life is in jeopardy. Too much fat will gradually increase susceptibility to everyday illnesses; you tire more easily and get depressed more often. It also makes it very likely you'll contend with major disease and die sooner than you'd care to.

Think of the public outcry if terrorists held an American city hostage and executed 3,000 to 4,000 people each day. Imagine this had somehow gone on for a whole year. Those 365 days of killing would result in maybe 1,400,000 dead.

It's an outrageous thought isn't it? But that's how many are killed every year by the three leading causes of death in the U.S. Roughly 750,000 of us die annually of heart disease, another 475,000 of us die of cancer and 150,000 of stroke.[3]

Our high-fat diet plays a decisive role in each of these diseases and is an important factor in others affecting millions upon millions of us (high blood pressure, diabetes, obesity).

Studies comparing the diets, diseases and death rates of 40 countries, as well as countless animal/human experiments and autopsies, all point to fat as a silent and relentless killer.

In 1988 Surgeon General C. Everett Koop reported he had examined over 20 years of research and found the trail to an obvious conclusion.[4] We Americans must change our eating habits. We've got to cut back on the fat in our diet and begin eating more vegetables, fruits and whole grain products. We've got to eat more fish and poultry, leaner meats and low-fat dairy products.

In 1989 a committee of the National Academy of Sciences submitted a 1200 page report on diet and health. In it they also made reducing the amount of fat we eat their highest priority recommendation.[5]

With the same sense of urgency, supporting recommendations have been made by a variety of health organizations such as the American Heart Association, Cancer Society, Diabetes Association and National Research Council.

How Much is Too Much?

Governmental agencies have recommended cutting the fat back to 30% of daily calories and they're being conservative. Understandably their recommendation is compromised by a powerful food industry and concerns about the impact a change in our eating habits would have on the economy.

Research tells us the 30% level of fat is still too high. For example, in one study it was found that a 30% fat diet slows but doesn't stop the development of heart disease.[6] Another found those eating a 27% fat diet had the same cancer rate as those eating 40% fat.[7] But a low-fat diet *does* boost our immunity to viral infections and cancer when fat is reduced to the 20% level.[8]

Few experts continue to support 30% as the best fat standard. Recently, *Consumer Reports* surveyed 68 nutrition experts who said they thought it would be far better in the 20–25% range. In fact, 27 of them wanted it to be 20% or less.[9] Some authorities are recommending that we keep our fat intake below 15% or even 10% of daily calories.[10]

How low can we safely go? According to the National Academy of Science's Recommended Dietary Allowances,

1% to 2% of total calories is sufficient to prevent a deficiency. A low-fat diet in the 10–20% fat range will certainly give us enough.[11]

The direction of diet change we need is clear and the many who tell us to at least get the fat under 20% are convincing.[12]

This, then, is the standard we chose for experimentation and recipe development.

Bottom Line: We eat twice as much fat as we should.

3

If We Cut Back on Fat, What Do We Eat Instead?

The foods we eat are composed of: *fats, proteins,* and *carbohydrates.* The typical American diet is about 40% fat, 10–15% protein and 45% carbohydrate. Many authorities now recommend we change this diet by lowering its proportion of fat from 40% to 20%, keeping the protein about the same and increasing the carbohydrate to more than 65%.

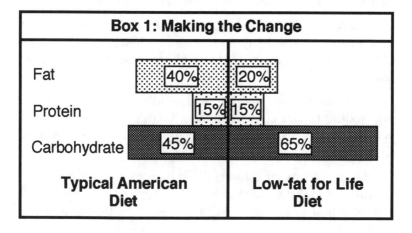

Box 1: Making the Change

	Typical American Diet	Low-fat for Life Diet
Fat	40%	20%
Protein	15%	15%
Carbohydrate	45%	65%

Less Fat but More Carbohydrate

To get out of the illness-prone fat lane, then, we need to cut down on red meats, take the skin off our chicken and shop at the non-fat end of the dairy cooler. We need to read labels, revamp our recipes and try new cooking techniques.

In these and many other ways we are trying to avert fat-related disease. But there's more to health than not getting sick. If we continue to eat the same total calories of food each day, keep the proportion of protein the same and lower the fat, we'll *automatically* be eating more carbohydrates *and* the health-enriching vitamins, minerals and fiber they contain.

For example, a muffin with 45% of its calories as fat would be considered a high-fat food. If you took the fat out of the muffin recipe it would automatically become a high-carbohydrate food because that's what would be left. And you'd probably have to eat two muffins to get the same calories as the one with the fat in it (oh no).

Imagine you're about to eat a slice of hot, whole-wheat bread. Spread butter or margarine on it and you're entering the fat lane. Make that jam, honey or *non-fat* margarine and you've got a high-carbohydrate snack in your hand.

Decreasing the fat and increasing the carbohydrate in our diet means we are changing it to more closely resemble that of cultures with a much longer and better health record than ours.

The Chinese, for example, still follow the same basic eating traditions that have kept them healthy for thousands of years. Indigenous hunting and gathering peoples continue similar ways of eating.

Though the specific foods differ, essentially the same basic low-fat and high-carbohydrate pattern of healthy eating can be found in different cultural traditions throughout the world.

Typically, it is a rural rather than urban diet. It consists of whole-grain bread or rice, beans, cooked vegetables, a smaller amount of meat, yogurt or milk, fresh fruits and vegetables. It is foraged, grown and prepared locally or at home. It is simple eating, "peasant" eating.

The diet characteristic of an urban life with an industrialized agriculture is very different. Here the emphasis is on domesticated meats, cheeses, refined-grain white breads and pastries, heavily processed convenience foods, snack foods, cooking oils and deep-fried, batter-coated foods. It has relatively small amounts of whole grains, vegetables and fruits and high levels of sugar, salt and chemical additives.

More Fiber in Our Food

Now, why is the rural diet healthier? For one thing it has more *fiber*. A diet rich in grains, vegetables, legumes and fruits is also rich in fiber, many kinds of fiber (pectin, cellulose, legimin). One of our most common fat-related diseases is colon cancer. Colon cancer is virtually unknown in places where people live on whole, unprocessed, high-fiber foods.

We used to eat a lot more fiber because we ate a lot more grain. One hundred years ago we ate five times as much as we do today. Now we use more of our grain to produce *meat* and refine the fiber out of most of the grain we still *do* eat.

Low-fat/high-carbohydrate eating means getting plenty of fiber back into our diet. Fiber is the undigested bulk and roughage part of plant foods. It prevents colon and other cancers because of the various ways it protects us from the poisons in our foods.

Fiber strengthens and conditions the entire gastrointestinal tract. The walls of the intestines become more effective barriers to the carcinogens in foods. They keep the carcinogens from passing into the bloodstream where they would circulate to organs and tissues throughout the body.

Fiber gives "push" and speed to the food materials moving through the intestines cutting down on the exposure time to the toxic chemicals in them. It also *absorbs* such chemicals and carries them out of the body in bowel movements. By retaining water, fiber keeps stool soft, meaning less trouble with constipation and hemorrhoids.

Diverticulitis is a painful and common disease in affluent cultures. Pockets form on the inner walls of the intestines trapping tiny seeds and food particles as they move through. With ample fiber, diverticulitis is uncommon. Fiber keeps the plumbing smooth and clean.

Some fiber is soluble. This type is especially known for its beneficial effects on the heart and circulatory system. It lowers blood pressure and cholesterol, which lowers the risk of heart disease. It helps maintain blood/sugar balances and lowers the diabetic need for insulin.

More Balance in Our Nutrients

In addition to the extra fiber it brings, an increase in vegetables, beans, fruits and whole grains in our diet also means we'll regain a balance of *nutrients* lost in high-fat eating.

Nutrients are, essentially, chemicals. Too much or too little of a food nutrient for too long creates biochemical imbalances. It puts body chemistry into a "dis-ease" condition. Fats are nutrients that we've been getting way too much of and complex carbohydrates are nutrients we've been getting far too little of.

Fats, carbohydrates and proteins are the "big three" of food nutrients. They make up 98% of what we eat each day. That's why we call them our *major* nutrients or the "macro-nutrients." But the bigger does not mean better or more important.

We need the macronutrients in large amounts because they are the fuel and building materials for our bodies. We also need very *small,* but crucially important amounts of a great variety of other food nutrients. These are the vitamins, minerals and trace elements we call the "micronutrients."

More Micronutrients for the Micro-World

Micronutrients are catalysts and key ingredients in the thousands of chemical concoctions our bodies use to protect and maintain their health. These biochemical activities are taking place at a microscopic level, where the stakes are often high as in fighting off a life-threatening infection.

In the world we perceive, our bodies seem to be solid, whole, wrapped in a protective layer of skin. But in the microscopic world our bodies are porous, open.

An endless parade of microorganisms freely enter and leave us. Many of them are pathogens, hostile parasites, hordes of tiny virus and bacteria invaders that come to raid and plunder us.

Poisonous chemicals also enter our bodies as easily as smoke drifts in through a window screen.

How do we survive the poisons and parasites? Our bodies have *defense systems.* In them, the micronutrients become part of some of our more magical powers.

Each of us has an army of "antibodies," an *immune system* of cells that fight off and destroy those virus invaders. We also have an *enzyme system* that de-toxifies those life-threatening chemicals.

But these defense systems can be overwhelmed. Toxic chemicals in our environment and foods accumulate in our bodies and impair our defenses. With our immune systems weakened, we are more susceptible to countless varieties of

viral infections and diseases—including the much-feared
AIDS.

Of those exposed to AIDS, individuals with an already
impaired immune system would be the most likely to come
down with it. Indeed, many scientists believe the AIDS epidemic is, in part, a result of our increased vulnerability from
chemical pollution.[1]

Anything we can do to strengthen our enzyme and immune defenses is obviously important in today's dangerous
world. Both systems rely upon a high level of nutrition.
Food nutrients are the "weapons and ammunition" of our resistance forces. Consider, for example, the importance of
micronutrient "antioxidants" in controlling "free radicals."

More Antioxidants to Fight Free Radicals

If you've ever tried to keep an aging automobile on the
road a little past its prime, you know the breakdown power
of oxidation and rust. A little moisture, road salt and time
will magically transform a high-gloss beauty into a disinte-
grating hulk of sagging doors, flapping fenders and rotting
floorboards.

In the human body the oxidation process is also a force to
be reckoned with. It forms highly unstable, toxic oxygen
molecules called "free radicals."

When it comes to disease, some consider these free radicals the most hazardous chemical agents in our bodies. It's
not difficult to see why. Body cells grow and function according to a genetic program of "instructions" (like a seed is
"instructed" to grow into a tomato plant). Free radicals
create conditions that eat away at cell membranes and
change these instructions causing cells to behave abnormally
(e.g., grow cancerous tumors).

In addition to this fundamental role in cancer, oxidation and free radicals also play an important part in heart disease. The fatty materials and cholesterol oxidized by the free radicals damage artery walls. White blood cells rush to the damage sites to defend against the free radicals attack. They stuff themselves with the oxidized fat and cholesterol materials and become "foam cells" that then clog our arteries.

High-fat foods, polyunsaturated oils, radiation, alcohol, cigarette smoke and many environmental chemicals (e.g., PCB's, agricultural pesticides) are known to increase free radicals.

Other foods contain nutrients that actually *decrease* free radicals. Guess what foods and nutrients we're talking about.

The mineral selenium, vitamin E, vitamin C and beta-carotene are some of the potent micronutrients called "antioxidants." They are found in many fruits and vegetables.

Carrots, sweet potatoes, squash, cantaloupe, apricots, broccoli and others are rich in beta-carotene. Vitamin C is, of course, abundant in citrus fruits, melons and berries. Vitamin E is found in many dark green leafy vegetables.

Studies consistently show the benefits of antioxidants in preventing a variety of cancers (e.g., colon, stomach, prostate, cervix, breast, lung and skin). For example, a recent report stated, essentially, the more vegetables, the less lung cancer. Another found antioxidants defend against abnormal cell growth in the breast and cervical cancers. Another found they block the cancer agents formed from the nitrites and nitrates in processed foods.[2]

Research on heart disease found beta-carotene cut the incidence of heart attacks in half.[3] Vitamin C and E were found to suppress the oxidation of cholesterol.[4] In fact, researchers reported white blood cells won't gorge themselves on cholesterol when vitamins C and E are present.[5]

Different lines of research show antioxidants enhance the immune system helping guard against infectious diseases. They also decrease the risk of rhumatoid arthritis and help prevent a leading cause of blindness, cataracts, which involves oxidation of the eye lens.[6]

More Cauliflower for Indole Power

The good news on vegetables doesn't end with the antioxidants. The crucifer family of vegetables (e.g., cabbage, cauliflower, kohlrabi, kale, turnips, brussel sprouts) has "indoles" that, like antioxidants, inhibit the effects of carcinogenic chemicals. Indoles have been found to protect against various digestive cancers and are also thought to affect the hormone system in ways that lower the risk of breast cancer.

In studies where animals are given indoles there is a significant increase in the rate at which the active form of estrogen (believed to trigger growth of breast tumors) is converted to a safer, inactive form of the hormone. The same results have been found with humans.[7]

The often heard "Eat your vegetables, they're good for you." seems a bit of an understatement, doesn't it? It was recently reported in *Nutrition and Cancer* that 128 of 156 studies found fruits and vegetables give significant protection for a long list of cancers.[8]

Study after study is telling us that those who eat the most fruits, vegetables, legumes and grains have the least cancer, heart and other diet-related diseases. The time bomb of disease in a high-fat diet can be defused with the nutrition and protective power of a diet high in complex carbohydrates.

Bottom Line: Less fat means more carbohydrates and that means more health-promoting fiber, vitamins and minerals.

4

Why Does Fat Give Us So Much Trouble?

Imagine a clock where each hour represents 100,000 years of past time. If the history of the human race began at midnight, the clock would just now be ready to strike the second midnight ending our first 24-hour day.

A few minutes ago, at five to 12:00, agriculture started in the Western world and we slowly began including more fat in our foods.

With the beginnings of industrialization, about seven seconds ago, the amount of that fat started increasing dramatically. High-fat eating is a very recent development in evolutionary history.

No Tigers in Our Family Tree

Our primate relatives, the apes and chimpanzees, ate fruits and vegetables. With nimble fingers and grasping hands they plucked lunch from trees and bushes. Their teeth were rounded molars, made for grinding fiber. Their extra long intestines held and gradually digested the slow-to-breakdown plant materials.

You won't find any meat-eaters in our family tree... no lions or tigers up there. We didn't inherit their long, pointed teeth and razor-sharp claws for ripping chunks of meat off a carcass. We didn't get their powerful stomach acids for quick digestion and short intestines to move the rapidly decaying material on out.

For hundreds of thousands of years we humans continued to eat primarily in the way of the primates. We were "hunters and gatherers." In small, family-based tribes we hunted and gathered wild plants and animals for our food.

We didn't grow and store food. When supplies got low, we moved on to new locations. We ate meat, fish and fowl along the way, but fruits, vegetables, leaves, roots, beans, seeds, nuts and flowers were our main sources of food. They were simply easier for us to find and gather.

So we always had plenty of bulk and fiber in our diet. But with the development of mills in the 19th century, we began grinding and refining grains and have steadily reduced our fiber intake ever since. The more we process our foods with canning, freezing and reconstituting, the more of its natural fibers are lost. We now eat about a fifth of the fiber we did just 100 years ago.

Our strong, active, hunting and gathering ancestors ate nearly five pounds of food a day. Our high-fat, refined and processed foods are "calorie-dense," so we get the same calories in only three pounds of food.[1] No wonder we're always hungry.

Further, the meat eaten by hunters and gatherers was *lean* wild game.[2] Domesticated meat animals have been bred, fed and penned to make them fat and tender. Lamb, ham, steak, hamburger, porkloin and similar "red" meats have considerably more fat than wild game (see Box 2).[3]

Box 2: Lower-Fat in Wild Game			
Domesticated Meats	**Calories**	**Fat grams**	**Fat percentage**
Ham	226	15g	60%
Hamburger	289	21g	64%
Porkloin	319	24g	68%
Sirloin steak	339	25g	65%
Wild Game	**Calories**	**Fat grams**	**Fat percentage**
Bison	109	1.8g	15%
Deer	120	2.4g	18%
Elk	111	1.4g	11%
Moose	102	0.7g	6%
Rabbit	114	2.3g	18%
Squirrel	120	3.2g	24%

* All portions 3.5 oz.

Human Information Service. *Composition of Foods, Raw, Processed, Prepared.* Agriculture Handbook No. 8-13, 8-17. Washington, D.C.: U.S. Department of Agriculture, 1986.

Our earliest ancestors, then, were charter members of the *Low-fat for Life* program. They ate little fat and a lot of complex carbohydrates and were on-the-move aerobic exercisers.

This was the human lifestyle for nearly all of the thousands and thousands of years of our history. It is what we were trained for in the patient process of evolution.

Our highly touted, modern and scientific way of doing things is but a blip on the historical record. The future will see it as a lesson learned...or not.

You Can't Fool Mother Nature

A low-fat/high-carbohydrate diet is natural to our human makeup. It fits the food processing system of the human body. The typical American diet *doesn't!* We simply were not designed to cope with the volume of fat we now eat. We were meant to thrive on the complex carbohydrates of fruits, vegetables, grains and legumes.

It would make sense, then, that those cultures that eat in harmony with evolutionary design would enjoy better health than those who don't. Cross-cultural studies consistently show this to be the case.

For example, consider the low-fat/high-carbohydrate diet of the Chinese. They eat lots of rice and vegetables with small amounts of meat and few, if any, dairy products. Only 10–15% of their calories come from fat, while 75–80% come from complex carbohydrates.

Compare this to the high-fat/low-carbohydrate American diet. Approximately 40% of our calories are fat and 45% carbohydrates. To make things worse, half the carbohydrates we get are the "simple" sugars and "refined," de-fibered flours. Both simple and refined carbohydrates are "empty" nutritionally. Eating too much sugar also throws off our body chemistry and has been linked to everything from tooth decay to hyperactivity in kids.

With a diet so low in fiber and complex carbohydrates, it shouldn't surprise us that American death rates due to heart disease are 17 times higher than those of the Chinese. Our death rates from breast cancer are 5 times higher and from cervical cancer are 8 times higher.[4]

Like the Chinese, the Japanese have low-fat/high-carbohydrate eating traditions. They've also enjoyed the lowest rates of cancer, heart disease and diabetes of any affluent country.

Recently, however, Japanese eating habits have been changing and their nutritionists are very concerned. Apparently the high-fat, low-fiber foods of the American fast food restaurants are becoming very popular in Japan. Japanese nutritionists know very well what will happen if this trend continues.

Studies show that those Japanese who move to America and adopt our ways of eating have higher rates of breast, colon and prostate cancer than people of the same age who remain in Japan. Their rate of heart disease also jumps to 10 times what it has been in their own country.[5]

What happens when a population *lowers* its fat intake? In World War I, grain imports to Denmark used to feed meat animals were severely cut back. The government decided to slaughter the animals and use what grains it could obtain for bread-making. This change of diet from meat to grain was associated with a dramatic drop in the death rate.[6]

In the same way, the rates of breast and colon cancer dropped dramatically in England during World War II when meat and fat intake was sharply reduced. With the return of peace (and fat) their rates returned to those before war.[7]

Bottom Line: The human body was designed to thrive on a low-fat and high-carbohydrate diet.

5

How Does Fat Give Us Heart Disease?

When food is eaten, it moves to the stomach and small intestines to be digested. Fats, proteins, carbohydrates, vitamins and minerals are extracted by the chemical actions of various enzymes and juices in what is called the digestive system.

These nutrients are then absorbed into the bloodstream. With fresh oxygen from the lungs, they are pumped by the heart through a vast network of arteries, veins and capillaries to nourish every cell in the body (see Box 3).

Evolution designed these digestive and circulatory systems to process low-fat, high-carbohydrate foods. They hum along just fine with bulky, fiber-rich vegetables, fruits and grains. They have a terrible time when overwhelmed with fat as in the current American diet.

The Bloodstream Blues

Excessive amounts of fat absorbed into the bloodstream clogs the circulatory system. Fat and the fat-like substance, cholesterol, deposit and build up on the inner walls of the

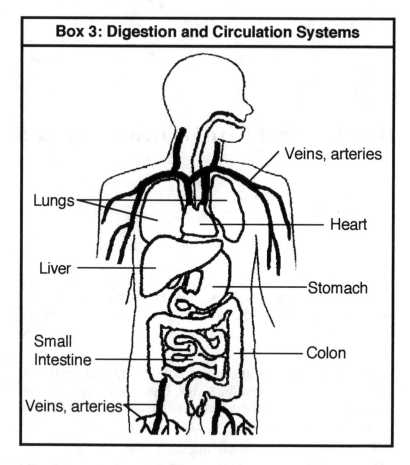

Box 3: Digestion and Circulation Systems

Veins, arteries

Lungs

Heart

Liver

Stomach

Small
Intestine

Colon

Veins, arteries

blood vessels. There is less and less room for circulating blood as the passageways within the blood vessels narrow. The heart has to work overtime, pumping harder to force the same amount of blood through a smaller space.

Blood pressure increases. Artery walls bulge, weaken and threaten to rupture. Blood circulation slows. Vital organs stop getting the nutrients they need to do their work. Muscles ache because they aren't getting enough fresh oxygen with the blood.

If a clot of blood or particle of fat blocks an already narrowed passage, blood flow stops. When blood can't get to our heart, a "heart attack" occurs. When it can't get to our brain, a "stroke" occurs. Without oxygen, brain cells die within minutes and the functions they controlled (speech, memory, body movement) are lost.

Hardening Gruel

The build-up of deposits and clogging of our blood vessels is called "atherosclerosis." The term came from the Greek words *athera* (meaning gruel) and *sklerosis* (meaning hardening). In other words, a cereal-like material is hardening in our arteries.

If you cut through a clean, healthy artery, its interior would be hollow like a drinking straw or garden hose. With atherosclerosis that artery begins to look more like a sausage stuffed with fat, dead cells, clotted blood, calcium deposits and chunks of cholesterol (see Box 4).

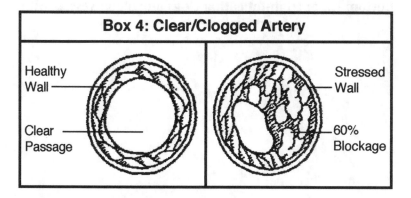

Box 4: Clear/Clogged Artery

Healthy Wall — Clear Passage

Stressed Wall — 60% Blockage

Now, don't think atherosclerosis is something that happens to us only when we are old and vulnerable. It robs our vitality throughout life.

- 25% of our kids already have high cholesterol and high blood pressure.[1]
- The American Heart Association recommends kids as young as two years old limit fat intake to avoid clogged arteries in adulthood.[2]
- A recent autopsy study of thirty-five 7–24 year olds who died of various causes found they *all* had atherosclerosis well underway.[3]
- Autopsies on Korean service personnel in their early 20's showed significant atherosclerosis.[4]
- Three out of five of us are expected to die from atherosclerosis.[5]

The message is clear. In the right amount, fat is an important and beneficial nutrient like protein and carbohydrate. In excess it is harmful. In the *Low-fat for Life* program, 20% or less is the right amount of fat for healthy living.

Bottom Line: High-fat eating clogs our blood vessels with fat and cholesterol.

6

What Does High-fat Eating Have to Do With Cholesterol?

Plenty. It makes sense that eating cholesterol-rich foods would lead to high levels of cholesterol in our blood paving the way for atherosclerosis, but this is only part of the story.

High-cholesterol foods *do* increase blood cholesterol levels. Generally, public health authorities tell us to keep our blood cholesterol level below 200 milligrams per deciliter (mg/dl) of blood by not eating more than 300 milligrams of cholesterol a day in our foods.

However, it's high-*fat* foods that are the real culprits. Total fat and saturated fat are what really boost blood cholesterol levels. How?

A Manufacturing Problem

While the human body does need a certain amount of cholesterol for making cell walls, nerve tissue and hormones, it *doesn't* need cholesterol brought in with food. The liver chemically manufactures whatever cholesterol the body requires.

High-fat eating interferes with body biochemistry and stimulates the liver to manufacture *excess* amounts of cholesterol which are then dumped into the bloodstream.[1]

Some studies suggest the cholesterol in food is less important than we've thought. For example, everyone knows egg yolks are a big deal when it comes to cholesterol, right? Well, a recent study of South African egg-farm workers raises a few questions about what they actually do to us.

Understandably, the egg-farm workers were found to be eating quite a few eggs. Their average cholesterol intake was over 1200mg a day, but get this—their blood cholesterol was still only 180mg/dl.

What's going on? It was found that less than 20% of the workers' daily calories were fat. These were *Low-fat for Life* egg eaters and the implication is that keeping our eye on the fat is the best way to avoid cholesterol problems.[2]

This can also be seen with Chinese men who average 127 mg/dl blood cholesterol levels eating a traditional low-fat/high-carbohydrate diet.[3] Understandably, then, in those regions of China, Japan and other countries where people still eat 10% or less of their daily calories in fat, clogged arteries are virtually *nonexistent.*[4]

Compare this to the results of the high-fat American diet. More than half of the middle-aged are above the 200 mg/dl limit and the average for men is 212 mg/dl.[5]

A Packaging and Shipping Problem

Fat is also a major player in the "good" and "bad" cholesterol we've been hearing so much about. These aren't really two kinds of cholesterol. They can't take the "bad" cholesterol out of our foods or put the "good" cholesterol in.

Any cholesterol *becomes* "good" or "bad" according to the way it gets "shipped" around the body. The body uses cholesterol for various jobs (e.g., building cell walls) at various locations. The liver manufactures and "ships" cholesterol throughout the body by means of the bloodstream transport system. "Good" and "bad" cholesterol refers to how it's "packaged" for shipping.

Cholesterol is shipped in packages made of protein and triglycerides (fat) called "lipoproteins." When shipped in a small, compact, "high-density lipoprotein" (HDL), it is called "HDL cholesterol." If, instead, it's shipped in a rather loose blob or "low-density lipoprotein" (LDL), it becomes "LDL cholesterol."

HDL cholesterol is the "good" type. It doesn't clog arteries. Instead it circulates in the bloodstream and works its way back to the liver where it may be shipped "out" with other body wastes via the commode. These HDL "good guys" even snag some of the LDL packages along the way, taking them along to the liver and then out the back door. We want this to happen because LDL cholesterol is the "bad" type.

LDL cholesterol sticks to artery walls and forms lumpy deposits of fat mixed with crusty, scablike chunks of crystalized cholesterol. These deposits are called "plaque." They are the "hardening gruel" of atherosclerosis that turn arteries into sausages.

Obviously, then, we want to keep our LDL cholesterol levels as low as possible. It's also obvious a high-fat diet works against us on this.

Remember, saturated fat affects body biochemistry. It not only stimulates the liver to manufacture excess cholesterol, it *also* gets it to package it as LDL cholesterol.

The more fat we eat, the more LDL cholesterol we produce. The more LDL cholesterol, the more barnacles in our blood vessels.

Want to keep the blood cholesterol levels down? Want to keep the LDL cholesterol down? Then keep the *fat* down! As fat content goes down (e.g., switching from whole milk to skim milk), cholesterol levels go down.

Bottom Line: Most of our cholesterol problems come from high-fat eating.

7

What About Fat and Cancer?

There are more than 100 different types of cancer and they all involve the rapid growth of abnormal cells. It is estimated that 40% of cancer in men and 60% of cancer in women stem from our high-fat/low-carbohydrate diet.[1]

Digestive Cancers

Understandably, diet is a key factor in cancers of the digestive system (stomach, pancreas, colon rectum). For example, in a recent study of 89,000 women, it was found that of the 61 foods they ate, beef, pork and lamb were the most strongly linked to colon cancer. Those eating skinless chicken and fish instead of the red meats cut their risk in half.[2]

Another study concluded a person who gets only 10 grams of saturated fat a day (about the amount in two cups of whole milk) is at risk for colon cancer.[3]

People in poor countries that cannot afford our diet emphasis on animal protein have much lower rates of cancer. Africa, for example, has a negligible amount of colon/rectal cancer.[4] In America this is our second most common cancer killing about 50,000 of us each year.[5]

Why the difference? It will take a lot of research to tell us *precisely* what's happening in the many types of cancer, but the underlying message is clear.

Just as fat clogs arteries by stimulating the liver to produce excess cholesterol, it also establishes conditions favorable to the growth of cancerous tumors. Once again, the fundamental effect of excess fat is biochemical interference.

In digestion, for example, enzymes break down the foods we eat to get at their nutrients. With high levels of fat this same process can increase the level of "carcinogens," cancer-causing chemicals.

As food materials move through the gastrointestinal tract, these carcinogens contact and irritate tissue (e.g., lining of colon). The longer the contact the more the chance for development of cancer growth.

And what do you know about the human digestive system that makes this especially problematic? That's right, evolution designed us to slowly process the fibrous materials of vegetables, fruits and grains. That's why our intestines are long (12 times the length of our trunk) compared to meat-eating animals (3 times the length of their trunk). [6]

It's estimated that 90% of our colon cancer deaths could be avoided by diet change.[7]

Hormone Cancers

In the hormone cancers, animal protein and fat are again implicated. The connection between fat intake and both breast and prostate cancer is often reported. International comparisons repeatedly show these cancers most occur in populations with the highest meat and dairy consumption.

What's happening? Biochemical imbalances. For example, the high-fat diet interferes with sexual development, encouraging earlier puberty in both men and women. This effect has, in turn, been associated with later breast and prostate cancers.[8]

Some believe high levels of fat interfere with the amount of prolactin (a milk-producing hormone) in the blood and promote breast cancer. Others theorize fat raises estrogen levels affecting breasts directly. Still others believe it effects the pituitary gland and generates hormones that stimulate abnormal cells in the breast.

Disagreements continue, but as the National Academy of Sciences and others report, the weight of evidence indicates high-fat diets are associated with a higher risk of breast, prostate, cervical, ovarian, uterin, colon and other cancers.[9]

Occasionally we hear contrary reports. Recently, for example, Harvard researchers said they had serious doubts that breast cancer was even related to fat. Of course, the National Institute of Health immediately responded that the jury was still out on breast cancer and we should watch for the results of their $600 million study before concluding anything.

The point here is *not* that dietary fat causes one specific cancer or another. Rather that it is related in one way or another to so *many* diseases. For example, fat cells in obese individuals have the capacity to change adrenal hormones in ways that promote uterine cancer. In the liver, fat stimulates an increase in the production of bile and promotes tumor growth.

Biochemical Dis-ease

When we consider the various diet-related diseases, we are reminded again and again of what happens when body biochemistry is continually overwhelmed by fat—any kind of fat.

The experts sometimes like to split hairs on which kind of fat causes what kind of effect in a specific disease. For example, a heart disease article tells us the "saturated" fat of our meats (beef, pork, lamb, poultry) and animal products (butter, cheese, eggs) is the *real* concern, not "unsaturated" (mono and poly) fat.

Evidence *does* suggest unsaturated fat (corn, sunflower, olive and canola oil, margarine) may be less risky with heart disease, but recent studies also show another type of fat present in margarine (trans fat) *does* increase cholesterol levels and heart disease risk.[10] Besides, unsaturated fat is known to promote *cancer*.[11] Don't split hairs. For our purposes fat is fat. It doesn't matter where it comes from. Keep it below 20%!

Excessive fat of any kind gives us trouble. It creates an overall condition of imbalance, disorder, dis-ease. And when an ailment develops it *amplifies* the dis-ease condition. For example, obesity dramatically increases the risk of developing atherosclerosis, diabetes, high-blood pressure and cancer. It's also strongly associated with the formation of gallstones which are in fact *made* of cholesterol.[12]

Having diabetes means you're more likely to get heart disease. The risk of heart disease doubles in diabetic men and triples in diabetic women.[13]

Breast and prostate cancer occur in countries that also have a high incidence of heart disease. A high incidence of heart disease in a population predicts high rates of colon cancer.

Bottom Line: High-fat eating creates biochemical conditions that pave the way for cancer, heart disease, stroke, obesity, diabetes, hypertension, and other health problems.

8

What About Discoveries and Scientific Breakthroughs?

Old habits die hard. That's why New Year's resolutions seldom make it past the first couple of weeks.

If our situation *demands* change, we look for the path of least resistance. We try to make the easiest and smallest adjustment possible.

And when it comes to lifelong eating habits, the rut is very deep. We are therefore inclined to overstate those discoveries, advances or new technologies that can be taken to suggest we might get away with eating pretty much the way we always have.

High-Tech Solutions

Some will stay with the high-fat American diet thinking that when the time comes they'll just have new arteries sewn in with a "bypass" operation. Or maybe they'll get an "angioplasty" where miniature balloons break through clogged arteries. Why, they even have "atherectomies" where they ream out clogs with rotary drills or lasers.

What do you think happens to the folks who get these high-tech solutions if they don't cut the fat?

- 320,000 Americans get bypass operations each year.[1] Half of the bypasses clog up in five years and 80% clog in seven years.[2]

- 200,000 of us undergo angioplasty each year. One-third of the arteries opened clog up again in four to six months.[3]

Omega-3's

A short time ago everyone was talking about the Greenland Eskimos. They have relatively high-fat diets, yet their incidence of heart disease is lower than ours. This was attributed to a type of fat (Omega-3 fatty acids) found in fish. Omega-3's are thought to affect Eskimo body chemistry in a way that reduces the stickiness of their blood platelets and provides anti-clotting protection.

Follow up studies established the fact that diets with a higher intake of fish have lower death rates from heart attacks. Fish oil capsules appeared in the marketplace and the desire for anti-clotting protection caused a near feeding frenzy.

However, there is a downside to this anti-clotting. You bleed easier when your blood is slow to clot. Heavy-dose users of the fish oil capsules soon reported problems with this. Apparently, Eskimos who eat very high quantities of fish also have to watch for this.

So our rush to capsules is premature. Though fish-eating is clearly associated with lower rates of heart disease, we still don't know enough about what's going on to get it in pill form.

In fact, some research questions the importance of the Omega-3's in fish. One study reported that people eating only 6–10 ounces of low-Omega-3 fish each week still had half the coronary heart disease of those who ate no fish.[4]

The point is we may not know enough to create the magic pill, but study after study *does* tell us the benefits of eating more fish.

For example, in one study, a group of meat-eaters were compared to a group who substituted fish for red meat three times a week. The meat-eaters had four times more fatal heart attacks than the fish-eaters.[5]

French Wine

More recently the French have been receiving a lot of attention for a similar reason and this time Americans are finding the breakthrough antidote for atherosclerosis even more compelling.

It seems the French eat more fat than we do, exercise less and smoke more, yet suffer fewer heart attacks. As with the Eskimos, something in the way they eat and live is protecting them.

A number of possible influences are under investigation, but for obvious reasons one has Americans already lining up for the cure—French wine-drinking.

Studies have suggested moderate alcohol use (e.g., one glass of wine each day) protects against coronary heart disease. Like the Omega-3's, alcohol is thought to reduce blood platelet stickiness and offer an anti-clotting protection.

Hearing about this on TV's "60 Minutes," our neighbor immediately drank three glasses of wine to flush away the clogs and get ready for a few pounds of pork at the dinner table.

But if preliminary findings are reassuring to regular imbibers and a boon to winemakers, other studies are less encouraging. They link alcohol use to cancer and a variety of other health problems, especially when drinking more than small medicinal amounts.

The American Cancer Society studied 275,000 middleaged men and found those who have four drinks a day are 30–35% more likely to die of cancer.[6] In a study of 89,000 women, those who took between three and nine drinks a *week* were 30% more likely than non-drinkers to develop breast cancer.[7] A recent Harvard study also found more than two drinks a day increases a woman's risk of colon or rectal cancer by 78%.[8]

The French have an unusually high incidence of mouth and throat cancer. Studies over the years consistently show heavy drinkers are 15 times as likely to develop mouth and throat cancers. Add the French love of strong cigarettes and the likelihood jumps to 50 times that of a non-smoking non-drinker.[9]

Our discoveries *are* important. Some become genuine medical milestones. A while back who'd have thought the ordinary aspirin would slow blood clotting? Some now consider it the single most important drug we have for preventing heart attacks.[10]

At the same time, we need to recognize that each discovery is only a *partial* solution. When a new drug or innovative medical procedure for one disease is getting a lot of the media spotlight, remember the cancers, diabetes, obesity and other fat-related diseases remaining in the shadows.

Bottom Line: High-fat eating promotes a variety of diseases. While celebrating a breakthrough on one, we could be headed for trouble with another.

9

What About All the Low-fat Foods Coming Out? Isn't the Food Industry Helping Us to Eat Healthier?

The eternal dream of a convenience addict is that someone or something else will do the hard work of change. Some advance or scientific breakthrough, some new governmental regulation or new products in the marketplace will make it easy for us.

Don't kid yourself. With increased public awareness and pressure, lower proportions of fat in more and more foods can be expected. Thus some of our food will at least become less *unhealthy*. But we want a healthy diet that is both low in fat *and* high in nutrient-rich carbohydrate foods.

Unfortunately, the forces of a profit-minded food industry and a convenience-minded public have combined over the last century to produce foods with fewer nutrients and more toxic chemicals than we'd ever have imagined.

Nutrients Needed

In Chapter 3 we talked about the importance of the fiber and micronutrients found in complex carbohydrate foods. Vitamins and minerals, for example, are crucial to body defense systems.

The chemical pollutants of modern life make excessive demands on micronutrient stores. Struggles with virus attacks deplete micronutrient stores. Excessive alcohol and sugar, a sudden crisis, chronic stress—all rob us of micronutrients and weaken our resistance to disease.

To replenish micronutrients each day our bodies must have highly nutritious foods. To maintain defenses and thrive in the often dangerous world we have created, they must have access to every basic micronutrient. We need the biotin, niacin, folic acid, beta carotene, riboflavin and many other substances we call vitamins. We need the potassium, calcium, phosphorous, zinc, magnesium, iodine and other materials we call minerals.

This isn't news. Every school child has heard about the thousands of sailors who died of scurvy until we discovered the link to vitamin C in fruits and vegetables.

That discovery took place in the 18th century, so we've been talking about the importance of nutrition for quite some time now.

So how are we doing? Are we making sure to get the nutrients our bodies need to protect our health? No.

Government study reports consistently warn us we are malnourished.[1] Here we are in this wonderful, rich, resourceful country of ours with food surpluses stacked up all around us and we suffer from *malnutrition*.

We're not just talking about the poor either. *All* segments of our society are getting less than enough nutrients in the foods we eat.

Does this have anything to do with our food industry? *Yes.*

Nutrients Lost

Before the Industrial Revolution most of us grew our own food, cooked it and ate it. Others bought food from local growers, cooked it and ate it. That was the old-fashioned way.

Throughout the 20th century we rushed to industrialize the way we grew food in America. We were proud of our achievements in other industries and wanted the *easier, faster* and *cheaper* foods promised in a factory approach to production.

So we centralized. We specialized. We used the techniques of mass-production. We transformed our small family farms into giant food factories incorporating all the latest biological and technological advances.

This transformation was powered by petroleum. With it we mechanized agriculture and created a vast armament of food production chemicals. We developed chemical fertilizers to speed growth, herbicides to kill weeds, pesticides to kill bugs, dyes to get the color right, preservatives to extend shelf life and enhancers to titillate our tastebuds.

We fell in love with the convenience of it all. We embraced the food factory and its petro-chemicals like we embraced the animal protein diet and its fat. And now we are discovering the tremendous hidden costs in both.

While we dramatically changed the way we produced our foods, we also dramatically changed their nutritional value.

Food nutrients are fragile substances. Many are lost in the long trek from some distant farm to the cells of our bodies.

To begin with, nutrients in the plants we eat (or feed to meat animals) come from the soil they grow in. Rich, fertile, productive soil has the nutrients that plants and, in turn, animals/humans need to thrive.

A healthy soil is a natural "community" teeming with life. The bacteria, fungi, algae, insects, decaying plants, worms, animal wastes—all are important contributors to its nutritional quality.

"Organic" farming methods work with this natural community and without pesticides and artificial fertilizers to produce vitamin- and mineral-rich foods. A recent study, for example, found organic corn had 20 times more calcium and manganese and 2 to 5 times more copper, magnesium, selenium, molybdenum and zinc than conventional corn.[2]

The petro-chemical fertilizers and pesticides used in conventional farming methods destroy the complex ecology of the soil community and deplete its nutrients.

An inert, lifeless soil requires great quantities of commercial fertilizer to produce foods with lower nutritional quality.

Factory methods of harvesting means crops are picked before they are ripe to prevent damage in shipping and storage. Unfortunately, the peak of nutrient value coincides with the peak of ripeness.

Time spent in transit and storage as well as shipping damage means further nutrient loss. Many vegetables, for example, lose more than half of their vitamin C before they reach the produce counter.[3]

From 70 to 80% of some nutrients are lost in different processing and refining operations. Whole grains are converted into tasteless, low-nutrition materials for fabricating heavily sweetened baked goods. Refined sugar, corn syrup and other sweeteners are routinely added to every kind of processed food and drink.[4]

Heating, drying and reconstituting, pre-cooking, canning, freezing, pasteurizing, condensing and all the other methods we use to process food result in tremendous nutrient losses.

Poisons Found

Our foods are far less nutritious than we want to believe and more dangerous than we want to hear about.

There are well over 25,000 pesticide products available to food producers. How long do you figure it will take to test each one? How long will it take to pull those from the market that don't meet standards of safety? Do you trust that the levels of chemical residue allowed in our food by current standards are indeed safe?

Recent research suggests by the time children are a year old, they have been exposed to a greater cancer risk from pesticides than the Environmental Protection Agency says they should have in a lifetime.[5]

Half our winter produce is shipped in from places like Chile and Brazil. Think we have a great system for monitoring *their* use of chemicals? Hardly. The FDA routinely inspects only 1% of all imported foods.[6] Ever wonder where these countries get the chemicals we're now trying so hard to avoid? U.S. companies are exporting 27 tons of pesticides every hour of every day.[7]

And get this: the stuff sprayed on fruits and vegetables is far less potent than what we get in our meats. All sorts of chemicals gradually *build up* in the fat of our meat animals.[8] What chemicals?

The insecticides and herbicides used to grow what we feed our meat animals, of course, concentrate in their fat. Use of such pesticides has increased from approximately 200,000 pounds a year in the 1950's to more than a billion pounds a year today.[9]

Dangerous industrial chemicals such as polychlorinated biphenyls (PCB's) and heavy metals such as lead and mercury contaminate our soils, plant life, water and air. They *also* accumulate in animal fat.

Hormone additives and slow-release implants are used extensively in meat production. They are cheap and dramatically increase growth and weight gains in livestock. Over the years we've had major problems with cancer-causing hormones such as diethylstilbestrol (DES), but food producers continue to fight restrictions every step of the way. When one product is eventually banned, they turn to new, less-researched hormone supplements.[10]

Beef cattle raised in crowded feedlots are continually stressed by swarms of flies. To producers stress means lost weight and lost profits. Therefore, toxic chemicals are routinely sprayed over entire feedlots. An alternative method is to submerge animals in tanks of fly-killing chemicals.

Ironically, stressed and diseased feedlot animals given antibiotics were found to make weight gains without increases in feed. As you might guess, we now feed *tons* of antibiotics to meat animals. We feed them more antibiotics for weight gain than all the antibiotics we use to treat both animal and human illness.[11]

The results are frightening. More and more we are encountering antibiotic-resistant diseases. For example, the dreaded salmonella food poisoning is not only on the increase, but becoming increasingly difficult to treat with antibiotics.

The U.S. General Accounting Office reported that 143 chemical residues were found in meat at higher levels than considered tolerable by government standards. At least 42 of these were thought to be carcinogenic.[12]

Through insecticides, hormones, drugs and medications we speed growth and treat disease in unhealthy meat animals. As a result, more sick animals make it to market.

Some of these are identified in government inspections, but the scope of the problem is far beyond the capacities of existing governmental programs. Only a fraction of deliberate violators are caught and their fines are insignificant compared to profits involved.

The FDA recently said of 600 chemical residues present in our meat only 10% are monitored by governmental agencies.[13]

Though advertising is continually telling us about all sorts of new fat-free products, don't expect our food industry to take the lead in changing our diet. Chemical food production methods are profitable and thoroughly entrenched.

The only change that matters to the food industry is the kind that rings in cash registers. An enlightened public, putting money where its mouth is, will bring the changes we want.

This means asking for low-fat, "organic," pesticide-free products at food stores and supporting the merchants that offer them.

Consumers have long avoided natural surface blemishes on fruits and vegetables. Now a cosmetic flaw can be viewed as an organic "badge of honor" for plants that made it to maturity without the help of toxic chemicals.

More and more low-fat items are showing up on restaurant menus. Choose them, comment on them when they taste good. Support the development of low-fat, healthy alternatives in the marketplace.

Changes in the marketplace will come as *we* change.

Bottom Line: Our food industry is more interested in profits than public health. Take care of yourself. No one else is going to do it for you.

10

What About Vitamin Pills?

The human body is remarkable in its ability to fight off invading microorganisms and toxic chemicals. This ability is built-in, natural. It was developed over eons of human life. But it was developed in a very different world than the one we now live in.

Needing More Nutrients and Getting Less

We need to face the fact that we simply were not designed for the kind of world we have created. We have enzyme systems, for example, that *are* able to de-toxify entering chemicals, but the living conditions that "trained" this ability in our ancestors could hardly prepare us for the chemical swamp we call modern life.

In the last chapter we talked about the many toxic chemicals that come with the way we now produce our food. Thousands of chemical fertilizers, herbicides, pesticides, colorants, preservatives, hormones and antibiotics contaminate our foods. Consider also those in the air we breathe, the water we drink and bathe in, the furniture we sit on, the clothing we wear.

We have accepted this chemicalized environment for many reasons. We long underestimated its dangers and were overly impressed with the achievements of modern science.

Smallpox and other killing infections of the past have left the idea of "enemy germs" deeply etched on our collective mind. We are obsessed with germs and odors and try to rid ourselves of them with potent chemicals. Given the chance, we would likely dip the entire planet in a vat of chemicals if it meant getting rid of germs once and for all.

Consider the billions we spend on chemical sprays for the illusion of germ and odor-free cleanliness. We spray artificial flower and pine tree scents throughout our homes to cover kitchen and bathroom odors. We spray our mouths and underarms with deodorants and have cabinets full of antiseptic sprays for every human orifice.

We spray chemical cleaners in our ovens and on our countertops. We spray stain-guard chemicals on our chair cushions and static-guard chemicals on our clothing. We spray lemon-scented wax on our end tables and ozone-eating lacquer on our hair.

And if some unwary quarter-inch bug of any species should happen into our view, we flood it and our surroundings with a few cans of aerosol poison.

If our bodies are to defend us in this overwhelming chemical assault we call modern life, they need *more* food nutrients than ever before. What a great time for nearly all of us to be hooked on low-nutrient foods and the convenience of a food production system that destroys nutrients in processing and refining.

Filling In as Best We Can

Many of us are turning to vitamin and mineral supplements. Should we? For quite some time it's been impossible to get agreement on an answer.

Research scientists, biochemists, physicians, various other mainstream and alternative health care practitioners, and, of course, vitamin companies say, "yes" we should.

The American health establishment (e.g., Food and Drug Administration, Department of Agriculture, American Medical Association), on the other hand, continues to harumph we don't need vitamin and mineral supplements. We are getting all we need in our food.

Accumulating evidence on the protective benefits of vitamins such as the antioxidants and the successes of experimental vitamin therapies in curing disease has eroded the "don't need them" position quite a bit. Taking vitamins and minerals to supplement our diet now makes sense pretty much across the board.

No Magic Pills and Potions

While it's time nutrients and their importance to our health received some attention, let's hope we don't miss the point. We've developed an obvious weakness for convenience. Taking magic pills and potions seems so much easier than learning about food nutrition and paying attention to what we eat.

Supplements are just that—*supplements*. We are taking extra vitamins and minerals to *supplement* the nutrition of our foods. Taking them will not magically make up for the sins of our food industry, the poisons in our environment, or the stresses in our life style. They won't make up for our lousy eating habits, lack of exercise, or excesses of alcohol, caffeine, sugar and salt.

Supplements *do* have an important role to play in our overall attempts to take better care of ourselves. They help us insure the nutrition we are already trying to get by eating the right foods. Taken in moderation they seem a low risk with high-potential benefits.

In a recent study of 100 people over the age of 65, half were given a multivitamin and mineral supplement and half were given a placebo. The group that took the supplements had half the colds and flus. When participants did get sick, those taking supplements got better twice as fast.[1]

Even if we think our level of nutrition has been okay, *optimum* nutrition might mean the difference between healthy vitality and a lifetime of endless colds, flus, headaches, and low-grade illnesses.

Until recently, many U.S. physicians seemed unaware of this. They assumed malnutrition was rare. But it is now thought nutrient deficiencies set the stage for a wide range of problems. A wound that doesn't heal properly, gum disease, nervousness, frequent minor infections, non-specific aches and pains, irritability, depression, fatigue, insomnia, anorexia—all may have their roots in nutrient deficiencies.[2]

The question, then, is "How much?" What is "moderate" supplementation? What is "optimum" nutrition? Again, there are no clear answers.

Suggested dosages range from "mega" to meager. There are many, many different vitamin/mineral formulations in the marketplace. Often they seem thrown together without any special logic or scientific rationale. They differ widely in the quantity and quality of ingredients and price.

Marketing claims, especially in mail-order catalogs, are full of medicine-show hype. They push high dosages with a lot of "bigger is better" arm-twisting. Remember, it's the *balance* of ingredients that's important in any formula, not the size of an individual ingredient.

Be wary of big doses. Vitamins and minerals *are,* after all, chemicals and do affect body chemistry. Shoveling in the supplements and self-medicating is risky business.

On the other hand, many believe formulas that stick to the government's "recommended dietary allowances" (RDA's) are at the meager end of the business. Nutrition scientists consistently recommend higher levels of vitamins and minerals. Anthropologists even tell us the diet of our hunting and gathering ancestors had nutrient levels much higher than the RDA's.[3]

The RDA's were introduced during World War II to prevent the malnutrition of soldiers. They were across-the-board minimum standards, not intended to maximize individual health.

The RDA's listed on vitamin and mineral products, then, are those the Food and Drug Administration (FDA) judges to be *adequate* for preventing deficiency diseases, such as scurvy, in healthy individuals.

They are conservative, standardized nutrient levels. They are not allowances established for achieving *optimal* health.

Each of us has unique nutritional needs because of differences in our genetics, metabolism, physiology, perceptions, emotions and moment-to-moment life circumstances.

The best nutrition, then, means having the right amount of the right nutrients available at the right times to fit our unique situation. It is something we work toward in daily life by eating for the best nutrition possible and "insuring" it as best as we can with supplements.

The Insurance Approach

Many of us take a moderate level of daily supplementation as an inexpensive "insurance"(see Box 5). We are try-

Box 5: RDA's, Toxic and Insurance Levels of Vitamins and Minerals

Vitamin/ Mineral	RDA's Men	RDA's Women	Toxic Levels	Insurance Levels
Vitamin A	5000 I.U.	5000 I.U.	20–50,000 I.U.	5–25,000 I.U.*
Vitamin B1	1.5 mg	1.0 mg	– – –	1.5–10 mg
Vitamin B2	1.7 mg	1.3 mg	– – –	1.7–10 mg
Vitamin B3	19 mg	15 mg	100 mg †	20–200 mg ◊
Vitamin B6	2 mg	1.6 mg	2,000 mg	2–20 mg
Vitamin B12	2 mcg	2 mcg	– – –	6–30 mcg
Biotin	30–100 mcg***		– – –	100–300 mcg
Folic Acid	200 mcg	180 mcg	– – –	200–400 mcg
Pantothenate	4–7 mg***		– – –	10–50 mg
Vitamin C	60 mg	60 mg	**	60–600 mg
Vitamin D	200 I.U.	200 I.U.	1000 I.U.	200–400 I.U.
Vitamin E	15 I.U.	12 I.U.	600 I.U.	30-200 I.U.
Vitamin K	80 mcg	65 mcg	500 mcg	– – –
Calcium	800 mg	800 mg	2500 mg	200–1000 mg
Chromium	50–200 mcg***		– – –	50–200 mcg
Copper	1.5–3 mg***		35 mg	1–2 mg
Iodine	150 mcg	150 mcg	50,000 mcg	75–150 mcg
Iron	10 mg	15 mg	– – –	10–15 mg
Magnesium	350 mg	280 mg	none ††	200–400 mg
Manganese	2–5 mg***		above 10 mg	5–10 mg
Molybdenum	75–250 mcg***		540 mcg	50-200 mcg

Box 5: Continued

Vitamin/	RDA's		Toxic	Insurance
Mineral	Men	Women	Levels	Levels
Phosphorus	800 mg	800 mg	over 1000 mg	– – –
Potassium	– – –	– – –	none ◊◊	– – –
Selenium	70 mcg	55 mcg	1000 mcg	50–200 mcg
Zinc	15 mg	12 mg	150 mg	10–15 mg

    * In the form of Beta-Carotene, which has less toxic potential than preformed Vitamin A

    † Niacin may cause "niacin flush," niacinamide doesn't

    ◊ In the form of niacinamide

    ** Some evidence of negative effects when 1500 mg is taken daily for two months

    †† Unless have renal failure or A.V. blocks

    ◊◊ Except if have kidney failure

    *** Estimated Safe and Adequate Daily Intake for Adults

– – – Not reported or not determined

National Academy of Sciences. *Recommended Dietary Allowances.* Washington DC:National Academy Press, 1989.

Hendler, S. *The Docter's Vitamin and Mineral Encyclopedia.* New York: Simon and Schuster, 1990.

ing to insure the availability of nutrients should our bodies require them for whatever reason. A recent *Newsweek* poll shows that 7 in 10 Americans now use vitamin supplements at least occasionally.[4]

The mounting evidence is that nutrients in amounts higher than the RDA's may help protect us from diseases such as heart disease and cancer. Consider, for example, several recent reports:

- A recent study found taking 600 I.U. of vitamin E (RDA 12–15 I.U.), 1000 milligrams of vitamin C (RDA 60 mg) and 50,000 I.U. of beta-carotene daily, prior to exercise, decreased cancer- and heart disease-causing free radicals by 17–36%.[5]

- Two studies, one of 87,000 women and another of 40,000 men, found taking 100 units of vitamin E daily (RDA 12–15 I.U.) cut the risk of heart disease by 41% in the women and 37% in the men.[6]

- A 10-year health survey found those consuming 300 mg of vitamin C a day (RDA 60 mg) had 40% fewer deaths from heart disease than those consuming 50 milligrams or less.[7]

- A review of 18 vitamin C studies showed people with the lowest intake had twice the rate of mouth, throat and stomach cancer.[8]

- Studies indicate women of childbearing age need two to four times the recommended amount of folic acid to prevent birth defects such as anencephaly and spina bifida.[9]

- A two-year study of 122 women found calcium supplementation of 1000 mg above the RDA (800 mg) slowed bone loss one-third to one-half of those not receiving the additional calcium supplement.[10]

Even so, the controversy over exactly what amounts we *should* take looks as though it will continue well into the next century.

What to do? For now, a more conservative approach would be to take a daily vitamin and mineral supplement that at least meets the RDA's and includes trace minerals.

But for three important reasons, higher-dosage insurance formulas are worth consideration:

1.) Authorities report many RDA dosages are too low.

2.) Dosages would have to be very high to reach toxic levels.

3.) There are many potentials for assorted health problems from even *minor* nutrient deficiencies over a period of time.

Bottom Line: Supplements are a kind of insurance when combined with high-nutrition eating and exercise.

11

What About Stress?

In ordinary conversations we often remind each other of the link between emotions and health.

"Boy, did my dad have a hemorrhage when I got in so late."

"And mine about had a heart attack over the dented fender."

Most of us remember the way our heart pounded when we were kids and thought we heard footsteps behind us or when our name was called to recite something difficult in a class. Whether the threat was imagined or real, significant or trivial, our heart thumped loudly in our ears.

That thumping heart has served us well since the dawn of time. For our most distant ancestors it was a tool for surviving the many dangerous circumstances they encountered.

The Fight-or-Flight Response

When clan mother met sabre-toothed tiger on the trail, her heart rate, breathing and metabolism shot up. Blood coursed into her arm and leg muscles.

In an instant her body was ready to react with everything she had. She might scream and throw rocks at that tiger or stab at him with a spear (fight). She might climb a tree, run or jump into a nearby river (flight).

She had no time for thoughtful consideration. Whether conflict or escape was ultimately her best choice, adrenalin was making the moves, not logic.

With danger past and action completed clan mother was free to relax. Her heart, breathing and metabolism could slow down while she savored her victory. At many camp-fires she would tell her story.

And the gift she passes along to us is that evolutionary tool of survival. It's that innate, automatic, heart-thumping, "fight-or-flight" response. For thousands of years it protected those before us. It protects us now.

Fortunately, most of us don't come up against the sabre-toothed kind of threat very often anymore. Twentieth century citizens traded them for day-to-day problems that are less acute, more chronic, nagging and bitchy.

Unfortunately, our bodies can't tell the difference. They react to late appointments, intimidating supervisors and lost car keys *as if* they are sabre-toothed problems.

They read the signals of our tension as a call to battle and respond out of the same straightforward, life-preserving habits that protected us through all the previous centuries of human life.

Over and over each day they rush to prepare for crisis. Over and over they jump to red alert, hypertensed for all hell to break loose.

We find comfort in having this primitive response in those times we are in danger and really need it. We celebrate, as well, those times it will leap into action for others, to lift an impossible weight from an injured child or grip a rope in icy water heroism.

But the fight-or-flight response gives us trouble when repeatedly aroused by the aggravations and intimidations of everyday life. Our bodies turn on themselves when forced to contend with the continual nitpicking, strain and drain we call "stress."

Chronic Stress and Tension

Noise, family and financial problems stress us. Even changes we would think of as *good* (finding a better apartment, getting a promotion) upset and stress us more than we think.

Changes requiring us to adjust our behavior in most any way stress us. Those who have the biggest and most life changes are found to suffer the most stress—and what describes 20th century life more than *change?*

Our relationships are fluid, impermanent, conditional. Our jobs are insecure, our schedules full and activities frantic. Always on the move, we eat while driving in heavy traffic. With a fax machine and cellular phone, we even do business from the front seat of a car.

Our lives have more affluence and convenience than ever before, but they are also chock full of stress and anxiety. Repeatedly we trigger the fight-or-flight response. Automatically our bodies are preparing us for those tigers on the trail.

We clench our fists and tense our muscles to protect ourselves from possible injury. We speed up our heart, breathing and metabolism to make more energy available for fighting or running. We shut our digestion down to divert energy to our muscles. We constrict the arteries in our arms and legs and clot our blood more quickly to prevent blood loss from possible wounds—but the tiger is paper. Fight-or-flight is not required and the tension is not resolved.

The effects of chronic stress and its unresolved tension are illness and disease. In the practicalities of daily life this means more colds, headaches and upset stomachs. But we are also learning some of the more serious effects of stress. For example, it sabotages the immune system and inhibits the body's ability to fight cancer cells.[1]

And while everybody knows that stress increases blood pressure, let's consider for a minute what actually happens when we do this repeatedly, day in and day out.

Chronically activated, the body *stays* tense (i.e., goes into a permanent state of hypertension).

Arteries remain constricted inside the heart. Blood remains more "clottable." The heart can't relax and in constant tension begins to break itself down, damaging its own fibers.

Now, add this state of hypertension to the fat and cholesterol in our arteries and what do you get? Right, hypertension compounds the risk of atherosclerosis, heart attacks and strokes. It packs cholesterol chunks deeper into artery walls, further weakening them. High blood pressure in already clogged, swollen and weakened arteries dramatically increases the risk of sudden death from their bursting and hemorrhaging.

But what can we do? In stressful situations the body's innate, fight-or-flight response *automatically* cranks up the heart rate, breathing and metabolism. We are told we should learn to relax more, but just how are we to do that?

Meditation and the Relaxation Response

There *is* something we can do. We can learn to work with *another* built-in response our bodies have available. It complements the fight-or-flight response, but has *opposite* effects. It *lowers* blood pressure. It *slows* breathing and metabolism.

Swiss physiologist Walter R. Hess was researching brain stimulation to produce the fight-or-flight response in animals. In the process he found that by stimulating a nearby brain site he could also produce an opposite pattern of reactions in what he called the "trophotropic" response.

Hess proposed this response was some sort of safety valve for over-stressed animals that quickly reversed an overstimulated fight-or-flight response.

Following this lead, Herbert Benson, M.D. searched for ways a person could learn to activate the trophotropic response when he or she needed to cope with stress. He found that with the daily practice of a simple meditation procedure an individual can learn to activate what he came to call the "relaxation response."

The various meditative disciplines (e.g., Zen, Yoga, Sufi, Christian, Jewish) emphasize different mental, spiritual and philosophical applications. Benson found, however, when it came to activating the relaxation response they all have four elements in common. All require a *quiet environment,* an *object to dwell upon,* a *passive attitude* and a *comfortable position.*[2]

Meditation and Relaxation

What happens when we meditate and elicit the relaxation response? Heart and breathing rates, of course, slow down. Brain waves shift from active "beta" to relaxed "alpha."

"Lactate" is a chemical associated with stress. The more lactate in our blood the higher our anxiety. Meditation significantly lowers blood lactate levels. It also lowers "catecholamines."

We've all heard the fight-or-flight, "adrenalin" stories such as where a mother is momentarily able to exert tremendous strength to save her child. The adrenalin and similar chemicals behind this special strength are produced by the adrenal gland and called "catecholamines."

Unfortunately, catecholamine chemicals also have powerful effects on the way our bodies control the fat and cholesterol in our blood. A stress stimulated increase of catacholamines in the blood is believed also to *raise* the levels of fat and cholesterol.

Studies show when subjects are taught to lower catecholamines with meditation, cholesterol levels fall an average of 20%, along with lowered blood pressure, heart rate and so on.[3]

In short, meditation practice helps us learn to "de-stress," to slow down, to quiet our anxieties. When a hassle pokes at our fight-or-flight response, we are able to relax, to substitute the relaxation response.

By routinely paying attention to our inner world we become more aware of the meaning of its signals. We open communications with ourselves.

We are able to sense arousal of the fight-or-flight response much earlier and can *choose* to continue it or gentle it down with signals practiced in daily meditation.

With this choice made available, we become better life managers. We are more able to deal with everyday pressures. We become more effective in the world and less the victims of circumstance.

And when we know how to relax we'll be able to avoid those stress reaction headaches, colds and bouts of insomnia. We'll also have a better shot at preventing serious problems like hypertension, heart disease and stroke.

Bottom Line: Meditation helps manage stress.

12

What About Exercise?

Throughout history, life has conditioned the human body for strength and endurance. We were designed for physical activity as we were designed for a low-fat/high-carbohydrate diet.

But with the advent of beasts of burden, slaves, servants and lower-class laborers, many of us came to believe success meant labor-saving convenience. Successful people had others and machines doing their physical work.

Killing Us Softly

A young America, eager to create its version of a better world, embraced this notion of success. We were rich in natural resources and had an ambitious people. We were the *new world* limited only by the extent of our imagination. We knew without question we would one day have prosperity and convenience beyond our wildest dreams. We were right.

Domesticated animals make protein more convenient by turning fields of grain into lockers of meat. Giant, corporate food-factories and coast-to-coast, fast-food restaurants conveniently raise and prepare our food for us.

Boy, this is really living isn't it? Our modern science and Yankee ingenuity have come up with labor-saving devices for every conceivable human effort.

Our world of convenience has been saving us so much labor, more than 60% of us are "sedentary," which means "accustomed to sit much or take little exercise."[1]

Electric can openers and car window openers are helping us save ourselves for something else. But while we wait for that something else we are becoming terribly unfit and unhealthy.

We have created a world where few of us are required to be physically active as an ordinary part of daily living and we now need to exercise or we won't live to enjoy what it is we've been saving ourselves for.

Everyone knows this. A recent analysis of 43 studies shows inactive individuals are at least twice as likely to get coronary artery disease as more active individuals *independent of other risk factors.*[2]

Study after study of thousands of men and women have clearly shown the most sedentary individuals have the highest death rates whether from heart disease, cancer or some other disease. So let's talk about exercise and being fit.

Exercise for Life

Essentially, there are two kinds of exercise, "aerobic" and "anaerobic." We'll tell you more about them in coming chapters, but here identify just several of their basic differences.

Aerobic exercise is longer-lasting, continuous, moderate exertion activity such as walking, jogging, swimming or bicycling. It uses oxygen, builds stamina and is often referred to as "endurance training."

Anaerobic exercise is more of a start and stop activity with short bursts of more intense effort as in weight-lifting, football and most other competitive sports. It develops muscle strength and is often called "strength training."

Going Longer With Aerobics

Common sense tells us being aerobically fit and active would encourage longer life. Research proves it. For example, a recent eight-year study of 13,000 people showed that by walking briskly for 30–60 minutes a day, death rates dropped 60% in the men and 48% in the women.[3]

Not only does a straightforward aerobic exercise such as walking extend life, it can dramatically improve its quality. Consider, for example, the cardiovascular fitness it's known to encourage.

The heart is a muscle that gets stronger with exercise. The stronger it gets the more forceful it is as a pump and the more it can move energy, oxygen and nutrients throughout the body with less effort. We feel healthier and more energetic as a result.

Now we're not talking buckets of sweat, either. In aerobic exercise such as walking the emphasis is on *longer* not *harder.* The more time you spend strutting your stuff, the more benefits you can expect. And it's worth getting out there even if you can only manage a couple of hours a week. You'll still be far less likely to have problems such as high cholesterol than non-walkers.

In one study of 3,600 people, walkers had one-half the prevalence of high cholesterol levels as those who didn't exercise. They also had significantly higher levels of HDL cholesterol.[4] Remember, HDL is the "good" cholesterol that helps clean the "bad" LDL cholesterol out of our arteries.

Aerobic exercise reduces blood-clotting, and lowers the risk of heart attack and stroke. It increases the size of arteries and lowers blood pressure.[5] Recently it's been found that aerobic exercise combined with a low-fat diet can even reverse atherosclerosis.[6]

Of course, aerobic exercise brings more than cardiovascular fitness. Studies show, for example, it increases lung capacity, reduces insulin requirements for diabetics and retards osteoporosis. It also increases blood flow to the brain for better mental functioning and alertness.[7]

But the benefit that undoubtedly caught everyone's attention is fat loss. Endurance training burns fat and helps us prevent a slew of obesity-related diseases.

According to the National Institute of Health, excess body fat is clearly associated with an increased risk of heart disease, various cancers, high blood pressure, diabetes, respiratory problems, arthritis and gallbladder disease.

It's estimated that 25% of cardiovascular disease can be attributed to excess fat and it doesn't take many extra pounds to increase our risk. Women only 15–29% over their ideal weight are thought to have an 80% higher risk of heart disease.[8]

No wonder walking is so popular. We need a simple, regular, aerobic, fat-burning activity to look and feel our best. But we should remember anaerobic exercise *also* plays an important role in our health.

Feeling Stronger With Anaerobics

Because anaerobic exercise builds muscle strength it offers very practical benefits. It makes our every day physical activities easier. Carrying groceries, changing a flat tire and shoveling snow become less a chore.

It also helps minimize injury when we slip on an icy sidewalk or stumble over toys in a dark hallway. Strength training conditions muscles, ligaments and tendons to better withstand sudden strain or sprain. The more muscle connecting our joints, the less likely we are to "throw out" a shoulder or knee.

More and more women are strength training for a similar kind of effect. It helps prevent osteoporosis, the debilitating bone-thinning disease. How does it do this?

Muscles create movement by contracting, thus pulling on the bones of our various bodyparts. For example, when you take a drink of water, the muscles of your arm and shoulder pull on your arm bones to move the glass to your mouth.

This tugging of muscle on bones seems to stimulate the bones to take in more calcium. They become stronger, harder and healthier in response to use and anaerobic exercise.

As mentioned earlier, aerobic exercise also helps prevent osteoporosis, but studies show anaerobic exercise has a greater bone-hardening effect. For example, one study found weightlifters had stronger bones than both swimmers and runners.[9] The stronger pull the muscles used to move the weight was more stimulating for the bones than simply moving bodyweight.

A final point. Strength training muscle workouts might seem an activity for the younger crowd, but improvement can be made at any age. A group of previously sedentary men with an average age of 59 were studied after 16 weeks of anaerobic exercise. Their strength increased by 45%.[10] In another study six women and four men between the ages of 86 and 96 increased their strength 174% with weight training.[11]

And those of us who have been around a while could use a little muscle-building. We need to regain what has slipped away over the years.

By mid-20's a sedentary person starts losing about a half-pound of muscle a year. The rate of loss gradually increases without us really noticing. Even if we stay at the same weight, our muscle gradually disappears to be replaced by fat.

So what's the big deal about losing a few pounds of muscle?

Body fat is burned off in aerobic muscle activity such as walking. Every decrease, no matter how small, means we become a little less efficient at burning fat. The same activity takes longer to burn the same amount of fat than it did when we had just a few more pounds of muscle.

The other side of the coin is the *more* muscle we have the *more* fat we burn. Aerobic exercise helps us burn fat; anaerobic exercise helps us build the muscle to burn it with.

Bottom Line: Exercise builds endurance and strength.

13

What About Body Fat?

Body fat and obesity have been a concern of Americans for the better part of this century. Recently, our understanding of how we get it has changed in important ways.

Old Thinking

For a long time we thought of the body as if it were a machine we learned to control. It was all a matter of eating (energy in) and activity (energy out). We were supposed to learn to maintain a balance between how many calories of energy we put in by eating and how many calories of energy we burned in daily activity.

If we put in *more* calories than we used to fuel our activities, the surplus would be stored in body fat. If we put in *less* calories than needed, our bodies would make withdrawals from their stored fat to supply the additional energy required.

In this line of reasoning those who get fat have failed to learn the balance between eating and activity. They aren't in control. They need to discipline themselves and restrict how much they eat until they find the right balance.

Such is the view that led so many to the "battle of the bulge." Usually it was a lifelong battle, a continual struggle to get the fat off and keep it off. The battle strategy was: less food (dieting) and more activity (exercising) until the bulge was defeated.

But with our limited understanding of how the body actually works, many made this a *choice* of eating less or exercising more. We assumed we could cut calories to force the body to use its stored fat for energy. *Or,* we could increase activity to burn more calories than we were eating.

Perhaps it seemed to many of us that cutting calories was somehow easier and less time-consuming than arranging for daily exercise. Whatever the reason, it was the *eat less* that really stuck in our culture with few paying much attention to the *exercise more*. Even our scientific community blamed excess body fat on overeating and emphasized dieting as the cure.

New Thinking

We now know our earlier view was an oversimplification. The body is *not* a simple machine. We had underestimated the very complex adaptive capacities of the human organism.

We misunderstood the problem of body fat and our solution of lifelong dieting wound up only making matters worse. We were wrong about how we get fat and we were wrong about how to get rid of it.

Until recently we misunderstood calories. We thought all calories were the *same*. It didn't matter whether they came from fat foods (cooking oils, butter, cheese, etc.), protein foods (fish, poultry, skim milk, etc.) or carbohydrate foods (breads, vegetables, fruits, etc.). We believed an excess of calories from *any* source would end up as body fat.

That's not how it works. Our body *uses* fat, protein, and carbohydrate calories differently and it *stores* them differently.

Fat

The body easily and efficiently saves the energy of the fat we get in our food by turning it into body fat. Body fat serves as long term storage of endurance energy, a "slow-burn" fuel. For example, if your car broke down in some isolated desert area, and you had to hike back to civilization, fat energy would keep you going.

Protein

When it comes to packing on those pounds of fat, protein is not of much concern. Protein energy is usually burned off on a daily basis for cell-building and repair and not put into long-term storage.[1]

Carbohydrate

The body is *able* to store carbohydrate energy as fat if necessary, but usually doesn't.[2] It would be a wasteful use of an important "fast-burn" fuel, "glucose." The carbohydrate energy of glucose fuel is necessary for brief, intense bursts of activity, such as lifting a heavy object out of your car trunk. Such activity burns up much of the carbohydrate energy we bring in each day by eating. Some of it is put in short-term storage in the liver and muscles as "glycogen" that the body converts into glucose when needed.

The foods we eat are *different* sources of *different* fuels our bodies use in *different* ways. A bulging waistline is stored fat that comes from the excess fat in our foods.

Studies show when you keep the amount of food you eat the same, but increase the proportion of *fat* in it, you develop body fat.[3] In other words, fat calories are the big culprits when it comes to body fat, not carbohydrate and protein calories.

Bottom Line: We get fat by eating too much fat.

14

So What Else is New?

If you're a seasoned dieter, you might wonder what all the fuss is about. After all, dieters have always had to stay away from fatty foods: all that french-fried stuff, rich desserts, ice cream, cheesy sauces.

Dieting means cutting your total calorie count. Fatty, rich foods are "calorie-dense." They have super high calories in very small packages. If you're struggling with a 1000 calories-a-day diet, you've had lots of going hungrys and growling stomachs. You'd hardly want to blow your whole day's allotment of calories with a waffles and ice cream breakfast.

An Essential Difference

In *Low-fat for Life* eating you'd likely not have the waffles and ice cream breakfast either. The calories might not bother you as much, but the *fat* certainly would. About 35% of the calories in most waffles are fat and we're talking 50–70% in most ice creams.

We keep our diet proportions to 20% or less fat, 10–15% protein and 65% or more carbohydrate. This means cutting back our fat intake from the usual 40% to less than 20% and staying about the same in terms of protein. It also means raising the carbohydrate level from 45% to more than 65%.

The essential difference, then, is we're not *cutting* calories. We're *substituting* carbohydrate calories for fat calories. We're *shifting* from high-fat/low-carbohydrate to low-fat/high-carbohydrate eating. We're *changing* from a meat and dairy emphasis to a fruit, vegetable, grain and legume (beans) emphasis.

And steady yourself while tying on your bib. You can be *Low-fat for Life* and still enjoy the taste treat of a "waffles and ice cream breakfast", but in a healthier, low-fat version. All you do is substitute our delicious low-fat waffle recipe for the conventional one. Substitute some non-fat frozen yogurt for the ice cream. And top it all off with our scrumptious Orangeberry Sauce.

Be Careful With Sugar

Now, if you're one of those folks with a gigantic sweet tooth, if you absolutely won't eat a waffle without a gallon of maple syrup poured over it, we'd better clarify something.

The healthy, nutritious carbohydrates are the *complex* carbohydrates found in fruits (Orangeberry Sauce), vegetables and grains (waffles). There are also carbohydrates on the other side of the family that, in excess, still might give us trouble. These are the *simple* carbohydrates found in sugars (e.g., maple syrup, corn syrup, honey, molasses, sorghum).

In the days of calorie-watching and dieting, we avoided sweets because they gave high calories in small packages. They didn't satisfy our hunger for their cost in calories.

Also, high sugar foods have a lot of "empty" calories. They lack vitamins, minerals and fiber. If you were cutting back on calories, you couldn't afford to spend your allotment on sweets and still have enough left to make sure of your nutritional needs.

With the understanding that body fat comes primarily from dietary fat, the calories of sugar no longer concern us in the same way—but don't go bonkers.

Questions about the relationship of sugar and body fat have not been answered to everyone's satisfaction. Some believe sugar and the artificial sweeteners affect body chemistry and increase fat storage.[1] Others argue a lack of evidence for this, and for that matter any link between sugar and body fat.[2]

The point is, if your diet is low in fat and high in complex carbohydrates, you can handle a little sugar now and then. Just take it easy. Moderation with the various sugars, syrups and artificial sweeteners is still the best rule-of-thumb.

The Big News

The really important news in all of this for those of us who tend to "pack it on" is that we get fat from eating too much fat. Carbohydrate calories are different and we can learn to keep the fat off without going hungry or giving up all our favorite taste treats.

Nearly a quarter (23%) of carbohydrate calories are spent turning them into body fat, so our bodies seldom go this route. It's much easier and cheaper storing *fat* calories. It costs only 3% of fat calories to get *them* into body fat storage.[3]

Hold out your hand. Imagine we just gave you a one-inch slice of hot, homemade bread. Let's make it our Light Wheat with our Strawberry Freezer Jam spread on it. Get the picture? This kind of eating can now be a regular, guilt-free part of your life.

The hot, homemade bread *won't* make you fat. The strawberry jam *won't* make you fat. Too many pats of butter or
margarine *will.*

A baked potato of 100 calories and 100 calories of french
fries are *not* the same. It's not the mashed potatoes, but the
butter, gravy grease and sour cream, that's putting the lard in
your bucket. Pizza and spaghetti are great, but gobs of high-
fat cheese and all those sausages will make waddles out of
twinkle toes.

Bottom Line: Carbohydrates are filling not fattening...
Wilma let's whip up some waffles!

15

What About Dieting?

Don't diet! Don't get on the dieting "roller-coaster" ever again. It just doesn't work.

Dieting Doesn't Work

If you've dieted, you already know this. Sure, you get a temporary weight loss when you starve yourself for a while. But as soon as you try to eat normally again you gain the fat right back.

So you diet again, but each round the fat is more difficult to lose and easier to gain back. And each round you're getting fatter on less food. Seems impossible, but it isn't.

Studies at Penn State showed that after animals lost weight on a low-calorie diet, they gained it right back. It then took them twice as long to lose it a second time on the same low-calorie diet and less than a third of the time to gain it back again.

You've heard those stories that sound like something right out of Ripley's "Believe it or Not." Like a 280-pound man who gets fat if he eats more than 1000 calories a day. Or a 130-pound woman who can't eat more than 600 calories a day without packing it on.

What's going on here? Surprisingly, studies show many fat people *do* eat less than thin people.[1] Through low-calorie dieting they have changed their body chemistry and require less food to maintain body weight.

Dieting Triggers the Starvation Response

The human body continually adapts to change and protects life with intricate systems and priorities. When you cut back too far on calories, your body slows down its fat-burning (metabolism) to protect its stored fat. It may slow metabolism to less than half its usual rate.

Why? Because your body "thinks" the dieting is a *famine*. It rushes to protect you from *starvation*. It slows you down, makes you feel tired more easily.

If you *do* manage to lose a few pounds, as soon as you try to return to "normal" eating, your body will "pack it on" again. It stays in its conserving, low rate of metabolism to get some fat back in the "savings account" as soon as possible. It "remembers" the famine and wants "insurance" fat in case you encounter another one—*which you will.*

As soon as you see the flab returning, you grit your teeth and start dieting again. Your body hunkers down in this new famine to protect you with the "starvation response." You are at war with yourself.

The starvation response is a body adaptation that evolved to protect the lives of our ancestors in seasonal food shortages and famines. The fat stores of slow-burn, endurance energy and slowed activity are as natural a response for us as hibernating is for bears.

When you cut back calories, you may be imagining yourself in one of those TV beach scenes with trim bodies frolicking in the surf. Your body doesn't see the commercial. Instead it senses danger and responds in the way it always has. Sure, it may let go of some fat at first, but then it will hang on to the rest in fierce determination—it *is* protecting your *life* after all.

Dieting Shrinks the Fat-burning Furnace

As part of its life-saving strategy, your body will do something else that really packs a whollop in the battle of the bulge. It burns *muscle* tissue rather than deplete *fat* stores. In some cases up to 75% of the weight lost in dieting is muscle.

In its starvation response your body makes metabolic, hormonal and enzymatic changes to conserve the endurance energy stored in its fat. Muscles are fat-burning furnaces. They burn fat calories even when at rest. The more muscle you have the more fat you burn.

To confront a famine, the human body wants to hang on to the endurance energy of fat, *not* muscle. It wants to *stop* fat-burning muscle activity. Sacrificing muscle tissue is an understandable, life-preserving strategy in the starvation response.

And here's the combination punch—when your body burns muscle to protect its fat, it's also doing what? That's right, it's *shrinking* your future fat-burning capacity!

As soon as you return to pre-diet eating, your body tries to replenish its fat stores as quickly as possible. And it's an easier job now. By getting rid of some of that muscle, you're burning *less* fat. So back comes the bulge and back comes the diet and out goes even *more* of that fat-burning muscle.

Lower metabolism and less muscle means you eat *less* and get *fatter*. With each round of dieting it gets worse. How can you possibly win the battle of the bulge?

Bottom Line: Dieting does more harm than good.

16

Then How Do We Get Rid of Fat?

To let go of its stores of fat, your body must have security. It must "know" it doesn't need the protection of extra fat.

Eat Enough Food

Food is energy, fuel for activity. Appetite is the way your body lets you know it's close to "empty" and asks that you "fuel up." When you respond by eating an ample amount of high-energy, carbohydrate food, you are telling your body the environment is life-supporting and abundant. Your body is secure in this happy state of affairs and you feel fullness and satisfaction.

How much will you be eating each day to let your body know all systems are secure on your end of the business? We'll give you some rules-of-thumb to figure this out later in Chapter 26.

Basically, you'll determine your target weight and the approximate daily calories you need to maintain this weight.

This figure, then, is what you use to guide the amount of food you eat each day.

You might hurry the process a little by eating fewer calories, but be careful. If the starvation response kicks in, you've got trouble. Sooner or later you'll need to bring those calories up to the right level. It'll be difficult doing this without picking up a few pounds if you hurried the process by cutting back too far on the calories.

Train to Your Target Weight

Set your sights on a target weight and train yourself to it. When you achieve your goal, you'll already be doing what you need to keep it.

Be patient. The excess fat pounds will gradually disappear. The process must be gradual if your body is to remain secure. If you're losing more than a pound a week, you're gambling against the starvation response. Remember, you're training your body and eating habits toward the weight you want. Take your time and do it right—once and for all.

The point is to get *enough* calories of the right *kind*. Make sure your body has its necessary protein (10–15%), lots of carbohydrates (over 65%), and keep fat calories under 20%.

Box 6: The 20% Solution

Researchers from the University of Vermont recently reported that chronically obese patients, who failed to lose weight on a variety of reducing programs, lost 20 to 30 pounds over the course of a year when they limited fat intake to **20%** of total calories.

Dept. of Health and Human Services
Publication No. (FDA) 92-1188

With this low-fat/high-carbohydrate eating you'll be surprised how full and satisfied you can feel while still trimming down. A gram of carbohydrate has four calories and a gram of fat has nine calories. This means when you eat fruits, vegetables, breads, pasta, rice and beans, you are actually getting food that weighs more than twice as much for the same number of calories. When it comes to body security this is a very desirable weight gain.

Drink Enough Water

While we're talking about body security and training yourself, there's something else that you can do. It's seldom mentioned, but very important. Drink plenty of water!

Water plays a critical role in getting rid of fat and keeping it off. Studies have shown a decrease in water will cause fat deposits to increase. An increase in water, on the other hand, will actually reduce fat deposits.[1]

With ample supplies of water, the liver converts fat into usable energy for our muscles. If water is limited, fat-burning is shut down and available water is diverted to priority jobs such as helping the kidneys cleanse the body of poisons.

To keep things running smoothly, the average person needs about two quarts of water a day. If you're trying to lose fat, your liver will be putting in some overtime, so better make that three quarts. Yes, you'll be visiting the bathroom more often at first, but you won't have to go as often once your body adjusts to its new supply of water.

Three quarts seems like quite a bit doesn't it? Sort of like sloshing your way into shape. When you spread it out over the day it really isn't a big deal. Recyle a milk jug or similar container. Mark the three-quart level on it. Fill it and drink it. Don't whine.

Help a Lifelong Friend

In the *Low-fat for Life* program, you're working with and supporting your body. This isn't a battle anymore. No more tricks and pills and bizarre dieting programs.

You're trying to understand and help a lifelong friend do a job that you very much want done. Your body works for you night and day. You want it to have job security, good working conditions and ample supplies of healthy food and water.

In these conditions your body will be secure enough to give up its stores of fat for your muscles to use in fat-burning activity.

Bottom Line: With the right eating and plenty of water, we get rid of fat with fat-burning activity.

17

What is Fat-burning Activity?

W e used to think calories were calories and exercise was exercise. If we got too many calories by overeating and/ or didn't exercise enough to burn those calories, our bodies would store the surplus calories in fat.

We were wrong. We now understand fat calories and carbohydrate calories are *different*. Excess fat calories are stored in body fat. Excess carbohydrate calories are stored in glycogen.

Both body fat and glycogen furnish fuel for the body. *Both* are burned in the muscles and used as energy for muscle activity.

But fat calories and carbohydrate calories burn *differently*. The body mixes them in *different* proportions to fit the requirements of *different* kinds of activity.

Aerobic Activity Burns Fat

Body fat needs *oxygen* to burn. With oxygen available it becomes a slow-burning, endurance fuel for moderate exertion activity over longer periods of time.

Less taxing, but continuous, long-lasting activities, such as jogging or bicycling, allow our bodies time to bring in oxygen for burning body fat as fuel. That's why we call these activities "aerobic" which means "with oxygen." In a brisk afternoon walk we'd likely be chugging along with more than 60% fat in our fuel mix.

Glycogen *doesn't* need oxygen to burn. On demand it instantly turns to glucose, a fast-burning, power fuel for brief periods of high exertion activity.

Vigorous, start and stop activities such as football or tennis rely on glucose as fuel because it will furnish energy before our bodies can get oxygen to our muscles. Such activities are "anaerobic" which means "without oxygen." In a strenuous weight-training session we'd probably be burning 70% or more glucose in our fuel mix.

Stay in the Aerobic Range

Aerobic exercise is often called "endurance training." It is an activity where you exert yourself *somewhat* but not a lot. Given the time, it is an activity you should be able to continue indefinitely. When walking, swimming or rowing, your heart and breathing rates go up a bit, level out and then stay there throughout the activity period.

What if you exert yourself too much? Your body will respond by changing the fuel mix. It will turn down the fat and turn up the glucose. Why? Because increasing the intensity of effort past a certain point begins to decrease the oxygen available for fat-burning.

This, of course, is not something you want to happen when you're out there in your sneakers and sweatsuit trying your best to fry a little flab. It's important, then, that you keep your activity in the "aerobic range" for maximum fat-burning.

In Chapter 24 we'll suggest exercise routines and will tell you about a precise way to monitor yourself and stay in the aerobic range. If you think about it, you'll see you already have a built-in gauge for a quick reading—your breath.

You *do* breathe a little harder in aerobic exercise, but you shouldn't get *out* of breath. You sometimes get a little tired, but shouldn't be exhausted. If you can talk to someone and be understood, or if you can sing, you're still burning fat.

If, on the other hand, your speech is gasping or your singing is pretty ragged, you're not burning much fat anymore. When you have trouble catching your breath, what's happening? Right, your body is getting less oxygen. And what does it do? Right again, it holds back on the fat and hauls in more glucose.

Strut Your Stuff Long Enough

The shifting proportions of fat and glucose in your fuel mix are part of the reason you need to continue an aerobic exercise for at least 20 minutes to get any fat-burning benefit and why it would be best if you would get out there an hour a day.

When you first start an aerobic exercise you are burning a lot of glucose in your fuel mix. After you continue at a steady pace for a while and oxygen is getting to your muscles, the fat kicks in. If you're going to do it, this is the time to do it. The longer you move now, the more fat you burn.

Remember, you're training for endurance and you'll find some nice rewards for the extra time and effort.

We used to think of exercise only in terms of calories burned during activity. There are about 3500 calories in a pound of fat. We generally burn about 350 calories in an hour of brisk walking. With everything else kept the same, this would mean 10 days to walk off a pound, right?

We now know differently. In earlier chapters we talked about how low-calorie dieting *lowers* the metabolic rate. Well, regular aerobic exercise *raises* the metabolic rate. It turns up the thermostat on that metabolic furnace of yours so you not only burn fat at a higher level *while* you exercise but for several hours afterward.

There's an "afterburn" that continues to burn fat at a higher metabolic rate even if you are resting in a hammock after your morning walk. It's said in some cases this after-burn can last up to 12 hours.[1]

And be sure to strut your stuff long enough. In a recent study of men riding stationary bicycles for differing lengths of time, it was found that the afterburn continued over 2 hours after a 30-minute ride, nearly 3 ½ hours after a 45 minute ride and over 7½ hours after a 60-minute ride.[2]

Aerobic exercise *changes* your body chemistry. It increases the enzymes known to help muscles burn fat more efficiently. Endurance athletes have been found to have greater numbers of these fat-burning enzymes than non-exercisers. After several months of regular aerobic exercise the body tunes its metabolic system to burn fat more efficiently—nifty.

Aerobic and Anaerobic Work Together

Aerobic exercise is fat-burning activity and would seem the answer to excess body fat. In truth, both aerobic *and* anaerobic exercise are important for getting rid of fat. They work together to do the job right.

It isn't what we *burn* in anaerobic exercise that helps in the body fat battle, it's what we *train*. Anaerobic exercise is often called "strength training." It is exercise that *increases* muscle strength and size.

Fat is burned in muscle. The more muscle you have, the more fat you burn with the same amount of aerobic activity. Strength training, then, increases your *capacity* to burn fat. It gives you a *bigger* fat-burning furnace.

In Part Three we'll show you how to get started with a strength training routine you practice for 20 minutes three times a week. With more muscle you'll burn more fat in your daily walk. You'll burn more fat while sneaking a little catnap. You'll burn more fat simply being alive.

Bottom Line: Aerobic exercise is fat-burning activity. Anaerobic exercise increases our fat-burning capacity.

18

In a Nutshell, What Do We Do to Be Healthier?

Evolution designed the human body over the millions of years we were hunters and gatherers and we're sabotaging our health with what we eat and the way we live in 20th century America.[1]

Designed for Hunting and Gathering

Science tells us the way our bodies work hasn't changed in the slightest for over 40,000 years. We are fully the same humans now as we were then. Our physiology, psychology, biology and chemistry remain the same. In effect, then, we remain hunters and gatherers but lead very different lives.

Our early ancestors lived shorter lives, perhaps half as long as they are now. Life in the wild had many opportunities for accident and injury. Childbirth complications and germ-spread illnesses also took a heavy toll.

But in other ways we were *healthier* then. We knew times of hunger, but usually had plenty. We foraged a wide variety of fruits and vegetables, roots, tubers, seeds and beans that

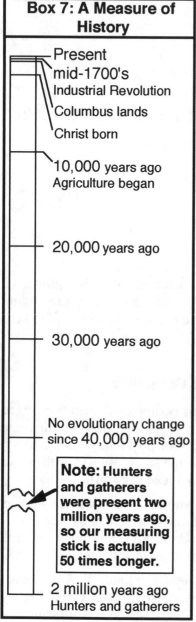

Box 7: A Measure of History

Present
mid-1700's
Industrial Revolution
Columbus lands
Christ born

10,000 years ago
Agriculture began

20,000 years ago

30,000 years ago

No evolutionary change
since 40,000 years ago

Note: Hunters and gatherers were present two million years ago, so our measuring stick is actually 50 times longer.

2 million years ago
Hunters and gatherers

were rich in vitamins, minerals and fiber. The wild game we hunted was very high in protein while much lower in fat than today's domesticated meat animals.

Our lives were vigorous, active. We were physically stronger. Our muscularity and fitness as hunters and gatherers were what we'd now expect only of our top athletes.

Modified With Farming

Our high level of nutritional health declined somewhat with the arrival of agriculture 10,000 years ago. We narrowed the variety of our foods considerably and subsisted more on the cereal grains we had learned to cultivate.

While grains helped furnish necessary fiber, they limited the range of our vitamins and minerals and lessened our protection against infectious diseases. Though we were hard working and strong, we had less low-fat protein from wild game and fish than our hunting and gathering ancestors. According to some anthropologists our average height decreased about four inches because of this.[2]

Changed With Industry

The Industrial Revolution brought dramatic changes. First, increased protein from domestic meats and dairy products is said to have helped us regain the height lost during the agricultural period.

Since 1900 we have also greatly reduced deaths from infectious diseases. With immunizations, medical treatments, sanitary conditions and various public health advances, we live longer, safer lives.

But *now* we suffer and die from *degenerative* diseases that were unknown to our ancestors throughout history.

Heart attacks, strokes, cancers, diabetes and hypertension now account for 75% of our deaths. These are *lifestyle* diseases. They come from the foods we now eat, the way we live with the abundance, comfort and convenience of modern, industrial life.

We Can Change Again

- We've been filling up on high-fat foods and not eating anywhere enough complex carbohydrates to get the health-promoting fiber, vitamins and minerals we need.

- We've been sitting too much and not exercising enough to keep our strength and vitality.

- Our lives are rushed and stressful and we seldom take time to relax.

We now know our habits of living are out of sync with our biology. The human body simply wasn't designed for the lifestyle we have thrust upon it.

But the nutshell point in this is that we can *change*. We can *prevent* our lifestyle diseases with an integrated program of nutrition, exercise and meditation. We can change with the daily routines of the *Low-fat for Life* program where we:

- Eat for the nutrients our bodies need to protect us, repair us and fuel our activity.

- Exercise for the strength and endurance to meet the challenges of an active life.

- Meditate to balance the stress and strain of modern life with regular periods of inner calm and relaxation.

Bottom Line: We can make the low-fat change.

Part Two:

Strategies for Dealing With Common Obstacles

Dominant values in our culture, entrenched personal habits, heckling friends and self-doubt may interfere with your attempts to practice a low-fat lifestyle. In this second part of the book we suggest general strategies and approaches that should help you get on with the business of change.

19

Obstacle: Our High-fat Culture

Most of us begin to think about eating differently and exercising more when we're out of shape. We don't like the way we look and feel. We want to burn off some fat, get some of our wind back, strengthen our heart, unplug our arteries and avoid as much disease down the line as possible. These are understandable and legitimate concerns, but our individual attempts to lead healthier lives are important for other reasons as well. They spark the desire to change in others and influence a culture that is clearly in need of some healthy changes.

Our Love of Convenience

Much has happened to us in the 20th century. Our country became the most powerful, industrial nation in the world. Our wealth brought conveniences we had never imagined. Sadly, these conveniences had hidden costs that robbed us of more than dollars. American life has become fat, sedentary, stressful and toxic.

Convenience has been our indicator of success. It let us and others know we were "making it." It was what we were working for. It was the prize, the "brass ring" we reached for every chance we got.

Each labor-saving convenience gave us a little of that royal power of command. A young and optimistic America wanted "all the modern conveniences" for everyone. Even ordinary folks could aspire to a "life fit for a king or queen" in America.

Convenience would do our bidding. Whether a kitchen gadget or diaper service, convenience meant something or someone would do our work for us.

The Costs of Convenience

The American dream of convenience grew up to become one of our worst nightmares. The convenient way of life we created is a disaster to our biology as humans and a disaster to the biological community in which we live.

Recent changes in our eating habits are central to the problem. From the early 1900's on, we turned away from a diet that was predominantly fresh produce, whole grains and foods rich in fiber. We came to prefer instead, a diet high in fats, sugars and the processed convenience foods produced by a rapidly expanding food industry.

This change led to the human diseases we've talked about in earlier chapters. It's also played an important part in our disappearing rain forests, the greenhouse effect, soil erosion, polluted surface and ground waters, acid rains and just about any symptoms of planetary disease you can think of.

When we thought a high-protein diet was the best guarantee of health, domesticating meat animals became a convenient way to get it. They turned our plant foods into meat protein. They did the work for us.

We now know we should have stayed with eating more of the plant foods ourselves. Eating too much high-fat meat sabotages our digestion and metabolism. And the demand we have created for meat sabotages our global ecology as well.

Tropical forests everywhere are being destroyed to provide land for meat production. By 1983 two decades of growth in beef exports reduced Costa Rica's tropical forests by 83 percent.[1]

In our own country more than half the 50 million acres of grassland opened for cattle grazing by the U.S. Forest Service is now considered to be in poor condition.[2]

Livestock on factory farms even contribute to the "greenhouse effect." Cattle, for example, produce a lot of methane gas. So do those huge piles of manure in feed lots. If you include the fuels burned to raise livestock, it turns out that a steak increases global warming about as much as driving 25 miles in an average American car.[3]

Farmland that once produced local food staples in poor countries such as Mexico, now grow grain for meats only the wealthy can afford.

We were wrong. There's more to the good life than money and the convenience it buys. We need to be alive and healthy in a healthy world if we are to enjoy it.

We simply cannot control, exploit and destroy the world around us without destroying ourselves in the process. Like it or not we are dependent on the natural world. We are connected to it, a part of it.

Health is Connection

Physical, social and psychological health are found in our relationship to the natural world. The natural world that surrounds us is the same world as that within us. It operates according to the same basic rules of healthy life—but we have lost our sense of this.

For 100,000 generations we were hunters and gatherers leading active, healthy lives. Our interactions with the natural world had the same sense of balance, connection and conservation anthropologists find in those indigenous peoples who continue traditional hunting and gathering practices.

The food we ate supported our physical health. The way in which we produced it supported our social and psychological health as well.

In family and tribal life harvesting plants, fishing and hunting were socially shared activities. In them we cooperated with others of our kind and learned the importance of social ties.

At the same time, our ways of gathering food encouraged in each of us a sense of connection to the rest of the natural world. In them we directly experienced taking life to nourish our own. Our daily activity continually reminded us that the life we took was the same kind of life we possessed. We understood "ecology" in our everyday experience of the give and take of nature. The life we ended in a plant or animal and took into ourselves was passed back to the plants and animals in our wastes and in our death.

Each day our work was immersed in a world where life was something shared. Life was something passed around, something all participated in. Each took its turn at this something called life.

All that has changed.

Severed Connections

Though industrial life has been our cultural bias for only 10 generations, we no longer see and relate to the natural world as we had for all our previous history.

We are modern, educated and advantaged, but we have lost awareness of our connections to the rest of our biological community.

Few of us directly experience taking life to sustain our own. Seldom does the magnitude of slaughter behind all those buckets of chicken and mountains of hamburger even dawn upon us. Those of us who *do* hunt, fish or garden view it as sport, hobby or leisure activity.

We no longer see our return to nature in our wastes and death. Instead we use tremendous amounts of water for the convenience of toilet-flushing our sewage into some distant and hopefully unseen place. We embalm our dead and lock them in vaults preventing nature from reclaiming them in decay.

Our solution to the eternal dilemma of having to kill in order to live is to pay for the convenience of having others do the killing for us.

But convenience always has its costs. By delegating our responsibility for producing food to industry, we have lost important intuitive connections and understandings.

No longer directly experiencing the taking of life to continue our own, nor even seeing others do it for us, we have lost the conserving, "primitive" inclination to take only what is needed from the natural world.

Free and Fat

Cut off, unaware and unaffected, we freed ourselves to indulge modern appetites which led *away* from health. We freed ourselves to overuse and disrespect the natural world which is the *source* of our health.

With the wealth, comfort and labor-saving convenience of industrialism we freed ourselves from the food-related tasks we thought were only time-consuming drudgeries.

At the same time we also freed ourselves from deciding the *quality* of what we ate. The food industry would decide that for us.

Now, what's the goal of the food industry? *Profit.* And what's been giving a lot of trouble to us and a lot of profit to the food industry? *Fat.*

Meat and dairy production in our food factories created huge amounts of surplus fat. Fat, then, became a very cheap food additive and the industry eagerly cultivated our taste for it.

Advances in refrigeration meant fatty foods that before would have quickly turned rancid, could now be kept for long periods of time.

Instead of turning animals out to pasture, we began keeping them in holding pens and feed lots. Unable to exercise, they got fatter, faster. Fat deposits "marbled" their unused muscles and made their meat so soft and tender it "melted in your mouth."

And isn't fatty meat convenient? It saves us so much labor in chewing.

We learned to efficiently get oil from seeds, nuts and palm trees to support an increasing demand for fried foods. Next came the convenience of fast food restaurants. They deep-fried everything, increasing its fat content—and ours.

Of course, our health problems run deeper than the effect of *what* we are eating. They include *how* we are eating.

The Ties That Bind

Health is in connection and participation. Studies show those who have close ties with others live longer and have fewer health problems than those who don't. For example, a study of 4700 men and women over a nine-year period found significantly higher death rates among those with fewer friends and relatives, less church or other support group participation.[4]

Health is not self-absorbed preoccupation. It is shared with others, it is communal. We have lost our ability to care for ourselves and we have lost our sense of community and caring for others.

Caring and attention are conditions of health, more powerful than we might suspect. Researchers studying the effects of feeding a high-fat/cholesterol diet to rabbits found the atherosclerosis they expected. They also found something they didn't expect.

One group of the test rabbits had 60% less atherosclerotic change. This, of course, astonished the researchers, but they finally found an explanation. One of the investigators had regularly taken rabbits from this group out of their cages, petted and talked to them.

They set up another study. This time they kept two groups of rabbits on the same high-fat/cholesterol diet and treated them exactly the same *except* one group was again petted, taken from their cages and talked to. The 60% difference in atherosclerosis again resulted.

Skeptical researchers at another university repeated the experiment and came up with the same results.[5]

In earlier times our physical, psychological and social health was rooted in our everyday activity with each other and the rest of the natural world. But in modern life we have progressively separated ourselves from both.

We have, to a large extent, even abandoned the daily activity of eating together in our families. Different members
of the family now eat different foods. Cereal boxes, pop-
tarts and microwave muffins have replaced the sit-down
breakfast in our "eat and run" lives.

Working parents have less time to prepare meals. Convenience foods, pre-prepared carry-in foods from deli-
counters, delivered pizzas and fast food carry-outs are the
fastest growing section of the food market.

In changing from eating with others to eating with a TV,
we are losing more than another "community" ritual. The
daily activity of food sharing affirms social ties found to be
so important to our health. Studies repeatedly show socially
connected individuals are physically healthier than loners.[6]

And What About Our Kids?

Children benefit a great deal from family meals. Coming
together, sharing food and caring for each other help develop emotional security. Even the simple habit of sitting down
with the family communicates an important message to a
child. Having a rightful place at the table translates into a
later confidence about having a rightful place in the world.

Psychologists have found the interactions between kids
and parents at meals are also very important. Studies show
the higher the quality of interactions, the more they enhance
a child's cognitive development and school achievement.[7]

In the absence of family meals and the influence of parents who understand nutritional needs, we are passing the
unhealthy legacy of convenience onto our kids.

They're hooked you know. They've been eating fast
foods from early on and the diseases of high-fat eating are
showing up in younger and younger children. Obesity in 6–

11 year olds has jumped more than 50% since the 1960's and roughly half of school aged kids can't perform a simple fitness test.[8]

It won't help to rush out and lynch some guy bagging french fries at the corner eatery. In one way or another we were all in on this. *We* wanted the convenience. *We* wanted a food industry to produce our foods. *We* traded the family meal table for a TV tray.

Convenient Health

For years we've denied what we've been doing to ourselves. We rationalized and procrastinated while the evidence kept piling up. But finally it's settled in. More and more of us across the country now know better. We know it's time to make healthy changes.

If our love of convenience helped lead us into trouble, it can also be a strategy to help lead us out. In a multitude of small ways we can arrange to make health convenient.

By keeping fresh fruit on hand we make healthy snacks more convenient. By parking the car in a new location we make a daily walk (to and from the job) more convenient.

Packing a lunch will make it more convenient than the fast food counter and free enough time to make a noon-hour meditation more convenient.

Windowsill herbs, a patio garden of lettuce, radishes and cherry tomatoes, a jar of sprouts on the kitchen counter, a log of shiitake mushrooms near the back door—all make healthy salads convenient.

Canning some locally grown tomatoes in the Fall will make terrific sauces, ketchups and salsas convenient all year long.

A stationary bicycle next to the TV makes "aerobic news" a convenient idea.

We are all inclined to follow a path of least resistance until it becomes habit. To acquire healthy habits, then, make healthy choices as convenient as possible.

Strategy: Making health convenient.

20

Obstacle: High-fat Habits

The essential activity of the *Low-fat for Life* program is the daily practice of eating, exercise and meditation routines. This activity establishes conditions favorable to increased health.

But initially, expect to hear plenty from your old habits. Obviously, they'll want you to do things the way you always have and will remind you of this every chance they get. Consistent practice will let them know you mean business and they'll respond by changing into the healthy new habits you want...but seldom without a fuss.

Creatures of Habit

More than most of us care to admit, we are creatures of habit. We fill our lives with them. They work hard for us and free us from having to think through everything we do.

Skillfully, habits drive our cars through rush-hour traffic while we gaze out the window and plan for some coming event or play back our lunch conversation with Harriet a few more times.

But there's another side to this handy little service. Once they're around for a while, habits get very persistent about discharging their duties. Getting them to *stop* becomes a real challenge. It takes effort and concentration to hold them back. If you're distracted, even for a minute, one will jump right up and do itself.

Evicting Habits

It would be nice if we could evict unwanted habits with a little "goodbye and good riddance" determination. Unfortunately, only the very small, very recent or seldom used habits would even consider leaving by simple request.

Troublesome, long-haul habits dig in for the duration. No matter how we go about serving notice, it'll take jackhammers and dynamite to send them packing.

Ever quit smoking? Then you know what it's like trying to get rid of a jackhammer habit. You'll swear it's gone forever. Then, something or other will upset you emotionally and..."Hey, who stuck the cigarette in my mouth?"

When you think about it, smoking is a fairly straightforward proposition. It's a distinct activity without easy substitutions. Chewing gum, even the stuff with nicotine in it, is hardly satisfying for those who enjoy the experience of inhaling smoke into their lungs.

So the range of choices on what to do about smoking is narrow. You smoke or you don't smoke. You smoke more or you smoke less. You continue or quit. If you decide to quit, you have to ask a very old habit to *stop,* to hit the road. You don't want it ever to do itself again. A rough goodbye to say the least.

Changing Habits

Low-fat for Life means working for healthy changes. It means working with habits. And let's face it, those afflicted with frequent "Big Mac Attacks" and "chronic couchpotatoitis" have habits of the jackhammer variety like smoking, but they can be dealt with differently.

To quit smoking you *stop* a habit. Eating to be healthier means eating *different* foods. You aren't asking your crew of habits to *stop* eating, but to change *what* they're eating.

With substituting, "Big Mac Attacks" can be changed into "Turkey Burger Tremors." A "couch potato" may continue to love TV, but by peddling a stationary bike through a few programs each day, can change into a "lean machine."

Sitting less, and exercising more, means *changing* habits. Getting out of bed a little earlier each morning to meditate, means *changing* habits.

You're not asking them to stop doing themselves, but to modify themselves. You're asking them to adapt to a new agenda. Emphasis shifts from *not doing* something to *doing* something.

Doing Something

In the *Low-fat for Life* program you're asking your habits to help you *do* something that you sincerely believe will benefit everyone engaged in the business of being you.

And *doing* something always seems a lot easier than *not doing* something.

Have you ever tried *not doing* the "white bear?" In the next two minutes do *not* think of a white polar bear. Do *not* picture a white bear in your mind. Keep that white bear *out* of your thoughts for two minutes.

Now, try *doing* something. Follow this lead and continue imagining for two minutes. It's a nice day and you're on a walk with a friend. You come upon a stretch of abandoned railroad track and decide to "walk the rail" like when you were kids. At first your balance is a little off, but soon you can go for long stretches. Imagine yourself with your arms outstretched, putting one foot ahead the other, showing off your childhood skill to a good friend.

Obviously there's more to it when you're changing habits, but you get the point. It's easier to imagine the rail walking than not to imagine the bear.

Doing the new thing, paying attention to it, is the best way to deal with even the most stubborn crew of habits. When you hold your attention on a new circumstance, they'll work like crazy to get things in some kind of order again.

You'll still hear some grumbling, but it'll quiet down if you don't pay too much attention—"Hey guys, will you keep it down a bit, I'm trying to *do* something here."

The Goggles Experiment

Charles Tart describes an experiment that demonstrates the power of a new circumstance to transform even our most fundamental habits. In the experiment, people wear special goggles that turn things upside down and reverse the right and left.[1]

At first, wearing them makes even ordinary, everyday tasks confusing and difficult. You have to watch everything you do very closely, because your old habits no longer work for you in the new circumstances.

If you see something on your right that you want to pick up, you must *think* to reach to your left. If you're distracted by something and stop paying attention, your old habits will do the reaching and WHAP, you just knocked a glass of orange juice across the room.

Surprisingly, after a few days of wearing the goggles, things no longer appear upside down and sideways. You are able to reach for things automatically again and don't have to *think* before every move.

You have adapted. You have responded to the requirements of new circumstances. You have established habits for living in the land of goggles.

What happens when you take the goggles off again? You guessed it. Now things actually seem cockeyed *without* them. For a time you have to be careful again until your old habits return.

The Force of Habit

The goggles experiment reminds us of the remarkable force of adaptation, the "force of habit" within each of us. It is built-in and automatically available whenever we encounter a new situation.

It will help us make important life changes if we have a mind to "stick with it." New habits will take hold if we patiently "keep the goggles on" through a sometimes difficult and clumsy period of transition.

Many people don't give their habit-forming capacity a chance. They don't stick with things. They give up. They "take the goggles off." They refuse to put up with the unsteadiness they feel while old habits try to pick up new routines.

Over and over they return to the old way. Over and over they "take the goggles off" until *this* becomes their habit. With it, they'll come to resist even the smallest changes.

They'll cling to the stability of old habits and severely limit their life experiences. They'll become a "slave to their habits."

Aim the Force of Habit

Others learn to work *with* the force of habit, to use it as a tool for living. They look for opportunities to flex this terrific capacity to learn, to adapt to new conditions and to make the strange familiar.

They become skillful at *aiming* the force of habit toward goals. They learn to set their mind to something and *practice* patiently while habits catch on to new routines. With practice things get easier and easier. And there's something you can do to make sure the easiers come faster. Consistently practice your eating, exercise *and* meditation routines. Don't slack off on any of them.

Some people think its okay to skimp on exercise. Others think the meditation stuff doesn't really do all that much. They're wrong!

A Synergistic Program

Eating, exercise and meditation routines fit together as interactive components in a system for training healthy habits.

Together, eating, exercise and meditation routines train mind and body habits simultaneously. Each area of activity energizes the others. They have beneficial effects on each other. They "cooperate" with each other to become far more than they could as separate activities. They are "synergistic."

Continuing work on *all* routines means whatever work you do in one area amplifies important changes taking place in the other two. In short, you're getting a lot more WHUMP for your effort.

In some ways the impact of eating, exercise and meditation routines on each other is obvious. For example, we know food is fuel for our bodies. It therefore makes sense that "high-octane" carbohydrate foods would give us more energy and increase our enthusiasm for physical exercise.

It *also* makes sense that fat foods turn us into couch potatoes.

Why do you want to nap after a high-fat meal? When fat hits your bloodstream, blood cells stick to each other and clump up. These clumps slow the flow of blood. Your brain and the various tissues and organs of your body receive less nutrients and oxygen.[2] You feel drained of energy and that couch pulls like a magnet.

And get this! Studies of appetite and food cravings show *dieting* increases our desire for high-fat foods. Know what decreases it? *Exercise!*[3] People who exercise regularly come to *prefer* the taste of high-carbohydrate foods.[4] Exercise actually changes our appetite.

A Few Suprises

How could it be that dieting and exercise would affect our food preferences? In earlier chapters we talked about what happens when we go on very low-calorie diets to lose weight. Our bodies come back with a "starvation response." They experience our dieting as a famine. To protect us from starving they turn up our appetite for the endurance fuel, fat. At the same time they shut down our fat-burning metabolism and get very stingy with our energy levels.

An "exercise response" works the same way, but in a different direction. A fit and routinely exercised body, experiencing ample supplies of food and the requirements of muscle exertion, "wants" the "high-octane" fuel of complex carbohydrates and turns up our taste buds accordingly.

So when we exercise, we're training more than muscles. We're even training our appetites. We'll then *want* to have the nutritious foods that support the active, energetic lifestyle we *also* want.

And at the same time we're synergistically training our emotions.

Studies show regular exercise promotes healthy emotions as well as bodies. It decreases anxiety and depression and increases self-esteem.[5] People who exercise feel better, more energetic. They have more vitality and their ordinary, everyday tasks seem easier to accomplish. Problems don't get them down as much because they have enough energy to work them through. They feel more competent at the job of living. They're happier.

Where does the extra energy come from? Exercise makes us more efficient energy *producers*.

Energy is created by chemical action in the "mitochondria" of our muscle cells. The bigger and more numerous our mitochondria, the more bursts of energy and "second winds" we feel throughout each day. And exercise increases our mitochondria.

Exercise also boosts energy by improving blood circulation and lung capacity. More oxygenated blood is pumped to the muscles and nervous system. And like blowing on hot coals, more oxygen means more fire! More oxygen means more fuel burned and more energy available.

The oxygen levels in our blood also affect our mental functioning. Studies often report decreases in memory, intelligence and perceptual judgement with aging. What's happening? Gradual increases in clogged arteries and sedentary living decreases oxygen to the brain. Understandably, aerobic (oxygen) exercise brings significant improvement and may prevent or reverse mental slowdown.[6] It also benefits younger as well as older folks. Researchers have found that regardless of age, active and fit individuals have higher intelligence scores than "unfit" individuals.[7]

Exercise also has a synergistic relationship with meditation for managing stress. Both stress and sedentary living create hormone imbalances. Sedentary people thus have higher than normal fight-or-flight hormones (e.g., adrenalin) in their blood.

Exercise is known to balance the body's hormone system, "tuning" it to more efficiently deal with the challenges of stress. With regular exercise a person both *reacts* more quickly to a stress situation and *relaxes* more quickly when it's over.[8]

Other research tells us certain kinds of exercise also stimulate the release of brain chemicals called "endorphins." It is thought these chemicals elevate our mood, make us feel happy and self-satisfied.[9] They give us the natural "high" runners talk about and speed up our getting the "habit" of exercise.

But when it comes to getting the habit of exercise, or *any* healthy habits for that matter, *meditation* is the real powerhouse.

The Healthy Habit-maker

Studies show meditators are able to form habits more quickly than non-meditators.[10] Meditation increases our ability to work with the force of habit and aim it where we want.

In experiments where loud, distracting noises are repeated at certain intervals, meditators are significantly faster at establishing a habit of "not hearing" the disrupting sound.

Even without meditation, we all have this ability to form a habit of "not hearing." If you moved next door to an emergency hospital, you'd eventually sleep through the night without noticing ambulance sirens. Your habit would automatically shut these disturbances off before they got to your conscious awareness. Meditators are simply *faster* and more effective at forming a habit such as this.

Meditation not only helps us establish healthy habits in eating and exercise, it helps make all transitions easier. It helps us adapt more quickly to necessary changes. We are able to adjust more quickly to a new set of "goggles."

Meditators are more able to rule out distractions and pay attention to what they want to do. They train their mind to stick with things. They are able to focus on what they *are* doing, rather than worrying over what they're *not* doing.

Essentially, meditation *is* practice in paying attention. With it we train ourselves to relax and listen quietly to our inner world while "not hearing" the distracting thoughts that continually pop into our mind. Meditation, then, increases our ability to *choose* where we pay attention and where we don't. It helps us persevere and achieve our goals.

In summary, to lead healthier lives we need to aim the force of habit in the direction of health. We set our mind to health, "keep the goggles on" and practice routines of healthy eating, exercise and meditation. Our practice is "on-the-job training" for promoting our habits to health. Things get easier and easier until doing the healthy thing becomes our "second nature."

Strategy: Keeping the goggles on.

21

Obstacle: High-fat Friends

While it's true that a growing number of individuals and families are trying to eat better and exercise more, we still live in a culture that's hooked on fat and convenience. When you start practicing your healthy routines people are bound to get on your case.

Most of us know what poor nutrition and sedentary lifestyles are doing to us. Most of us know our diet-related diseases are at epidemic levels. Books, articles and TV talk shows warn us nonstop that we absolutely *must* change.

Are We Changing?

At this stage of the game it seems we're still doing a lot more knowing and talking than changing.

Sure, we're eating less beef and more chicken and fish. But what kinds of chicken and fish do you figure we're talking about? Most of it's that Kentucky-fried and "nugget" stuff.

Yes, we seem to be switching from whole milk to lower fat versions. At the same time we've dramatically increased our consumption of the highest fat, premium ice creams. Are we eating less fat? Yes and no.

And what about exercise? Sure, we know we should be more active. We try to *look* as if we are. We wear sweatclothes and sneakers everywhere, but we never walk if we can drive.

Again, we *talk* a lot about fitness, but our lifestyles remain essentially sedentary. Our jobs are sedentary, our home lives are sedentary. Even our recreation is more sedentary than we'd care to admit.

We're nuts about spectator sports where we pay money to watch someone *else* burn energy. We watch TV. We go to the movies. We read. We play cards. We invite friends to dinner. We eat. We drink. We sit and talk to each other in our sweatclothes and sneakers.

Doers and Talkers

Making healthy changes means you'll be doing what others are just talking about. It may sometimes seem as if everyone is getting on the healthy lifestyle bandwagon, but don't kid yourself.

Yes, people want to look and feel better, but they *don't* want to do the necessary changing. They *don't* want to struggle with the obstacles of a pro-fat world. But unfortunately, they *do* want to defend what they're not doing.

If they notice your healthy efforts, they'll insist you listen as they explain their *right* to eat and live the way they want. Fair enough, *if* they stop complaining about the everyday illnesses that come with high-fat eating and promise not to consume ten times their share of medical resources on the way out.

Just keep your goggles on (ears plugged) and you'll do
fine. But remember, others *aren't* doing so fine. With all the
half-hearted attempts, backsliding and guilt feelings, you
shouldn't expect much enthusiasm for your efforts to be
healthy.

What About Friends?

Unless they're making changes with you, even friends
won't be very supportive. Their often-repeated suggestion
that you "lighten up a bit" because "life's too short," will get
old in a hurry.

You'll be surprised how often you'll be treated as if it's
you that needs saving. Some food cult or something has tak-
en control of your mind. What's the matter with you? You
used to be so much fun. What difference could a little more
beer and pizza make? Lighten up a bit. Life's too short.

You'll be tempted to explain. Forget it. Nothing needs ex-
plaining. You're doing what they should be doing but aren't.

Don't bother telling them how great you've been feeling.
It will only make things worse. For heavens sake, don't let
them see how eager you are to taste that new pinto bean recipe.

Just keep your goggles on, stick with the program and be
patient with your friends. After all, you've become a new
circumstance in their lives and all their habits are grumbling
about it.

Loaded Questions

Everyone will seem to notice your eating changes. You'll
be asked a thousand times a day what you're doing and why.
Again, quite a few of those asking will be privately unhappy

about their *own* health and appearance, so the questions may be "loaded."

You might think it best to simply answer that you want to "eat healthier" or "lose a few pounds," but this seems, instead, to stimulate endless tabloid health advice, dieting folklore, heckling and sabotage.

If you're with people who know you're trying to make healthy choices, the implication is you think their differing choices are less healthy. It's a set up and no matter how much you yammer about individual freedom and how their choices are their business, you're going to get some flack.

Going home from the party before midnight, saying "no" to someone's special dessert or meditating during lunch break are grounds for public ridicule and flogging when you say you're trying to be healthy.

Be in Training

Prepare yourself. When someone asks what you're up to, try coming at the whole business from a different angle. Quiet down on the health and appearance stuff and remember—you're in *training*.

This *is* what you're doing after all. The eating, exercise and meditation routines *are* training for a low-fat lifestyle. With them we're training our bodies to be fit and trim. We're training our habits, training our muscles, training our minds, training our appetites.

Being in training makes sense to people. They understand following the rules when someone's training to learn something or achieve a goal.

At one time or another most everyone signs up for *some* kind of training: voice-training, job-training, computer-training, scuba-training. Everyone's had to "listen to the teacher," "practice the lesson" and "follow the instructions" along the way.

It also helps if you're preparing for some sort of coming performance activity. It doesn't matter whether you're headed for the Olympics, a local walkathon, birdwatching jamboree, cooking contest or annual tug-of-war—people will be more tolerant of your *training behaviors* than they would be of your *healthy choices.*

Be in a Program

You'll carve out even more room for yourself if you're in some sort of *program*. Understandably, if you paid for it, you'd want to "stick with the program" to get your money's worth.

Membership in an ongoing, flexible, multi-level training program could easily become a consistent and acceptable explanation for what you're doing.

Be in Our Program

Now, where do you find such a program? You already have. *Low-fat for Life* is a program of routines where you train healthy habits by:

1. *Eating* for nutrients.

2. *Exercising* for strength and endurance.

3. *Meditating* for stress management.

You paid for the program when you bought this book. Now get your money's worth—practice your routines.

Strategy: Being in a training program.

22

Obstacle: Doubting Yourself

Typically, those wanting healthy changes join a fitness outfit, buy exercise equipment, read books or take classes to launch a shaping up campaign.

Seldom does the campaign last very long. The changes seem too hard, or the results don't come fast enough.

Seasoned couch potatoes have a lot of trouble. When it comes right down to it, they really don't like anything that would help them be healthier. They don't like vegetables. They don't like working out. They don't like to grumble, but their knees hurt, their sneakers don't fit and they got gas from that bean salad at lunch.

Even if they try simple exercise such as a leisurely walk, it'll touch off an avalanche of reasons to stop. They just knew they should've waited till they had more time. They'll try again later when they can really get into it. Did they happen to mention that their sneakers don't fit? Walking's really terrible when you've got gas. Maybe they'll just find ways to enjoy life while they still have the chance. With the zillions of diseases around they're bound to catch one of them anyhow...pass the gravy please.

The "quick-fix" crowd doesn't last too long either. They make a lot of high-powered start up noises and seem willing to try anything—as long as it promises *fast* results. They're "taking their medicine" and "biting the bullet" to "get the job done."

This, of course, makes them ripe and ready for the fitness hustlers who come loaded with gimmicks and promises. Soon that quick-fix desire is churned into a costly and short-lived frenzy of diet fads, protein supplements, support groups, herbal tonics, workout paraphernalia, dance videos and stress-relief weekends.

Lasting Change

It does take effort to make lasting changes. It does take patience to continue eating, exercise and meditation routines until they become your new healthy habits.

But it *is* do-able. It *needs* doing. It's *worth* doing.

Day in and day out we are reminded of sensational and complex problems that we feel helpless, as individuals, to really do much of anything about. Drugs, crime, poverty, homelessness, the list is long. When it comes to what we can do to change things, the list is short: "You can help. Send money!"

This time there's more we can do. This time each of us can participate in turning things around. We'll be changing for the better no matter how small our beginning steps may seem.

Practicing eating, exercise and meditation routines may seem awfully David considering the Goliath-sized mess we've made. But like David's well-aimed rock, there's a powerful and typically underestimated ingredient here...*health!*

The Force of Health

Given a chance to do its work, health is a potent force for bringing about the changes we need. Somehow, we seem to have forgotten this.

We *do* worry about our individual health problems. We *do* worry about wrecking our environment. We pay so much attention to what could go wrong with us or already is going wrong with us, that we end up with a very limited view of what health actually is.

Most often we think of health in terms of what it *isn't*. You're healthy when you're *not sick*.

When health is in the news someone is typically telling us about some new chemical hazard, something that spilled somewhere, some lurking disease virus, some expensive treatment technology that no one can afford—unless they get on the Oprah Show and everyone sends in money.

Commercials blab away about an endless list of products for an endless list of aches, pains and ailments that they tell us we'll all get at one time or another.

A health examination is checking to see if anything's wrong. A report of good health means nothing was found.

Health insurance really insures our ability to pay the health care people to try to fix us when something goes wrong.

No wonder so many forget being healthy is *more* than not being sick.

The Experience of Health

The *Low-fat for Life* types chugging along out there haven't forgotten what health is. They made healthy lifestyle changes and they're sticking with them.

They know something about health that gets them over the hump of their old habits. Something that motivates them. Something that convinces them to continue taking better care of themselves than ever before. They know the *experience* of increased health.

The strength that comes with increasing health is experienced subjectively. We *feel* it.

Appearance and disease prevention are logical reasons for change. They help us *decide* to change. But it's the *experience* of health that helps us stick with eating, exercise and meditation routines to lock in healthy habits.

Health is a dynamic, energetic force. We feel it as energy. We can tell when it weakens or grows stronger.

Illness or chronic stress are experienced as a drain on our energy. We feel tired and run down. But when someone says "Wow, I have a lot of energy today", we know they're feeling healthy. It feels *good* to be charged up and ready to go.

The Habit of Health

Beginnings always take gumption. Trying to start eating, exercise and meditation routines is no different. All the old habits will be moaning, groaning and making excuses. But continuing effort is soon offset by the feelings that come with increasing health.

The healthier someone gets, the more energy and enthusiasm they feel and the more of it they want. They get the *habit* of health. They get greedy about it. They get hooked on the vim that comes with vigor and vitality.

Increased health, then, translates into having more energy available for the active enjoyment of life. But it will also be there when illness, injury or disease knocks at the door.

We all get clobbered by life circumstances. Health doesn't make us invincible. It *does,* however, make us more *resilient.* The healthier we are, the more able we are to "roll with the punches" and "snap back."

A healthy body demonstrates resilience over and over. It "knows" what health is. Every part of us is *organized* for health.

The human body has always had the habit of health. We see it in the fundamental fact of the body's ability to heal itself. We watch this magical process through all the cuts, bumps and bruises of childhood and it remains vigilant for a multitude of breakdowns and repairs that will come during our life.

Again and again our bodies bring us back to health. With each rebound they "learn" and grow stronger. A skirmish with chicken pox is "remembered." Stored in a complex immune system, it becomes a strategy of defense in case that virus ever tries again.

Conditions for Health

It's in our *nature* to be healthy. Our bodies sense prevailing conditions and respond in ways to achieve the best health possible. It's in *all* of nature to be healthy. It's built-in, automatic and ready to go.

Healthy life is a natural process. With the right *conditions* of moisture and warmth, life comes to a planted seed and it sprouts. The tiny sprout continues to grow into a strong, healthy plant if conditions continue to be favorable.

The reach for health is natural. It is in a tomato plant, it is in us. The health of our bodies, minds and relationships grow stronger *when conditions are favorable.* We tend to our health needs as we would tend to our garden by arranging those favorable conditions and "letting nature take its course."

Anticipating, planning and arranging are special abilities of the human mind. Optimum health requires that we use these abilities to arrange the healthiest conditions we possibly can.

The thinking you that is reading this is fully capable of arranging these conditions. When you do, your body will *automatically* use them to your best and healthiest advantage—how *convenient!*

The Life Within

In everything you do, in every activity you engage, in every moment-to-moment circumstance you help create, you are influencing the life that resides within you as you influence the life outside yourself.

Consider, for example, insights offered by Rudolph Ballentine about some of the life conditions in just one small part of your interior geography.[1]

Hundreds of different kinds of bacteria, fungi, yeasts and viruses live and interact in the colon of your digestive tract.

Entirely different microbe communities live on one side of your colon wall than at the same elevation on the other side. And these communities are both different than those living on the "valley" floor between them.

What you eat, do, and feel, affects these colon citizens in dramatic ways. You are their environment and the differing conditions you create encourage or discourage the growth of very different microbe populations.

Your body provides colon residents with nourishment and a home. In turn they help you in tasks such as processing fiber, destroying dangerous toxins and getting rid of wastes.

Of course, not all residents are so helpful. You may also provide conditions that promote the rapid growth of less friendly microorganisms. These may, for example, inflame your intestines, cause chronic diarrhea or constipation and lead to disease.

The life within us reflects our personality, our habits, behaviors and preferences. The choices we make in living attract the microscopic life within us toward our health or illness.

If the enzymes produced by our emotions nourish some and poison others, what colon microbes might a person invite who continually feels hatred or fear?

Doing Your Part

Taking care of ourselves is a notion more profound than we typically assume. It includes establishing conditions that invite the right participants to the enterprise we like to call "our" life.

We are far more than human intellects driving around in biological machines of just so many gears, tubes and switches. We are complex, living organizations of cooperating life.

You and every cell, every microbe in your body, are in this together. Training your habits with eating, exercise and meditation routines to take better care of your "self," then, is simply the *thinking* you doing *its* part, doing *its* job in the business of the *total* you.

It's asking the thinking you to participate in something the rest of you has been trying to do all along: going after the best health possible in whatever the circumstances.

Strategy: Taking care of yourself.

Part Three:

Routines for Training Healthy Habits

Health grows when conditions are "right." Training healthy habits with daily eating, exercise and meditation routines creates and maintains these "right" conditions. Part Three shows how to do it.

23

Eating Routines

In the *Low-fat for Life* program we don't provide a structured meal-by-meal menu. Rather, we give you many examples and suggestions you can adapt to suit your circumstances. This isn't a "crash diet" you follow for a month and then drop to return to your old eating habits. It's important that you take the time to work through your choices and develop the habit of paying attention to what you eat. Choose well for a new, healthier lifestyle.

Eat for the Nutrients in Food

Low-fat for Life eating is eating for nutrients. It's being concerned about both the "macro" and "micro" nutrients in our foods.

Fat, protein and carbohydrates are the "big three" of food nutrients. They make up most of what we eat each day and are used by our bodies in large amounts for building materials and to fuel activity. These are the "macronutrients."

We also need small, but regular amounts of other nutrients that are extremely important to the disease prevention
and self-healing actions of our bodies. These are the vitamins, minerals and trace elements we call the "micronutrients."

Nutrients are, in essence, chemicals. Too much or too little of a food nutrient for too long creates unhealthy chemical
imbalances in our bodies which lead to illness and disease.

We now recognize the nutrients in the typical American
diet are poorly balanced. Though its level of protein is okay,
it is an unhealthy diet because it has too much fat and too little complex carbohydrate.

Too much fat encourages degenerative disease. Too little
complex carbohydrate weakens our defenses. It deprives us
of the disease-preventing vitamin and mineral micronutrients and fiber found in complex carbohydrate foods.

The American diet emphasizes high-fat meats and cheeses, refined-grain white breads and pastries, heavily processed convenience foods, snack foods, cooking oils and
deep-fried, batter-coated foods. It's loaded with sugar, salt
and chemical additives, and offers little in the way of vitamins, minerals and fiber.

The healthy diet is low-fat/high-carbohydrate eating (see
Box 8). It emphasizes whole-grain breads, cereals and pasta,
brown rice, a wide variety of beans, cooked and fresh vegetables and fruits. It's supplemented by lean meats, fish, low-
fat yogurts and cheeses. This is a diet loaded with the vitamins, minerals (see Box 9) and fiber (see Box 10) so critical
to our health.

Box 8: Low-Fat and High-Carbohydrate Foods

Cereals

- Farina(Cream of Wheat)
- Malt-o-meal
- Shredded Wheat
- Multi-grain cooked cereal
- Nutrigrain
- Special K

- Grape Nuts
- Cream of Rice
- Cheerios
- Bran Flakes
- Corn Flakes

- Oatmeal
- All-Bran
- Granola
- Wheat Chex
- Total

Breads

- Tortilla (corn, whole-wheat)
- Muffins
- Whole-wheat bread
- Bagels
- Rye bread
- Breadsticks
- Corn bread

- Pancakes (whole-grain)
- Pita bread
- Oatmeal bread
- Banana bread
- Whole-wheat rolls
- Waffles (whole-grain)

Legumes

- White kidney beans
- Garbanzo beans
- Great northern beans
- Refried beans
- Fava beans

- Split peas
- Pinto beans
- Navy beans
- Mung beans

- Lentils
- Adzuki beans
- Black beans
- Kidney beans

Fruit

- Plums
- Apricots
- Kiwi
- Cantaloupe
- Grapefruit
- Tangerine

- Apples
- Oranges
- Peaches
- Papaya
- Rasberries
- Grapes

- Nectarines
- Bananas
- Pineapple
- Cherries
- Watermelon

- Blackberries
- Blueberries
- Pears
- Honeydew
- Strawberries

Continued...

Box 8: Continued

Grains

- Barley
- Amaranth
- Millet
- Buckwheat
- Rye
- Wheat
- Rice
- Basmati
- Oats
- Wheat bulgur
- Wild rice

Pasta

- Macaroni
- Buckwheat soba
- Wheat noodles
- Spaghetti
- Somen
- Rice noodles
- Spinach pasta

Vegetables

- Asparagus
- Beets
- Potatoes
- Rutabaga
- Chard
- Yams
- Leeks
- Mushrooms
- Onions
- Cabbage
- Cauliflower
- Squash
- Tomatoes
- Watercress
- Lettuce
- Broccoli
- Pumpkin
- Spinach
- Corn
- Kale
- Turnip greens
- Sweet potatoes
- Peppers
- Carrots
- Lima beans
- Green beans
- Brussels sprouts

Box 9: Vitamin and Mineral Foods

Vitamin/Mineral **Best Food Sources**

Vitamin/Mineral	Best Food Sources
A/Beta-Carotene	Liver, carrots, sweet potatoes, broccoli, spinach, collards, turnip greens, kale, squash, cantaloupe, mustard greens, beet greens, papayas, tomatoes, lettuce, apricots
Thiamin (B1)	Whole-grain products, brown rice, seafood, dried beans
Riboflavin (B2)	Dairy products, green vegetables, fruits, whole-grain products, meats
Niacin (B3)	Meats, fish, poultry, eggs
Vitamin B6	Meats, whole-grain products, brewer's yeast
Vitamin B12	Fish, dairy products, beef, organ meats
Biotin	Nuts, whole-grain products, milk, vegetables, brewer's yeast
Folic Acid	Green vegetables, oranges, dried beans, rice, brewer's yeast, liver
Pantothenic Acid	Whole-grain products, organ meats
Vitamin C	Citrus fruits, peppers, cabbage family, tomato, strawberries, acerola cherries
Vitamin D	Fortified milk, liver, body produces with sunlight
Vitamin E	Whole-grain products, green vegetables

Continued…

Box 9: Continued	
Vitamin/Mineral	**Best food sources**
Vitamin K	Dairy products, green vegetables, cabbage
Calcium	Dairy products, green vegetables, tofu, salmon
Chromium	Whole-grain products, black pepper, thyme, meat
Copper	Shellfish, nuts, fruit, oysters, dried beans
Iron	Lean beef, poultry, fish, soybean hulls
Magnesium	Lean meat, seafood, green vegetables, dairy products
Manganese	Whole-grain products, nuts
Molybdenum	Whole-grain products, legumes, leafy vegetables, milk, dried beans
Phosphorus	Dairy products
Potassium	Fresh vegetables and fruits (banana, cantaloupe, orange, spinach, cabbage)
Selenium	Broccoli, mushrooms, cabbage, celery, onions, cucumbers, garlic, radishes, brewer's yeast, whole-grain products (depending on regional soil conditions), fish
Silicon	Vegetables, whole grains, seafood
Zinc	Whole-grain products, brewer's yeast, wheat bran and germ, seafood, meat

Box 10: Fiber Foods

Food	Dietary Fiber
• Oat bran, 1/4 cup	14.0g
• Kellog's All Bran, 1/3 cup	8.5g
• Wheat bran, 1/4 cup	8.0g
• Lentils, boiled, 1 cup	7.9g
• Black beans, boiled, 1 cup	7.2g
• Oatmeal, dry, 1/2 cup	7.0g
• Pinto beans, boiled, 1 cup	6.8g
• Kidney beans, boiled, 1 cup	6.4g
• Lima beans, boiled, 1 cup	6.2g
• Rasberries, 1 cup	5.8g
• Garbanzo beans, boiled, 1 cup	5.7g
• Post Bran Flakes, 2/3 cup	5.6g
• Peas, raw, 1 cup	5.4g
• Dates, dried, 10	4.2g
• Pear, 1 medium	4.1g
• Grape Nuts, 1/2 cup	3.6g
• Corn, boiled, 1 cup	3.4g
• Apple, 1 medium	2.8g
• Strawberries, 1 cup	2.8g
• Banana, 1 medium	2.7g
• Pineapple, 1 cup	2.4g
• Green beans, boiled, 1 cup	2.2g
• Sweet potato, baked, 1 medium	2.1g
• Spinach, raw, 1 cup	1.8g
• Broccoli, chopped, 1 cup	1.2g
• Carrot, raw, 1 medium	1.1g

Adapted from Pennington, J. *Food Values of Portions Commonly Used.* New York: Harper and Row, 1989.

Follow the Nutrient Guidelines

Low-fat for Life eating is low-fat/high-carbohydrate eating. You don't just eat whatever you happen to find in the refrigerator, or what you think might taste okay, or what your friends are eating, or what you saw advertised on TV last night.

You are choosing what you put in your mouth according to the nutrients your body needs for optimal health.

Your body is a complex organization of participating microscopic life forms that we call your "inner crew." It includes all the folks in your various nutrient-processing departments such as those specialized in stomach, small intestine and liver operations. It includes those who participate in the nutrient and waste transportation systems circulating throughout your body. It includes those who work in your defense systems, fuel and cell-building systems.

You are eating for nutrients to do your part in taking better care of yourself. You're supporting your crew by bringing in the best food nutrients possible.

Following the nutrient guidelines we've mentioned throughout this book is the bottom line of eating for nutrients.

Keeping fat calories under 20% of total calories, protein calories between 10–15% of total calories and carbohydrate calories above 65% of total calories is the goal that influences what foods we buy, meals we plan, cooking techniques we use and foods we eat.

Get Lots of Nutrient Calories Every Day

The amount of food nutrients a person needs each day is usually stated in calories. You should know what your approximate calorie requirements are.

Remember, we're not talking about calories as the bad things that make you fat. From years of hearing that we eat too much, many of us have been conditioned to the idea that low-calorie eating is healthy eating.

Advertising likes to push this idea. "Our frozen sparrow legs taste great and they're low-calorie too!" We should applaud them for giving us small amounts of the nutrients we need?

We do want low-fat calories, but we also want an abundance of the vitamin, mineral and fiber-rich *carbohydrate* calories.

How many calories? It depends upon how much you weigh, how physically active you are and your rate of metabolism.

If you need to lose weight see Chapter 26 to estimate your "target" weight and calorie requirements for fat loss. But if your weight is about right, you can figure calorie needs by paying attention to what you eat in a day. Write *everything* down, check labels and use the appendix food values to find calories. Add them up to get your approximate daily requirement. It would make sense to monitor yourself for several days to find your average calorie intake, since it may vary from day to day.

To keep your calories straight, at first you'll be doing a lot of measuring and weighing. Food labels and the nutrition analysis we have in the appendix will tell you how many calories are in certain amounts of food.

Measuring cups and an inexpensive food scale are a *must*. We use measuring cups as serving spoons and ladles. Let's see now: a *cup* of rice (230 calories) with a *cup* of stir-fry vegetables (say, 120 calories) and a *three-ounce* piece of grilled chicken breast (150 calories)...

Spread Calories Out With Three Main Meals and Snacks

Your inner crew works 24 hours a day. They need a continuous supply of high-quality, food nutrients to do their best work.

That's why nutrition experts tell us to spread out our daily intake of nutrient calories by eating at least three main meals and including between meal snacks.

So if you need, say, 1500 calories a day, you could furnish them in the following installments:

breakfast	—	300 calories (oatmeal and fruit)
lunch	—	350 calories (soup and sandwich)
snack	—	100 calories (fruit or muffin)
dinner	—	550 calories (stir-fries over rice)
snack	—	200 calories (popcorn)
		1500 total calories

Don't skip any meals! Considering what's at stake, it's amazing to hear people say with great conviction that they simply refuse to eat breakfast or that they skip lunch whenever they're too busy.

They're wrong and you know better. Take care of yourself and support your inner crew. Give your body a consistent supply of nutrients throughout the day.

By routinely eating all meals and snacks you are developing an important habit for healthy living. You are learning to maintain the conditions of health. You are following a daily pattern of eating that smoothes out high- and low-calorie periods and avoids body fat problems that come with "starve and stuff" eating cycles.

Your crew will appreciate the steady supply of nutrient materials you furnish. They'll quickly respond to the rhythm of a regular eating pattern. You'll feel better and notice your energy levels are more consistent throughout the day.

Keep Your Eye on the Fat Calories

Making sure less than 20% of your nutrient calories are fat, 10-15% are protein and more than 65% are carbohydrate would seem to involve a lot of complicated figuring—it doesn't.

We found if you keep your eye on the *fat* end of the business everything else will pretty much fall into place. This is important because making changes means paying close attention to what you're doing. At the same time you want to make every effort to keep things as simple as possible to avoid confusion.

Keeping your eye on the fat doesn't mean cutting fat is more important than increasing the complex carbohydrates. Rather, keeping the fat below 20% *results* in the equally important carbohydrate increase.

The foods we eat are composed of fat, protein and carbohydrate. Authorities now agree that we really don't have to worry about getting enough protein in our diet as long as we're getting enough daily calories. So that leaves the fat and carbohydrate to think about. When you cut back on the fat, you have to eat *something* and there's only one thing left—carbohydrate.

Check the numbers in the following table. Assume you require 1500 calories a day. When you cut the 600 fat calo-

ries (40%) back to 300 fat calories (20%), where do the 300
calories go? To carbohydrate calories.

	High-fat Calories		Low-fat Calories	
Fat	600	(40%)	300	(20%)
Protein	225	(15%)	225	(15%)
Carbohydrate	675	(45%)	975	(65%)
Totals	1500	(100%)	1500	(100%)

If you stopped eating the three pats of butter or margarine
you ordinarily had each day, you'd cut approximately 300
fat calories. Putting these calories into several carbohydrate
snacks would be easy. For example, a large apple is 100 calories. One of our muffins would be about 100 calories. How
about a cinnamon-raisin bagel for 200 calories?

When you eat *less* high-fat meat, butter, cheeses and
foods with too much cooking oil, you'll "automatically" be
eating *more* fruits, cereals, breads, rice, pasta, beans and
vegetables to satisfy your hunger.

Keeping your eye on the fat means you don't have to pay
as much attention to some other things as well. Less fat
means less cholesterol, less saturated fat (heart disease), less
unsaturated fat (cancer).

At the same time filling up on fruits, grains, legumes, and
vegetables means you're increasing the soluble and insoluble fiber, antioxidants, indoles and other vitamins and minerals known to *prevent* cancer and heart disease.

And keeping your eye on the fat also clears up a lot of the
label confusion in shopping, but we'll tell you more about
that later.

Keep Your Eye on the Fat in All Meals and Snacks

In the *Low-fat for Life* program you eat less than 20% fat at *every* meal. This is different than "budgeting" your fat on a day-long basis. Fat-budgeting, in our experience, is self-defeating.

If you required 1500 calories a day and kept below the 20% limit you'd wind up with 300 fat calories a day, right?

Some writers suggest you can *choose* when and where you got your fat as long as you ended up within your 300-fat-calorie budget for the day.

They say not to worry about the extra fat you might eat at any one time. You can adjust for it in other meals and still stay within your fat budget for the day.

They suggest you can spread it out evenly over the meals of the day or have more at some times, less at others: it's yours to decide according to the fat-budget suggestions.

In other words, with a fat budget of 300 calories, you could choose to have a high-fat "Big Mac" lunch (315 fat calories) and then balance your fat budget by having a no-fat dinner.

But wait a minute. Isn't the point in this learning to take better care of ourselves? Do you really believe it's okay to lard up your system at lunch and somehow make up for it with a no-fat dinner?

Box 11: Greased Lightning

Think the effects of fat come slowly? Think again! Just *one* high-fat meal may cause the body to produce "thromboxane," a hormone that constricts arteries and clots blood. According to well-known health specialist Dr. Dean Ornish, this is a reason why heart patients often get chest pains after a fatty meal and why so many of them end up in the hospital after holiday excesses.

This kind of thinking offers the illusion of choice, when in fact it would continually sabotage what it is you're trying so hard to do.

That "freedom" to lard up at lunch spells *trouble* when it comes to those old habits you have to contend with. They'll never settle down if you keep reminding them of the good old days in fat land.

Stick with the program! Hold the fat to 20% at *every* meal. Those habits will come around after they consistently experience the effects of healthy eating for a while.

You'll soon have the habit of making meals under 20% fat. You'll *know* without thinking what food combinations will keep you under the 20% cut off. You'll have the habit of making meals that taste delicious to your new appetite...that's now "hooked" on enjoying healthy foods.

This is what you want, isn't it—to *change* the way you eat and *change* your eating habits?

Well, new eating habits are only going to emerge if you consistently eat the way you know you should.

On the other hand, if you consistently vacillate between high-fat and low-fat eating, know what you'll get? The habit of *vacillating!* That's the way it works, isn't it?

And let's not be silly about this. An occasional meal over the 20% limit doesn't matter. An invitation or happenstance is bound to corner you into one now and then—but don't play games with yourself. These occasional wanderings into fat land won't kill you, but too many side trips and you'll never get where it is you want to go.

You already know how it works. If you want to do something, you have to *do* it. You're either eating the *Low-fat for Life* way or you're *not,* every time you stick something into your mouth.

For many reasons, most of them money, everyone seems to soft-peddle what we have to do to be healthier. Magazine articles are very careful not to push us too hard, or offend us or depress us in any way that might give us cause to quit buying their magazines.

They hedge a lot. They suggest we "limit" high-fat sauces, gravies and desserts and "consider" a meatless meal now and then. Come on...we've been "limiting" and "considering" for a long time now. If it's working so well, what are you doing reading this?

It's time to make the change to healthy eating once and for all. Keeping every meal under the 20% fat limit is the way to get the job done right. This approach establishes a consistent routine to train your habits to healthy eating. Once new habits are in place, you won't need to count calories or figure fat very often. With a dozen or so of your favorite recipes at hand you'll *know* you're eating low-fat, high-carbohydrate in harmony with your biological design.

Keep It Simple Until Your New Routines Settle In

Making changes means paying attention. You'll get new habits in place faster if you have less demands on your attention.

In the beginning, limiting your choices frees attention to get the change done and helps hold down the confusion. Establish a simple routine pattern from the start, so that your habits get a clear and consistent message about the changes you want. You'll be able to add all sorts of choices later on when your habits have made the changeover to healthier eating.

To start, then, choose a few meals under the 20% limit and stick with them a while. This is what we mean by "no-think," "some-think" and "adventure" eating. With a little planning you'll have a basic supply of low-fat meals for starting your routines. Consider having a no-think at breakfast, some-think at lunch and adventure at dinner.

A no-think breakfast doesn't mean you have to eat exactly the same thing every morning. You might make, say, three breakfast choices and then keep recycling them. But the point is most of us don't have much time to fool around at breakfast anyhow, so it's a great place to repeat a basic choice into a habit right away.

A no-think breakfast is also an easy opportunity to practice aiming the power of habit. When you do something that clearly lets your habits know what you want, they'll stop grumbling and change over fast.

If you're like many others, hot oatmeal or farina with sliced banana, raisins or blueberries mixed in will taste good breakfast after breakfast.

At lunchtime you may appreciate some variability, but don't need a lot. Try a some-think soup and sandwich lunch. In other words, you stick with the idea of soup and sandwich but vary the *kind* of soup and sandwich you choose each day.

Morning and afternoon snacks are easy to manage as some- or no-thinks. If you have access to a steady supply of a favorite fruit, you might never tire of it.

Dinner is the obvious time for adventure eating. It's usually the best meal for planning and experimenting. Same goes for the evening snack.

In the beginning, of course, it might also make sense to work with some-think dinners during the week and save the adventures for weekends. Work out a main meal pattern for Monday through Thursday such as stew, stir-fries, spaghetti and casserole and recycle it for a while.

Your habits will appreciate such simple, consistent meal choices especially when busy times crowd your mind with other things.

In our family the weekend eating routine is different from the weekday routine, anyhow. Having people over, attending social gatherings, enjoying leisurely brunches and other spontaneous events encourage a lot more adventure eating.

Do routines such as no-think and some-think regiment us? That certainly hasn't been our experience. If anything, a solid, healthy routine establishes some of the regularity, rhythm and coherence we could all use a little more of in our lives.

Our bodies come to rely on a timely supply of healthy food nutrients. Our inner crews are down there chugging away night and day. Makes sense to give them the best working conditions we can possibly arrange.

Cut Down on Some Foods, Get Rid of Others

A surprising number of writers tell us we don't have to eliminate the super high-fat foods, we just need to eat them in smaller amounts or less frequently. Like the idea of budgeting our daily fat calories, this *sounds* great but works against habit change.

It's true we can manage a few high-fat foods, but reducing their amounts to get a 20% fat meal might take some fancy footwork.

If chicken dinner for you has meant eating a bushel basket of heavily-battered, deep-fried chicken parts with a dab of potatoes and a dab of vegetables, a three- or four-ounce broiled, skinless chicken breast is bound to cause a commotion with your habits.

To *reduce* a portion of meat successfully, you need to *expand* other enjoyable parts of the meal pattern. Much of this shift in emphasis will depend on your particular taste directions, but we'll give a couple of examples to explain.

Like most folks our family always enjoyed french-fried potatoes. When we changed our eating habits, we came up with a non-fat version we call "oven-fries." We're crazy about them.

So when we have chicken in smaller portions, we also have huge portions of oven-fries and other favorites like baked beans. In this pattern the amount of chicken is not an issue.

For years beef roast with carrots, potatoes and plenty of gravy was a regular around our house. Now that same basic taste combination is captured in our beef stew. The smaller portions of beef are irrelevant because the portions of stew and the pile of fresh whole-wheat rolls are so large.

The strategy of reducing portions by changing the pattern of food in the meal has worked well for us. It's what we mean when we talk about shifting the *emphasis* from meat to vegetables, breads, beans, fruit and so on.

When you do, you'll immediately recognize how much *more* food you get for your calories in low-fat eating. That's because carbohydrates and protein have less than *half* the calories of the same amount (weight) of fat. This is obvious in many single food substitutions. For example, you'll get about three ounces of non-fat cheddar cheese for the same calories you'd get in one ounce of the regular version.

The same thing happens when you reduce the fat in your recipes. A commercial muffin with oil in its recipe might have 250 calories with 40 percent of them fat. If you bake your own muffins and take the oil out, you could have two muffins for the same calories with only 5 percent of them fat.

And reducing the fat in recipes is especially easy. Taking the oil out of muffins, pancakes and quick breads has everyone asking why it was ever there in the first place. You'll find this true in "defatting" many of your recipes.

But it's more difficult reducing some of the high-fat single item foods. *Peanuts* are a good example. A two-ounce handful of dry roasted peanuts would be gone in a flash if it showed up in one of our snacktimes. Peanuts are 79% fat. Those two ounces would be 253 fat calories out the window.

Again, if we're talking about 1500 calories a day and 300 fat calories, that little pile of peanuts would mean nothing else we ate in a day could be over 4% fat. Peanuts taste great, but they're not worth blowing a whole day's eating.

We *could* try eating just one ounce of those peanuts and then sit there all depressed, remembering the good old high-fat days when we'd pig out on peanuts without a care in the world.

Reducing works fine for portions in a meal or oil in a muffin batter, but you'd be better off *replacing* that peanut snack with a low-fat alternative.

Snacks must trip up a lot of people who are trying to eat better. On a Super Bowl Sunday the food industry expects us to eat something like 6 million *tons* of potato chips.

When it comes to fat, most snack foods aren't bad, they're terrible. Set your sights on finding new snack materials. Hunt for low-fat chips and party mixes. Try muffins, bagels, fruit, popcorn or pretzels.

The cost of making a change is losing some of those old favorites. Its reward is in finding the new ones. You're simply replacing good tastes that are unhealthy with good tastes that are healthy.

Box 12: Low-Fat Choices	
Instead of these...	**Choose these:**
Doughnuts, pastries, sweet rolls	Muffins, banana bread, bagels, angel food cake, cinnamon rolls (homemade)
Ice cream, sundaes, dream bars	Non-fat frozen yogurt sundae, sherbet, fruit ice, fruit juice bar, frozen banana, waffles and frozen yogurt
Milkshake, malt	Homemade malt (i.e., non-fat frozen yogurt, chocolate syrup, powdered malt)
Potato chips	No-oil potato or corn chips, pretzels, whole-grain crackers, rice cakes, popcorn
Nuts, peanuts	Popcorn, pretzels, dried fruit, crackers with non-fat cheese, vegetables and non-fat cream cheese
Chocolate chip cookies	Ginger snaps, fig bar, homemade oatmeal raisin cookie
Chocolate and various candy bars	Non-fat chocolate pudding, chocolate non-fat frozen yogurt, chocolate skim milk, granola bar, dried fruit

New tastes that become new favorites are blessings. They *pull* your appetite in the direction of eating you want to go in. Whenever you find one, make a big deal about it.

Sometimes even obvious replacements give you a giant psychological boost. Our family loves ice cream. Giving it up seemed one of the higher costs of healthy eating. Then we tasted non-fat frozen yogurt—all right!

Be Fussy Until Your Habits Come Around

People often assume they're "eating pretty well" and don't need to "go overboard" on following nutrient guidelines. They "common sense" their way through meals and "watch themselves" enough to think they're healthy eaters. A little analyzing often surprises them.

For example, let's follow Tara through a day of eating. There she is just waking up. She's late and worried about getting to work. Now she's grabbing a muffin for breakfast as she runs out the door. Look, she didn't put any butter on it.

At midmorning snack time Tara's hungry. No problem. Her desk is well-stocked with granola bars, so she chomps one down.

For lunch Tara microwaves a Weight Watchers Chicken Enchilada. This keeps her happy until late afternoon when a friend offers her some potato chips. She figures she's done well so far and the chips *are* a "light" brand so she eats a few.

Home for dinner Tara makes herself a ground turkey burger and salad for supper. She figures the turkey is low-fat, and she's using low-calorie dressing and reduced-fat cheese on her salad.

Before bed Tara snacks on some microwave popcorn while watching a favorite TV program. As usual, she didn't put extra butter, cheese, caramel, salt or anything else on it. It seems to her she ate healthy for the day. Did she?

The figures (see Box 13) say she didn't. Tara's been "watching herself" eat a typical high-fat American diet. She just finished a 45% fat day. She's making an effort, but her choices aren't fussy enough. Not only is she eating high fat, but she's low in complex carbohydrates too.

Box 13: Fussy Choosing	
Tara's Choice	**Fussy Choice**
Breakfast	
Banana Muffin (commercial) 242 cal., 10.3 g fat 38% fat	Banana Muffin (homemade) 114 cal., 0.7g fat 5.5% fat Skim Milk, 1 cup 86 cal., 0.4g fat 4% fat Orange 65 cal., 0.1g fat 1% fat
Mid-morning Snack	
Granola Bar 120 cal., 5.1g fat 38% fat	Apple 100 cal., 0.5g fat 4.5% fat
Lunch	
Chicken Enchilada (Weight Watchers) 360 cal., 18g fat 45% fat	Chicken Enchilada (Homemade) plus ½ c. Rice 336 cal., 4.2g fat 11% fat
Mid-afternoon Snack	
Potato Chips, 1 oz. (Pringle's Light) 147 cal., 8.2g fat 50% fat	Bagel (Cinnamon Raisin) plus 1 T. Kraft strawberry jam 224 cal., 1g fat 4% fat
Supper	
Turkey Burger, 3.5 oz. (Louis Rich) plus hamb. bun 327.5 cal., 14.4g fat 39% fat	Turkey Burger, 3.5 oz. (skinless ground) plus wheat bun 230 cal., 4g fat 15.6% fat

continued...

Box 13: Continued		
	Tara's Choice	**Fussy Choice**

Supper continued	Lettuce Salad, 1½ c.
	3 T. low-cal dressing
	1 oz. light cheese
	   156 cal., 9.2g fat
	   53% fat
		Lettuce Salad, 1½ c.
		3 T. non-fat dressing
		1 oz. non-fat cheese
		   112 cal., 0.3g fat
		   2.4% fat
		Minestrone Soup, 1 c.
		   86 cal., 0.3g fat
		   6% fat
		Oven Fries
		(homemade)
		   145 cal., 0.2g fat
		   1.2% fat

Evening Snack	Microwave Popcorn,
	4 c.
	   230 cal., 13.5g fat
	   53% fat
		Air-popped Popcorn,
		4 c.
		   92 cal., 1.2g fat
		   12% fat

Days' Totals:	1582 cal., 78.7g fat 45% Fat	1590 cal., 13.2g fat 7.5% Fat

With just a few changes and a little of her own cooking, Tara's eating for the day could have easily stayed below the 20% fat level (only 7.5%), had more carbohydrates and actually had *more* food for the same calories.

Instead of someone else's high-fat banana muffin, she could have made her own ahead of time. How about our banana muffin with 0.7 grams of fat and 114 calories, for example. Then she'd still have room for a cup of milk and an orange.

There are plenty of low-fat granola bars available. If Tara had read the label she could have picked one with 1 gram of fat and 100 calories. A big 100 calorie apple with 0.5 grams of fat would have been better yet.

What about that enchilada? Just because a product says Weight Watchers doesn't mean it will always be low in fat. This is another example of why cooking for yourself is so important. If Tara had made a big batch of our enchiladas on the weekend, she could have saved the "deliberate leftovers" to take to work. And here again, by cutting the fat she'd be able to eat *more* food for the same calories. How about a half cup of rice to round out the meal?

And the potato chips? Like peanuts they'd be easier to re-place than reduce. They're too high in fat and too hard to eat in small amounts. How about a bagel instead? Put some jelly on it for 1 gram of fat and 224 calories.

The ground turkey continues to fool a lot of people. If she'd have hunted, Tara might have found some low enough in fat, but most of the prepackaged stuff has the skin ground up with it. That makes it as fat as regular hamburger. She could have asked her butcher or deli counter to grind some skinless turkey breast for her.

The hamburger bun was a chance to pick up some com-plex carbohydrates had Tara chosen a whole wheat bun. The lettuce salad is fine, but she should be using a non-fat cheese and non-fat dressing instead of the "reduced" versions. This would bring the turkey burger and salad in at 4.3 grams of fat and 342 calories.

Of course, less fat means more carbohydrates. This time there was enough room to slide in a bowl of minestrone soup and a serving of oven-fries.

Popcorn is a healthy snack unless coated with oil to pop in the microwave. If Tara had popped her own she could have four cups of it for 1.2 grams of fat and 92 calories.

The total with changes would be 13.2 grams of fat for 1590 calories or less than 8% fat. Same calories, less fat, more carbohydrates, more food—not bad!

If you start watching what people eat you'll find many who think they are trying, but are worse off than Tara. One bad habit, like putting butter on everything, will keep them in the fat lane day-in and day-out. Our pro-fat world has many of us thinking "just a little won't hurt" too often each day.

Both butter and margarine (unless a non-fat version) are 100% fat. Two pats of butter have 25 grams of fat in them or 225 fat calories. If you eat, say, 1500 calories of food a day, you've got to stay under 300 fat calories to make 20%. Your chances are zip if you insist on those "a little won't hurt" habits.

Box 14: "Little" Additions

A 20% fat, 1500 calorie day...

Plus:	Becomes:
2 T of butter or margarine	1700 calories, 29% fat
3 T peanut butter	1785 calories, 29% fat
3 oz potato chips	2000 calories, 34% fat
3.5 oz chedder cheese	1900 calories, 30% fat
3 T mayonaise	1710 calories, 29% fat

Read Labels and Figure the Fat

To know how much fat is in the foods we buy we have to read labels. To make them more accurate and understandable, Congress passed the Nutrition Labeling and Education Act in 1990. It mandated the U. S. Food and Drug Administration (FDA) to develop a new system of food labeling.

After two years of haggling among the involved governmental agencies and various consumer, health profession and food industry groups, the new labeling rules were announced in December of 1992.

The new regulations were hailed as a major victory for health conscious shoppers. Louis Sullivan, Health and Human Services Secretary, at the time said, "The Tower of Babel in food labels has come down."

Standard serving sizes were established for many food categories that are closer to what people actually serve (e.g., the serving size for fruit juice is eight fluid ounces). This prevents the previous sort of deception where a product would be advertised as having, "Only 50 calories per serving," then indicating a serving size half that of competing brands.

Label health claims were also tightened up. Terms such as "light," "low," "less," "lean" and "free" are now strictly defined, cutting back on their misuse in sales hype.

New labels list the grams of fat, carbohydrate, protein, cholesterol, sodium and fiber in the product and tell the percent of a sample daily diet the numbers represent. The idea is to show how much of a recommended daily amount of nutrients are in the product.

So did the Tower of Babel come down? Did the new regulations clear up label confusion?

Though it's likely the new labels have curbed some of the dishonesty in advertising, they have done little to dispel confusion. Indeed it seems worse.

Terms *are* strictly defined, but they're also difficult to understand and remember (see Box 15).

Box 15: Examples of New Label Terms

Free
Contains under: 5 calories; 5 mg sodium; 1/2 g sugar, fat or saturated fat; and 2 mg cholesterol.

Low
Contains no more than: 40 calories; 140 mg sodium; 3 g fat; 1 g and 15% total calories saturated fat; and 20 mg cholesterol.

Reduced
A nutritionally altered product contains 25% fewer calories than a reference food. Cannot be used with the term "low."

Light
An altered product contains 1/3 fewer calories or 50% of the fat in a reference food; if 50% or more of the calories came from fat, the reduction must be 50% of the fat; the sodium content has been reduced by 50%; and may describe properties such as texture and color as long as intent is clear (e.g., light brown sugar).

And there are other problems. Look at the label in Box 16. It represents a macaroni and cheese product. Notice the percents listed. It says total fat is 20% of "Daily Value." Does that mean it's 20% fat? No such luck.

The label says the amount of fat in a serving of the macaroni and cheese is 20% of *the amount government agencies recommend you eat in a day.*

Box 16: Food Label

Nutrition Facts

Serving size $^1\!/_2$ cup (114g)
Servings per container 4

Amount per serving

Calories 260   Calories from Fat 120

	% Daily Value*
Total fat 13g	**20**%
Saturated Fat 5g	**25**%
Cholesterol 30mg	**10**%
Sodium 660mg	**28**%
Total Carbohydrate 31g	**11**%
Sugars 5g	
Dietary Fiber 0g	**0**%
Protein 5g	

Vitamin A 4% • Vitamin C 2%
Calcium 15% • Iron 4%

*Percents (%) of a Daily Value are based on a 2000 calorie diet. Your Daily Values may vary higher or lower depending on your calorie needs.

	Calories	2,000	2,500
Total Fat	Less Than	65g	80g
Sat Fat	Less Than	20g	25g
Cholesterol	Less Than	300mg	300mg
Sodium	Less Than	2400mg	2400mg
Total Carbohydrate		300g	375g
Dietary Fiber		25g	30g

Calories per gram:
Fat 9 – Carbohydrate 4 – Protein 4

Now, there are a number of reasons why the "% Daily Value" recommendations aren't helpful to us:

1. Government recommendations on nutrition are compromised by other concerns—the effects on food sales and the economy, political ramifications and powerful special interest groups. The government recommendation for fat intake is 30% of total calories. This is too high. It's got to be 20% or less.

2. Label recommendations are based on an average diet of 2000 calories a day. Calorie needs vary quite a bit from person to person. Many women require only 1500 calories a day, which would make for very different percentages.

3. Label recommendations are based on the assumption that following a daily fat budget is the way to go. Earlier, we explained this approach as cumbersome and self-defeating. We advocate keeping all meals and snacks below the 20% fat level as the best and quickest way to lock in healthy habits.

Healthy living means *taking charge* of our health. It means *taking care* of ourselves by *paying attention* to the foods we eat. It means knowing enough about nutrition to choose food products according to the *facts* on labels, rather than advertising or even governmental recommendations about what we should eat.

The *key* fact we want to know about a food product is its proportion of fat. One easy calculation will tell us:

Fat calories ÷ total calories = proportion (%) of fat.

Look at the top of the label in Box 16. Listed under "Amount Per Serving" are the fat calories (120) that you divide by the total calories (260), which tells us the macaroni and cheese is 46% fat. This one calculation puts you in charge.

Now, 46% fat is awfully high, isn't it? It's the cheese that's doing it. If it's meat or dairy, that's where the fat is at.

To get this half-cup of macaroni and cheese squeezed into a meal under the 20% fat rule will take a little doing. You have to add enough non-fat calories (in this case 350–400) to bring the proportion of fat under the 20% wire.

A cup of rice with a little salsa (240 calories), a cup of steamed vegetables (50 calories) and a cup of skim milk (90 calories) would work out fine. So:

> 240 + 50 + 90 + the 260 calories in the macaroni and cheese = 640 total calories.
>
> 120 fat calories ÷ 640 total calories = 18.75% fat.

Get the idea? This is why we figure the fat percent right away. It's our top priority in label reading. With this one calculation we may start figuring the rest of the meal.

This approach is much less confusing than trying to relate the label information on one product to an entire day of budgeted meals and snacks.

The fat percent also serves as a quick rule-of-thumb indicator for carbohydrates. What's low in fat is usually high in carbohydrates.

In the high-carbohydrate foods you, of course, want the complex variety. Labels don't tell you this directly, so you have to do a little figuring. They list "Dietary Fiber" and "Sugars" which do indicate the amount of the carbohydrates that are complex. High-fiber and low-sugar tell you the carbohydrates are more complex.

You don't want too many of the refined, processed carbohydrates such as in white flour or the "simple" sugar carbohydrates because they're "empty calories." They don't have the fiber, vitamins and minerals found in whole grains, vegetables, beans and fruits.

Look at the macaroni and cheese label again. The sugars are reasonable (4 grams), but they have 0 fiber. This means the fiber in the macaroni flour was refined out (white flour) rather than kept whole (whole-wheat flour).

When you're eating for health you want to get your calories' worth of *nutrition* and it would be hard *not* to get your daily allotment of *empty* calories.

Experts tell us to limit refined sugars/sweeteners to 10% of total calories. On 1500 calories a day that would be 150 calories, which aren't many. You can use up your day's allotment on a single bottle of soda, which averages about 10 teaspoons (150 calories) of sugar carbohydrates.

Look for complex carbohydrates wherever you can find them. Emphasize fresh produce and whole grains as much as possible in your stir-fries, casseroles, soups and stews, snack foods, pastas, breads, cereals and juices. They are foods that help balance a higher fat portion of the meal like a serving of macaroni and cheese.

When purchasing food, check the *ingredients list* as well as the nutritional facts. The first item on the ingredients list is the main ingredient.

Is that white flour or sugar in the top spot? Even if they say "unbleached" or "enriched" flours, they're still refined carbohydrates. They may say brown sugar, corn syrup, sucrose or honey, but we're still talking about simple carbohydrates.

If the first ingredient says "whole wheat" or "100% pure fruit juice" you're on the right track. You may find simple or processed carbohydrates farther down the list. But using fat, sugar, white flour, salt and so on in *moderation* to enhance the flavor of complex carbohydrates is all right. Just make sure the main ingredients are packed with the nutrients you need.

Box 17: Hidden Sugar

Even when sugar isn't the first listed ingredient it may be hidden in a product. Producers are able to hide sugar by spreading it through a variety of refined sweeteners. Each has smaller amounts and can be listed separately near the bottom. Together they still comprise a high sugar total.

Look for other "sugar" words like:

• Brown Sugar	• Mannitol	• Maple Syrup
• Corn Syrup	• Molasses	• Natural Sweeteners
• Dextrose	• Dextrin	• Raw Sugar
• Fructose	• Sorbital	• Glucose
• Sucrose	• Honey	• Turbinado Sugar
• Maltose	• Xylitol	• Confectioner's Sugar

What do you do when foods don't have labels? Use our food values list in Appendix A—we've already figured the fat percentage for you. If a food isn't listed check a food values book such as Jean Pennington's *Food Values of Portions Commonly Used*. It doesn't list fat calories, but fat grams. A gram of fat equals nine calories, so you can figure the fat percentage using this calculation:

Fat grams x 9 ÷ total calories = proportion (%) of fat.

Get Your Calories' Worth of Nutrients

Reasonably tasty, low-fat products *are* showing up in the marketplace, but be careful. Heaven only knows what chemical concoctions will be offered as fat replacements.

Even the more expensive "healthy" product lines leave a lot to be desired. Frozen dinners claim to be low-calorie, low-cholesterol, low-fat and low-sodium. Sounds pretty good until you think about it.

They're saying they're low in the bad things. Calories aren't bad things. We're not looking for low-calorie food. We need calories, plenty of them. But they've got to be the right kind.

- We *don't* want too many *fat* calories.
- We *do* want lots of *complex carbohydrate* calories.

Most low-calorie frozen dinners have less than 300 total calories. How many of these calories do you figure are in that little pile of green beans they gave you? Maybe 10–15 calories? There are only 44 calories in a whole *cup* of green beans.

Now, let's say (again) you eat 1500 calories a day. Two-thirds or more of them are supposed to be complex carbohydrates. That's 1000 calories of fruits, vegetables, grains and beans you're supposed to be eating every day.

This is why our government agencies are telling us to increase our servings of these foods. The USDA's dietary guidelines, for example, tell us we should get 6–11 servings of grains, 2–4 servings of fruit and 3–5 servings of vegetables.

Think that little pile of green beans would even qualify as *one* serving?

Again, why do we *want* more of those green beans? Because *healthy* eating is eating for the *nutrients* in food. We need the vitamins, minerals and fiber that are found in vegetables, fruits, grains and beans.

Calories, cholesterol, fat and sodium, then, aren't the only things many "healthy" product lines are "low" in. They're also typically low in vitamins, minerals and fiber.

Additionally, our food factories lose important nutrients at every step of production. Why?

Box 18: Serving Sizes	
USDA Daily Recommendations:	**One serving is:**
Grains 6–11 servings	1 slice bread • $\frac{1}{2}$ bagel • 1 tortilla, 6" $\frac{3}{4}$ cup flake cereal • $\frac{1}{4}$ cup granola $\frac{1}{2}$ cup rice, grits, couscous (cooked)
Vegetables 3–5 servings	$\frac{1}{2}$ cup broccoli, carrots, string beans, etc 1 potato (size of large egg) • $\frac{1}{3}$ cup yams 1 leafy salad (in small bowl or plate)
Fruits 2–4 servings	$\frac{1}{2}$ cup raw, canned, cooked fruit 1 apple, orange, banana (medium) $\frac{3}{4}$ cup fruit juice • $\frac{1}{4}$ cup dried fruit
Dairy 2–3 servings	8 oz low-fat, skim milk • 1 cup yogurt 1 $\frac{1}{2}$ oz cheese • 2 cups cottage cheese
Meat 2–3 servings	3 oz poultry, lean beef, veal, fish
Newsweek. May 3, 1993.	

First, the way in which a plant is grown is very important when it comes to its nutrients. The condition of the soil, weather and the type of fertilizing obviously affect the chemical composition and nutrient development of plants.

Those foods grown organically in deep, rich, naturally fertile soil are nutritionally superior to those grown in the over-used, deficient soils of many factory farms. Heavy doses of commercial fertilizers may help increase the *amount* of food produced, but they also lower its nutritional *quality*.

To gain time and make sure produce is tough enough for shipping, the industry likes to harvest plants long before they are ripe—and long before nutrients have fully developed.

Handling and hauling further deplete whatever nutrients *do* manage to develop. However, the most serious nutrient losses of all come with the many ways in which the industry finally conditions, processes and prepares the food that ends up on our dinner plates.

All that slicing, peeling, grinding, mixing, whipping, mashing, fabricating and extruding...all that frying, boiling, baking, pressure-cooking, homogenizing and pasteurizing...the *more* a food is processed, the *higher* are its nutrient losses.

Some even believe overprocessing our food is the *main* reason why so many Americans have serious nutritional deficiencies.

That pre-cooked convenience food may look good. It may even taste good. But is it supplying the nutrients your body needs?

There *are* ways to produce and prepare foods that conserve nutrients. Unfortunately, nutrient loss hasn't been a priority concern in the food industry. Public pressure is rapidly changing this, but what can you do right now?

We asked ourselves that sort of question in the mid-1970's. The answer led to a rural lifestyle and producing most of our food at home. We learned to tend our gardens, fruit trees, berry patches, mushroom logs, poultry and meat animals. We learned to process an annual supply of food through canning, freezing, drying and root-cellaring.

For us, growing our food and insuring its nutrition has been an important way to enjoy the good life. We wouldn't be true to ourselves if we failed to at least encourage you to consider a similar direction.

This may seem a laughable propositon if a frantic work life leaves you with barely enough time to read a menu or frozen dinner package, but let's be honest. Attention, involvement and participation are the words of health, not fast, easy and convenient. The *ideal* routine for assuring healthy foods for yourself and your family would be to somehow *grow* your own, *cook* it and *eat* it!

You don't have to move to the country to produce at least *some* of your own food. Even a small window garden of herbs and lettuce will reward you in taste and encourage you to learn more. Methods are available that make patio and apartment gardening feasible. Acres of lawn in suburbs everywhere beg to be put into family food gardens. Community gardening programs are more and more popular.

You want to obtain the most nutritious foods you can. If you don't grow your own, you'll have to get out there and track down the best you can find for your money. Be a modern "hunter and gatherer"—high-quality, organically-grown foods can be found through natural and health food stores, food co-ops, farmer's markets, buyer's clubs and pick-your-owns.

Organic certification programs in most states require that farmers use no chemicals or pesticides for three full years before approving their food.

Yes, they'll cost more at the checkout, but how much will you save in future doctor bills? The world around you will be healthier, too. Studies show, for example, that organic farming has significantly less soil erosion, ground water pollution and uses about half the energy required in conventional farming. [1]

Depending on where you live, you might be able to buy organic foods directly from a local farmer. "Contract-growing" or "community-supported agriculture" is becoming quite popular in some parts of the country. In this, small farm operations raise organic vegetables, grains, fruit, mushrooms, herbs, even meats for a membership of individuals and families.

Typically, such grower-buyer arrangements encourage face-to-face relationships and opportunities to pick-your-

Box 19: Shopping Tips

- Make your menu plan and shopping list for the week. It will keep you on track and save time.
- Shop after you've eaten to be less tempted by high-fat favorites.
- Be prepared to read labels. Don't rely on label claims, check the nutritional information for yourself.
- Buy staple items (dried beans, flour, rice, oats, pasta) in large quantities. Saves money and trips to the store.
- Get to know the butcher for special requests.
- Watch for labeling claims on prepackaged ground turkey and luncheon meats (look for fat percentage by calories, not weight).
- Use the sniff test when purchasing fish—no smell means freshness.
- Shop at the non- or low-fat end of the dairy case.
- Check egg substitute packages for fat-free brands.
- Shop at smaller, whole-foods cooperatives (or natural food stores) for a wide selection of whole-grain and legume products, bulk herbs and spices, organic foods.
- Support farmers' markets, contract growers and pick-your-owns for locally grown fresh produce.
- Ask your store to stock non- and low-fat products.
- Check the ingredient list on commercial breads, crackers, boxed cake mixes, cookies, cereals (avoid white flour, fats, sugars and high sodium content).
- Be careful in the snack food aisle (e.g., stick to pretzels and popcorn and look for baked, non-fat chips).
- Avoid products with lard, palm oil, coconut oil and partially hydrogenated vegetable oils.

own, attend pot-luck meetings, swap recipes and learn from other enlightened eaters. Growers have the security of knowing what foods to produce for a guaranteed market and network members have a secure source of nutrient-rich foods.

If you can't find local growers in your area and or a reasonable selection of organic foods where you shop, you might consider ordering by mail. Many organic farms will now ship directly to your door.

Prepare Top Quality Meals and Still Save Money

Whatever your level of cooking skill, you can prepare and eat great tasting, healthy meals right from the start. Cooking healthy isn't cooking complicated.

Whole foods, fresh foods and basic ingredient combinations, whether in a stir-fry dish or slow-cook stew, are delicious, nutritious and require only minimal preparation.

Cooking is an important doorway to healthy living. Eating for the nutrients in food is much easier when you get to choose the ingredients and cooking methods.

If you feel lost in the kitchen, start with the simplest preparations you can think of and take it from there. Instead of going to the ice cream shop for a malt, buy some frozen non-fat yogurt, malt flavoring and chocolate to prepare your own at home.

Maybe you're not ready to make a pizza from "scratch," but you could purchase the ingredients separately and put them together at home. Be sure to keep the crust, sauce and other ingredients low-fat right through to the non-fat cheese on top your favorite vegetables.

Start with small "from scratch" cooking projects. Experiment with our different muffin recipes and become a muffin

Box 20: Cooking Tips

Remember to:

- Use non-stick cooking spray instead of butter or oil.
- Use non-stick cookware and bakeware.
- Bake, broil, grill, poach or microwave meats and fish rather than fry or deep-fry.
- Trim all visible fat from meats.
- Remove skin from chicken and turkey.
- Skim fat from chilled stocks, soups and stews.
- Use de-fatted meat broth, dry wine or plain water instead of butter or oil when sautéing, gravy and sauce making.
- Use non- or low-fat dairy products.
- Use two egg whites in the place of one whole egg.
- Top vegetables and baked potatoes with herb seasonings, non-fat margarine, butter-flavor granules or non-fat dairy products rather than butter or regular margarine.
- Look for baked goods recipes that replace the oil with apple juice, apple sauce, milk or yogurt.
- Prepare several meatless meals in your weekly menu.
- Spread your toast with jelly or honey rather than butter.
- Spread your bagel with non-fat cream cheese.
- Spread your bread with non-fat mayonnaise, non-fat margarine or mustard.
- Fill the sandwich with water-packed tuna, bean spreads or skinless chicken breast rather than luncheon meats.

expert. Then step up to bagel-making. Rainy Saturday blahs perk right up with bagels hot from the oven.

For main meals from scratch, the crock-pot is a great starter-outer. Try our soup, stew and chowder recipes. Add some hot, whole-grain bread or buns, and a salad from your window garden. Then listen to the cheers of your inner crew.

Most of us wind up with a dozen or so favorite recipes that we enjoy over and over. Experiment, find your favorites, use the most nutritious ingredients you can obtain and cook for high-quality health.

Perhaps it seems the higher nutrition foods are going to cost you more. Not really.

Box 21: Useful Kitchen Tools

- food scale (weighs in ounces)
- measuring cups and spoons
- knives and chopping board
- mixing bowls
- wisk, spatula, ladle, rolling pin
- colander, strainer
- casserole dish
- large soup or stock pot
- vegetable steamer
- non-stick pots and pans
- microwave containers, freezer containers
- microwave oven
- blender
- food processor
- crock-pot/slow cooker
- wok

The higher prices on new low- and non-fat products make it seem that healthier eating is going to be more expensive. If you've located a source for organically grown, pesticide-free foods you'll pay more than you would at the supermarket.

At the same time low-fat/high-carbohydrate eating also offers tremendous opportunities for *cutting* costs. Essentially it is a shift from more expensive meat eating to less expensive vegetarian eating, from more expensive refined and processed foods to less expensive unrefined and unprocessed foods.

Researchers at the George Washington University Lipid Research Clinic, for example, recently reported a family with two grade-school children that ate at a 10% fat level spent $40 a week less on groceries than another family eating at a 37% fat level. That's a savings of more than $2000 a year.[2]

Fast and convenient is, of course, more expensive. The convenient portion, convenient package, convenient preparation, convenient restaurant—all add to the costs.

The grains, beans and pasta of a healthier diet may be purchased in bulk, which saves you plenty. These foods don't require refrigeration, which saves you plenty. Cooking them yourself saves you plenty, and certainly *eating* them saves you plenty. Consider, for example, the importance of low-fat eating in cancer prevention.

For a long time our country has been pouring vast amounts of money (over $4 million a day[3]) into the search for cancer cures, but we're simply not succeeding. Cancer death rates continue to climb year after year.

But if we're failing to cure cancer, we *do* know how to prevent much of it from happening in the first place. The National Cancer Institute estimates roughly 80% of cancer cases could be prevented, up to 60% of these by diet change alone.

By cutting our fat intake in half and doubling our intake of the cancer-preventing fiber, vitamins and minerals found in vegetables, fruits and grains we're saving *plenty*.

Be Ready for Fat Food Invites

All of us get cornered into a high-fat/low-carbohydrate eating situation now and then.

Say you've just started your healthy eating routines. Someone in the car hollers "It's time to eat." Next thing you know you're staring at a menu. You want to do it right but aren't sure about making quick and accurate choices.

Now, *Low-fat for Life* eating isn't strictly vegetarian, but it *does* shift from the typical meat and dairy emphasis to more of a vegetarian emphasis. So, when eating out and in doubt, go the vegetarian route. Order a meatless meal. It may not be the best choice possible, but it will get you through with minimal hassle and a good chance at healthy eating.

This is one of many little strategies you'll come up with to make it in a high-fat world.

All of us encounter fat food situations. Weddings, holidays, reunions, meetings, parties, eating out, an invite to friends or family—all challenge your ability to keep the fat out of your food.

The "in training" strategy we talked about in Chapter 21 is useful in many such situations. And there are other strategies you can develop as well.

The point is to prepare yourself so you don't get caught off guard. Are you just going to take it as it comes, try to hold it down by picking and choosing or not eat much of anything at all?

Don't wait until you're at the wedding to think about it. Have a plan of action in place. For the rare event like a special reunion, you might want to prepare for high-fat eating with extra low-fat meals the week beforehand. At a local wedding you might eat at home and then take small portions at the reception.

When invited to an unfamiliar restaurant you could phone to ask about their menu. Order in advance and make low-fat arrangements such as having your food baked not fried and not buttering your food or covering it with sauce. Keep a list of restaurants offering low-fat choices. Support them and encourage expanded low-fat menus.

If you're with a group of friends or co-workers watch out for those fast food, "Let's grab a bite." times. Some of the most popular menus are loaded with fat.

Box 22: Fast Foods		
Food	**Calories**	**Fat**
Mc D.L.T.	680	58%
McDonald's Big Mac	570	55%
Burger King Double Beef w/ cheese	950	57%
Burger King Onion Rings	274	53%
McDonald's French Fries, regular	220	47%
K.F.C. thigh, extra crispy	371	64%
K.F.C. Chicken Nuggets, 10	460	57%
Burger King Croissandwich	538	69%
Pizza Hut Super Supreme, thick crust, 2 slices	590	40%

Pennington, J. *Food Values of Portions Commonly Used.*
New York: Harper and Row, 1989.

Again, have a plan of action ready before hand. More and more low-fat alternatives are showing up in fast food restaurants. If you hunt you'll find a few already (e.g., muffins, fresh and frozen yogurts, fruit juices, cold cereals, salad bar vegetables).

And remember, we may all enjoy eating out, but the "at home" alternative could be suggested more often. TV commercials make it seem family ties and friendships are only strengthened by being waited on. But people also enjoy working together to achieve a great meal. Slicing vegetables for Szechuan Shrimp or Mandarin Orange Chicken is enjoyable with friends talking around the table.

If you often go out for pizza with friends, start an at-home "pizza night." With informed friends organize low-fat potlucks and exchange new recipe ideas.

Make Healthy Eating Convenient

Most of us lead busy, sometimes hectic lives. In particularly tight scheduling, even minor changes seem like major hassles. Our efforts, then, to change something as fundamental as the way we eat would stand to benefit from a little planning and organizing.

Obviously we want to get our new healthy eating routines practiced into habits as quickly as possible. The key to this in terms of planning is to recognize the powerful role of *convenience* in habit-forming behaviors (see Chapter 19).

The convenient lunch counter saves us time that we then spend shopping in the stores. The new apartment that's so convenient to our job has a tiny kitchen perfect for the heat and eat convenience foods. The spiffy little car has a long list of convenience options that we're able to afford with a long list of convenient monthly payments.

The more frenzied our schedules, the more ready we are for the promises of labor and time-saving conveniences.

Everybody in the whole world is doing their utmost to make it convenient for us to do what *they* want. The trick in planning is to make it convenient to do what *we* want.

We want to be healthier. We want to take better care of ourselves by changing what we eat. To successfully avoid the wrong but very convenient foods, we need to make the right foods as convenient as possible.

This means cooking, baking and shopping for food on weekends to make microwave portions convenient all week long. It means baking or buying those whole-grain rolls and breads for soup and sandwich lunches. It means stocking up with apples, oranges, bananas, plums, cherries and other fruits for convenient snacks.

Don't forget the fresh vegetables. Carrots, celery sticks, sliced zucchini and cucumbers are great for snacking, too. Ever tried sunchokes or kohlrabi?

Many think they don't like vegetables. What they don't like is the way vegetables are *prepared* for eating. "Plain" vegetables sitting next to a reduced meat portion has them looking glum. But woking them in oriental seasonings, souping and stewing them perhaps with cajun zing makes for appealing tastes.

We need to eat more vegetables to get our fiber, vitamins and minerals. Soups, stews and stir-fries make eating more vegetables *convenient!*

Have a hard time getting breakfast ready in the morning? Make it more convenient. Put the ingredients for a "Fiber 20" breakfast (see Box 23) together before you go to bed. Hot cereal ingredients in the bowl are ready for a four minute microwave in the morning.

Box 23: Fiber Insurance

The typical American diet contains 10–15 grams of fiber daily. Nutrition experts recommend we eat 20–40 grams a day, while a range of 40–60 grams is better yet. A convenient way to insure the minimum amount is with our **Fiber 20 Breakfast** (see Chapter 29 for the recipe).

Fiber 20 Ingredients	Fiber	Insoluble	Soluble
1/2 c. Oatmeal	7g	3g	4g
2 T. Oat Bran	7g	3.5g	3.5g
2 T. Wheat Bran	4g	4g	0g
1 Banana	2.7g	1.5	1.2g
Fiber 20 Totals	**20.7g**	12g	8.7g

Prefer fruit? Have a bowl of mixed fruits sliced up and ready in the refrigerator. Prefer muffins? Have a batch of them in the freezer waiting for a morning heat up. Take a couple along for later snacks.

Pre-made sauce is the convenient way to a spaghetti dinner. A crock-pot stew simmering during the day seems awfully convenient at evening mealtime. It's also a convenient way to eat a lot of vegetables, isn't it?

Do everything you can think of to make your new routines *convenient* to practice. Make food preparation and eating as much the center of your attention as you can. For example, no matter what your kitchen is like it can be made more convenient for preparing and storing foods.

No room for a freezer? Don't be embarassed by having one in your bedroom. Be proud of how well stocked it is.

Create a work/eating area that makes it more convenient to prepare foods. Put shelves at one or both ends of a table. Stock them with glass jars full of different beans, cereal

Box 24: Deliberate Leftovers

A little extra planning makes healthy food convenient.

- Bake extra bread, muffins, bagels, pancakes or waffles on the weekend to toast or microwave during the week.

- Pre-cut bread into slices and store in the freezer. Pop off a slice as you need it for a quick snack.

- Bake a whole chicken, skin and bone it, freeze in small containers. Use in casseroles, soups and sandwiches all week.

- Cook a large pot of soup and freeze in small microwave containers to heat when you need a quick meal.

- Cook several pots of beans at the same time to use for soups, refried beans, cold salads, etc. Freeze extra.

- Make up a variety of stir-fry sauces that are ready-to-go with rice and vegetables.

- Sandwich spreads such as egg, tuna, chicken or bean mashes can be made in large enough quantities to last a few days.

- Cook or steam more vegetables than you plan to eat. Reheat later or use in soups and salads.

- Double your casserole recipe. Freeze one.

- When you clean vegetables for a salad, prepare extra for snacks and lunch bags.

- Make extra burgers to heat the next day for lunch.

- Surplus baked or boiled potatoes can be made into hash browns, home fries or oven fries.

- Double your spaghetti sauce recipe for additional meals-in-a-hurry.

- Double your bread recipes. Store extra in freezer.

- Get into the habit of cooking for more than one meal at a time.

grains, flours, pasta, herbs, teas, raisins, dates, seeds. Hang often-used pans and utensils. Add a few plants, cookbooks and a good overhead light.

What else do you need for you and a friend to do a little cooking or baking on your next "free" evening?

Checklist: Eating Routines.

❏   Daily calories estimated.

❏   Daily calories divided into meals and snacks.

❏   No-think and some-think meals identified.

❏   List of meal and snack choices or possibilities written out.

❏   Listed meals and snacks are all below 20% fat and provide a variety of fruit, vegetables, grains and legumes.

❏   Organic, high-quality food sources found.

❏   Strategies for fat-food invites identified.

❏   Times to shop, prepare and eat meals and snacks scheduled (see Week-at-a-Glance example in Appendix B).

24

Exercise Routines

Exercise is an important part of the low-fat lifestyle. Earlier in the book we discussed its role in looking and feeling your best. Now we want to take you beyond the theoretical perspective and show you how to make exercise part of your daily routine.

Note: If you have a history of heart, back, knee or other physical problems, consult your physician before attempting these exercise routines.

There are basically two types of exercise to consider, endurance and strength. Each sets specific conditions in your body and each has its importance in a healthy lifestyle. Let's look first at endurance, or aerobic, training.

Endurance Training

Aerobic exercise, combined with a low-fat diet and creative meditation, is simply the best way to get rid of excess body fat. Fat is burned in your muscles. You've got to move it if you want to lose it.

The more you exercise aerobically, the better. With consistent training your body will develop a greater number of fat-burning enzymes, increasing its ability to use fat for energy. Endurance exercise makes you a better fat burner over the long haul.

Aerobic activity also helps prevent many of our culture's diseases and health problems. In time, you can expect a rise in HDL's, a drop in LDL's, decreased blood pressure, greater lung capacity, increased insulin sensitivity, stronger bones, and a lower risk of a heart attack or stroke.

Endurance exercise can take many forms. Cross-country skiing, biking, running and aerobic dance classes are all fine possibilities. If you prefer the convenience of in-home training you can purchase a treadmill, rowing machine, stationary bike or step machine.

Walking for Endurance

Of all the possibilities, we choose walking as our overall favorite endurance routine. Why?

In "Eating Routines" we suggested you make healthy eating a convenient thing to do. The same goes for exercise. The more convenient an exercise is, the more likely you will do it.

Walking is convenient. You can walk anytime, day or night, indoors or out. You can do it pretty much where you want. Mall walking, for example, is becoming very popular.

You don't need any special equipment either. You can walk down a street in ordinary clothing at a very business-like pace. No one will guess you're really exercising. Of course, if you prefer, you can strut around in your sweat pants and let everyone know just how healthy and vigorous you're getting.

It's easy to combine walking with all sorts of other activities like listening to music, talking with a friend, reading or walking your dog. Practice a foreign language with audio cassettes.

Maybe you'd like to join a walking club or go on a walking tour vacation. The magazines on walking are loaded with ideas.

Another big point in walking's favor is its effectiveness as an aerobic exercise. Even Dr. Kenneth Cooper, one of the original proponents of running and jogging, has suggested that people should walk more and run less.[1]

Recent research from Cooper's Institute for Aerobics has shown that walking can produce the same improvements in aerobic conditioning and calorie burning as running or jogging with less chance of injury.[2]

It should be easy to see why walking is the bottom line exercise for our endurance routine. It's convenient, effective and can be modified to fit your needs, circumstances and fitness level.

The Aerobic Range

You remember from earlier discussion that aerobic (endurance) exercise requires oxygen to burn fat as fuel. Anaerobic (strength) exercise doesn't require oxygen to burn glucose as fuel.

When exercising aerobically you therefore keep your exertion level *moderate* to make sure you're able to bring in enough oxygen to continue burning fat. If you're pushing too hard you'll start burning more glucose in your fuel mix. You want to keep things chugging along within the optimum *aerobic* (oxygenating) range.

After you've walked in the aerobic range several times, you'll learn to recognize it by your breathing. *Shallow breathing* tells you to increase the pace; *heavy breathing* tells you to decrease the pace.

However, when starting out it's best to check your heart rate to know you're doing it right. Your aerobic range is from 60–80% of your maximum heart rate.

You can find your estimated maximum heart rate by subtracting your age from 220. If, for example, you're 50 years old, your estimated maximum heart rate would be 220 minus 50 or 170 beats per minute.

The 60–80% aerobic range (170 X .60 and 170 X .80) would then be 102–136 beats per minute. Box 25 gives you the aerobic training range by age.

Box 25: Aerobic Training Range

Age	20	25	30	35	40
Training Range*	120–160	117–156	114–152	111–148	108–144
Age	45	50	55	60	65
Training Range*	105–140	102–136	99–132	96–128	93–124
Age	70	75	80	85	90
Training Range*	90–120	87–116	84–112	81–108	78–104

*Training range in heart beats-per-minute

So to check your heart rate you count the number of times it beats in a minute, right? Well you can, but there's a better way. For now let's just label this as helpful background information. We'll show you how to use it in the four steps of our endurance routine.

Walking in the Aerobic Range

1. Start Walking, Find Your Pulse

First get your heart rate going by walking. After 10 minutes or so locate your pulse on the inside wrist or on the large artery on either side of your Adam's apple.

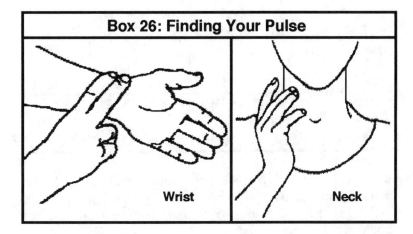

Box 26: Finding Your Pulse

Wrist   Neck

Try to keep moving while you do this. If you come to a complete stop, your heart rate will drop quickly and you won't be as accurate. If its too difficult to find while walking at your normal pace, try slowing down until you get it.

2. Determine Your Heart Rate

Now that you've found your pulse, start counting and use a stopwatch to time yourself. But don't follow the heart rate guidelines of beats-per-*minute*. Its hard to accurately count pulse beats for this length of time, especially while you're walking.

All you have to do is count the number of beats you get in 10 *seconds*. Box 27 gives you a list of 10-second beat counts for different ages.

To match this with your beats-per-minute figure, multiply your 10-second count by six. For example, the above 50

Box 27: Aerobic Training Range-10 second count				
Age	20	25	30	35	40
Training Range*	20–27	19.5–26	19–25	18.5–24.5	18–24
Age	45	50	55	60	65
Training Range*	17.5–23	17–22.5	16.5–22	16–21.5	15.5–20.5
Age	70	75	80	85	90
Training Range*	15–20	14.5–19.5	14–18.5	13.5–18	13–17.5

*Training range in heart beats-per-10-second count

year old should have a 10-second count somewhere between 17 (60%) and 22.5 (80%) beats. If you multiply these by six you'll get the 102 and 136 beats-per-minute our walker should aim for.

3. Adjust Your Pace

When you find your heart rate, adjust your pace to get it in the aerobic range. If you're under 60%, speed up a little. If you're over 80% slow it down. Check things periodically to make sure your pace is consistent.

Remember what we said earlier. Once you get the basic feel for it, you won't need to check any longer. Pay attention to your *breathing*. You'll know when to speed up and when to slow down and you can just concentrate on enjoying your walk.

4. Walk For 20-60 Minutes

Build up gradually. Begin with a brisk 20-minute walk. You could simply walk away from your starting point for 10 minutes and then return. Increase the walking time 5 or 10 minutes each week until you are walking an hour each day. On level ground without interruptions many walkers hustle along at about four miles an hour.

Authorities suggest walking a minimum of three times a week, but every day if possible. We walk every day except Sunday, our official day of rest.

When you first begin a walking program emphasize longer, not harder. Your body needs time to adapt and develop the aerobic capacity of your heart, lungs, and fat burning enzymes. If you increase your walking intensity too early, you won't be ready and you'll switch over to anaerobic, glucose-burning metabolism.

So stick to the lower (60%) end of the heartbeat range while you get yourself up to 60 minutes. After that you can increase your speed and heart rate as you feel ready.

Walking Equipment

If you start putting on a lot of miles you may want to purchase some walking shoes. Research has found that regular running shoes don't work well for walking because they're designed for *shock absorption*.

They have a thick, cushioned heel that makes it hard to walk effectively. Casey Meyers describes it like walking in sand. Your foot "sinks" at the same time it tries to push off, fatiguing your legs before your workout is done.

A walking shoe needs a *firm* heel between 1/2 and 3/4 of an inch thick. The platform, or sole, must be flexible, not rigid, near the ball of the foot. And you need plenty of room around your toes for the natural "push-off" motion of walking.

Today there are many walking shoes available in a wide range of quality and price. You should be able to pick up a good pair for forty to sixty dollars, less on sale. Check the walking magazines for helpful shoe reviews and product information.

Some consideration must also be given to the clothing you wear on a walk.

A good winter routine should consist of numerous light layers of clothing rather than a single, heavy coat. You can regulate your temperature by removing a jacket as you heat up, or putting it back on if you cool down. In severe cold you'll probably want to add a hat, gloves or even an insulated ski mask.

Warm weather is different. A summer routine is concerned with keeping cool. Drink lots of water and wear something light that allows plenty of air circulation and comfort. Of course the summer heat often brings insect pests, so wear a hat or bandana to keep them at bay.

If you can, walk at night or in the early morning when temperatures are cooler and you can avoid the direct sun. If it's dark be sure to wear reflective clothing.

A walking endurance routine is an easy way to burn fat and increase your aerobic health. Just start walking, monitor your heart rate or your breathing, adjust your pace to the aerobic range and stay out there for an hour or so.

Strength Training

The changes created by strength exercise are important for optimum fitness and physical health. They complement and enhance the benefits of an endurance routine by increasing fat-burning capacity, bone and joint strength, and the ease with which we go about our daily physical activities.

We know that endurance activities like walking and biking are aerobic. Their continuous, moderate intensity burns fat for fuel.

In contrast, strength training is "anaerobic". The intense, short bursts of activity are performed *without* oxygen and therefore require glucose or glycogen as an energy source.

Strength exercise is usually performed against an outside resistance or force like weights, hydraulics or gravity. By progressively increasing this resistance over time, you create the conditions to which your muscles respond by growing larger and stronger.

We're not talking about any complicated or time-consuming program, either. A bottom line commitment of three 15–20 minute sessions each week will help you strengthen your muscles and balance your aerobic training for a lifetime of fitness.

To get you started we offer two beginning strength routines that suit different goals and circumstances. The first version utilizes *bodyweight*. It has you working with the push-up and pull-up exercises you are likely familiar with. Its main attraction is that it is easy to habituate to, like walking is for aerobic exercise. This is the choice for those who primarily want to firm up muscles, keep strength up and prevent gradual muscle loss.

Those who wish to *increase* muscle size should consider the dumbbell routine. It's easier to work with and fine tune for individual differences in "progressive resistance" training. We'll talk more about this shortly, but first let's nail down some of the language of strength training.

Definitions

Repetition: one full movement of an exercise from the start position to the finish position and back again. For example, do you remember doing push-ups in gym class? When you did one push-up, you did one repetition.

Set: a group of repetitions done one right after the other. If you did 10 repetitions (10 push-ups) in a row and then stopped to rest, it was a set.

Rest Period: the time between sets that you let your muscles rest and recover their energy. We suggest about 45–60 second rests.

Full Range of Motion: each repetition of an exercise should be performed all the way through, from the start position to the finish and back again, in a continuous motion without any lengthy pauses. This full range is important to ensure the development of strength at every point in an exercise, the maintenance of flexibility in your muscles, and the full benefit for your work.

Repetition Speed: this means a slow to moderate repetition speed with no bouncing or jerking. Rather than developing conditions for muscle growth, fast movements allow momentum to take over and transfer the stress to your joints and connective tissue. A two-second count up and a two-second count down will be effective.

Now let's put some of this into a hypothetical situation. If your workout called for two sets of push-ups for 10–15 repetitions, what would you do? First you'd complete one set of 10–15 repetitions (do 10–15 push-ups) in controlled form through a full range of motion. *All* the way up and *all* the way down without bouncing at the bottom, for as many as you can in good form. Then rest for 60 seconds to allow your muscles to recover. Follow this with a second set of push-ups for 10–15 repetitions. That's it. You'd rest again and likely move on to another exercise.

What happens if you can't stay in the right repetition range? What if you can't do 10 push-ups and you only get 8? Or maybe 15 is really easy and you can keep going to 20 repetitions?

What you need to do is adjust the resistance, the force against which your muscles are working, until you are exercising in the 10–15 repetition range.

With bodyweight exercises this is a little tricky. You can't just change your weight (the resistance) at a moment's notice. What you *can* do is modify the exercise a little.

If, for example, you can only do 8 push-ups and you want to do at least 10, you can make things easier by doing them with bent knees. If, on the other hand, you can do more than called for, say 20 repetitions, you can try to make the exercise harder by putting your feet up on a chair or slowing down the speed of each repetition.

Dumbbells are easier to adjust for individual needs. With them, you correct resistance directly. By simply changing the weight on the bar you'll be able to keep your exercises in the strength-building range of 10–15 repetitions.

If 10 is too hard and you can only get 7 or 8 repetitions, you're using too much weight on your dumbbells. Reduce it enough to bring you back into the 10–15 range.

If 15 is too easy and you manage to get 18 or 20 repetitions, you need to put extra weight on the dumbbells.

It will take a little practice and experimentation to find the right amount of resistance for each exercise, but you'll get the hang of it. Simply adjust things up or down until your repetitions fall in the correct range.

Progressive Resistance

For increasing muscle the key training concept is "progressive resistance." This means gradually increasing resistance to encourage muscle growth. Again, it is a matter of arranging conditions that will elicit a healthy growth response.

In adapting to the increased weight put on a dumbbell, for example, our muscles respond with complex biochemical and structural changes that make them bigger and stronger.

With training, a muscle that originally managed 10 repetitions will, in time, be able to complete 13 or 14. Strength building will continue until this muscle is at the top of its desirable repetition range at 15.

Increasing repetitions beyond 15 would further strengthen the muscle somewhat, but would more and more shift over from strength training to the endurance training sought in aerobic exercise.

So, to stay in the right training range of repetitions, you need to add weight to your dumbbells to the point where you can just manage 10 or 11 repetitions again.

Your muscles will then gradually adapt to the new resistance by getting stronger, enabling you to complete more repetitions. When you again are putting out the 15, it's time to increase that resistance—and so the story goes.

Continue increasing resistance to encourage continued muscle growth. This is progressive resistance training in a nutshell.

No Such Thing as a Lazy Muscle

It's still popular to describe strength training in "macho power" terms where you are *forcing* and *shocking* your "lazy" muscles into growth.

The continual emphasis on "paining muscles to gain muscles" certainly helped pave the way for the abusive use of steroids and other drugs in athletics.

A more enlightened view recognizes there is no such thing as a lazy muscle that must be whipped into growth. Laziness is something your mind and habits need to sit down and talk about.

In well-planned training conditions, muscles will often respond to the challenge of maximum exertion with feelings of healthy *exhileration*. This is what athletes mean with popular terms like *pump, burn* and *second wind*.

It is your responsibility to arrange the best possible environment for the healthy, invigorating life you and your body want. You don't have to use *force* to be healthy. Work *with* your body. Maximize growth by coaching, guiding and supporting.

When you furnish nutritious foods, meditative attention, and both endurance and strength exercise, your body *will* become healthier, stronger, and more fit.

Additionally, as we explained earlier in the book, by carefully arranging your eating, exercise and meditation routines, they'll have a synergistic effect to help you achieve a greater overall growth response.

You Are Unique

Remember, each of us is unique in how our growth proceeds. We each have our assets and liabilities.

Don't worry about how others do their workouts. Some individuals are able to increase the weight on their dumbbells in 5 pound increments. Others should only add ½ pound at a time. You are unique and your body will respond in its own unique way.

You're not a machine, so it won't be all steady uphill gains. Some days you'll feel as if you could pull a telephone pole out of the ground. On others a 20-pound weight will act like it's 200 pounds. One day it's an easy 14 push-ups, the next it's a grunting 11.

These are necessary, normal, natural differences. Your body has energy cycles and rhythms that will clearly affect your workouts.

Sometimes you'll have to lower resistance to stay within your repetition range. This isn't losing ground. You're looking for an overall healthy effect and the ups and downs of individual sessions are poor indicators of what's going on. For every "low" day you have, there's a "high" one in which you'll feel new strength and improvement.

It's a good idea to keep a notebook for a written record of what you've done. Instead of seeing just the ups and downs of the day-to-day workouts, you can look back and be inspired by the progress you've made over time.

Remember to Warm Up

Light exercise to warm up is important. It allows your body to get ready for more strenuous work. It helps prevent injuries like sprains, strains, and muscle pulls.

Cold muscles are unprepared. Think of it this way. A rubber band put in the freezer gets brittle and stiff. If you pull it hard it may snap. But if you warm it up in a glass of hot water it becomes soft and pliable and can easily be stretched to different lengths.

How do you warm up? Simply do 5–10 minutes of aerobic exercise prior to your strength training session. You'll know you're ready when you feel a little sweat on your forehead and your body feels "loose."

If time is a problem, you might consider combining endurance and strength training. Reduce the length of your walks to 30–40 minutes three days a week and schedule your strength sessions right afterward. Your muscles will be warm and ready to go. The other three days walk for the full hour.

Putting It All Together

These strength routines are designed for someone begin-ning an exercise lifestyle. They each consist of basic exercis-es that use the major muscles of your body in the shortest time possible while still establishing conditions in which they adapt and grow in strength and tone.

Choose the version that best suits you. Read through it and make sure you're comfortable with the exercise descrip-tions and accompanying illustrations prior to trying them.

Normally, you will do two sets for every exercise, but in the first two weeks we recommend you only do one set each. This will give your body time to adjust and prevent too much soreness.

The days you schedule your strength training are also im-portant. You'll need three non-consecutive days like Mon–Wed–Fri, Tues–Thurs–Sat or Sun–Tues–Thurs because the rest days in between are essential for the recuperation of the muscles.

During strength exercise you are encouraging or stimulat-ing your muscles to grow. It's in the 48 hours *after* training that your muscles actually grow to adapt to those previous exercise conditions.

This is the cycle of growth: challenge and response, chal-lenge and response. The rhythm of your schedule is impor-tant for optimal progress. Aerobic training can and should be done daily. It develops the *endurance* capacity of your mus-cles in lower intensity activity. Maximum muscle effort in anaerobic training for *strength* requires rest periods.

Strength Routines

Before starting your strength routine, read through Boxes 28 and 29. They provide some training tips that apply to both versions.

Box 28: Do's and Don'ts of Strength Training

Do
- Tighten your stomach muscles as you lift to support your lower back
- Keep your back in its natural curve (the lordotic position)
- Control the resistance, don't let it control you
- Keep breathing
- Warm up
- Keep your head and neck straight
- Keep your knees from going out past your toes when training legs (stick your butt out back rather than your knees out front)
- Use safety collars on barbells and dumbbells
- Use proper form and position on all exercises

Don't
- Jerk or bounce to complete a repetition
- Try to lift more weight than you can handle in good form
- Hold your breath
- Let your knees come out past your toes when training legs

Box 29: How to Breath While Strength Training

- Never hold your breath while strength training. The internal build up of pressure could stop the flow of oxygen to your brain (the Valsalva Maneuver) causing you to pass out.

- Inhale during the relaxation or "down" half of an exercise. Exhale with the exertion.

- When doing a push-up, for example, inhale as you lower your body to the floor. Exhale as you press yourself back up.

Version A—Bodyweight Exercises
Push-Up
—develops the chest, shoulders and triceps

Position
- Lie face down on the floor.
- Place your hands 2–3 inches outside your shoulders.
- Elbows should stick out away from your body.

Performance
- Keeping your body straight (don't sag or arch), push up until your arms are straight.
- Lower slowly.
- Repeat for 10–15 repetitions.
- Rest 45–60 seconds and repeat for a second set.

Modifications

Start   **Finish**

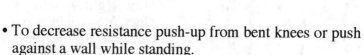

- To decrease resistance push-up from bent knees or push against a wall while standing.
- To increase resistance push-up between two chairs, with feet elevated on chair or have a friend place a book or household item on your shoulders.

Pull-Up

—develops the upper back, shoulders and biceps

Position

• Hang from a bar with a comfortable grip, about 6"–18" between hands.

• Hands can face palms-in or palms-away, whichever is more comfortable.

Performance

• From the start position, pull yourself up until your neck is level with bar (Don't jerk or use leg swing to help you).

• Lower slowly.

• Repeat for 10–15 repetitions.

• Rest 45–60 seconds and repeat for a second set.

Start   **Finish**

Modifications

• To decrease resistance, place a chair below and slightly behind you and assist yourself by pushing lightly with your legs. You could also have a friend lift up lightly on your waist or feet.

• To increase resistance, wear heavy boots or hold a heavy household item with your feet or tied around your belt.

Lunge—develops the legs and hips

Position

- Place your hands on your hips or let your arms hang freely at your side.
- Step forward with one leg until there are about 2–3 feet between it and your back leg.
- Your upper body should remain upright throughout the exercise.

Performance

- From the start position, slowly lower your body by bending your knees until your front leg forms a 90 degree angle.
- Lower yourself straight up and down, not forward and backward.
- Push back up using your legs until they are straight again.
- Repeat for 10–15 repetitions.
- Step forward with your other leg and repeat.
- Rest 45–60 seconds and repeat each leg for a second set.

Start   **Finish**

*Note—To prevent excess strain on the knees, be certain your shin and knee remain relatively upright and don't go out over your toes. We suggest standing next to a mirror to check this. If you do the movement correctly, i.e., straight up and down, this shouldn't be a problem.

Abdominal Crunches

—develops the abdominal (stomach) muscles

Position

- Lie face up on the floor.
- Legs should rest bent across a chair or hang freely with thighs perpendicular to the floor.
- Arms should be across the chest or behind your head.
- Lower back should touch the floor.

Performance

- Curl or "crunch" your shoulders toward your legs.
- Do not try to "sit-up" completely. Just let your shoulders come off the floor a few inches. Don't worry if the motion seems very short.
- Your lower back should stay in contact with the floor and not lift off.
- Un-curl to starting position.
- Repeat for 10–15 repetitions.
- Rest 45–60 seconds and repeat for a second set.

Start   **Finish**

Modifications

- To decrease resistance place your hands on your knees and give yourself a *slight* pull up.
- To increase resistance, hold a household item on your chest or do your repetitions more slowly.

Lying Back Arch

—develops the low-back muscles

Position

- Lie face down on the floor.
- Keep your legs straight and pressed together.
- Place your arms straight overhead.

Performance

- Raise your arms, trunk and legs off the floor simultaneously.
- Lower slowly.
- Repeat for 10–15 repetitions.
- Rest 45–60 seconds and repeat for a second set.

Start

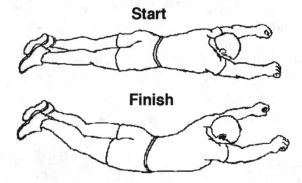

Finish

Modifications

- To decrease resistance, try raising only one of your body parts (trunk or legs) or decrease the weight of your trunk by placing your arms alongside your body. If you still have difficulty, you may assist yourself by pushing lightly with your arms.
- To increase resistance, hold a book or household item in your hands or between your feet.

*Note: If you have a history of low-back problems, consult your physician before trying this exercise.

Version B—Dumbbell Exercises

Dumbbell Bench Press—develops the chest, shoulders and triceps

Position
- Lie face up on a bench with your feet on the floor, dumbbells in hand.
- Elbows should stick out away from your body, not in close to your sides.
- Forearms should be straight up and down with your palms facing your feet.
- Dumbbells should start in line with your lower-chest area and finish over your shoulder/upper-chest area.

Performance
- From the start position push the dumbbells up until your arms are straight.
- Lower the dumbbells slowly and in control back to the start position until you feel a slight stretch across the chest muscles.
- Repeat for 10–15 repetitions.
- Rest 45–60 seconds and repeat for a second set.

Start

Finish

*Note: Don't worry if this exercise feels shaky and uncoordinated at first. With practice you'll develop the balance necessary for smooth control of the dumbbells.

Dumbbell Row

—develops the upper back, shoulders and biceps

Position

• Hold a dumbbell in one hand, letting it hang straight down.

• Stand next to a bench and place your opposite arm and knee on it to support your body.

• The dumbbell hand should face palm in toward the body.

• Upper body should be parallel to the floor.

Performance

• From the start position pull the dumbbell until it touches the side of your waist (not your chest).

• Once you reach the finish point, lower the dumbbell slowly until your arm is straight.

• Repeat for 10–15 repetitions.

• Move to other side of bench and repeat for opposite arm.

• Rest 45–60 seconds and repeat each side for a second set.

Start   **Finish**

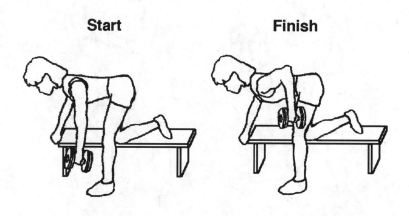

Dumbbell Shoulder Press
—develops the shoulders and triceps

Position
• Sit upright on a bench.
• Keep your abdominal (stomach) muscles tight to keep your back from over-arching or sit in a sturdy chair with a back support.
• Hold a dumbbell in each hand at shoulder level.
• Palms face the front.

Performance
• From the start position, press the dumbbells overhead.
• Lower slowly back to the start position.
• Repeat for 10–15 repetitions.
• Rest 45–60 seconds and repeat for a second set.

*Note: You may want to watch yourself in a mirror until you are comfortable with your balance and performance.

start   **finish**

Dumbbell Lunge—develops the legs and hips

Position

- Hold a dumbbell in each hand. Let them hang freely at your side.
- Step forward with one leg until there are about 2-3 feet between it and your back leg.
- Your upper body should remain upright throughout the exercise.

Performance

- From the start position, slowly lower your body by bending your knees until your front leg forms a 90 degree angle.
- Lower yourself straight up and down, not forward and backward.
- Push back up using your legs until they are straight again.
- Repeat for 10–15 repetitions.
- Step forward with your other leg and repeat.
- Rest 45–60 seconds and repeat each leg for a second set.

start   **finish**

*Note—To prevent excess strain on the knees, be certain your shin and knee remain relatively upright and don't go out over your toes. We suggest standing next to a mirror to check this. If you do the movement correctly (straight up and down), this shouldn't be a problem.

Abdominal Crunches

—develops the abdominal (stomach) muscles

Position

• Lie face up on the floor.

• Legs should rest bent across a chair or hang freely with thighs perpendicular to the floor.

• Arms should be across the chest or behind your head.

• Lower back should touch the floor.

Performance

• Curl or "crunch" your shoulders toward your legs.

• Do not try to "sit-up" completely. Just let your shoulders come off the floor a few inches. Don't worry if the motion seems very short.

• Your lower back should stay in contact with the floor and not lift off.

• Un-curl to starting position.

• Repeat for 10–15 repetitions.

• Rest 45–60 seconds and repeat for a second set.

Start   **Finish**

Modifications

• To decrease resistance place your hands on your knees and give yourself a *slight* pull up.

• To increase resistance, hold a household item on your chest or do your repetitions more slowly.

Lying Back Arch

—develops the low-back muscles

Position

• Lie face down on the floor.
• Keep your legs straight and pressed together.
• Place your arms straight overhead.

Performance

• Raise your arms, trunk and legs off the floor simultaneously.
• Lower slowly.
• Repeat for 10–15 repetitions.
• Rest 45–60 seconds and repeat for a second set.

Start

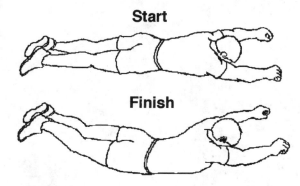

Finish

Modifications

• To decrease resistance, try raising only one of your body parts (trunk or legs) or decrease the weight of your trunk by placing your arms alongside your body. If you still have difficulty, you may assist yourself by pushing lightly with your arms.
• To increase resistance, hold a dumbbell in your hands or between your feet.

*Note: If you have a history of low-back problems, consult your physician before trying this exercise.

Checklist: Exercise Routines.

❑ Endurance routine(s) selected.

❑ Aerobic range identified.

❑ Endurance training equipment acquired.

❑ Strength routine selected.

❑ Strength training equipment acquired.

❑ A week of exercise routines scheduled (see Week-at-a-Glance example in Appendix B).

25

Meditation Routines

How Do You Meditate?

In a basic meditation routine, such as we are suggesting, you sit, relax yourself and count your breaths or repeat a special word with each exhale for 20 minutes or so.

Simple instructions, but not that easy to accomplish. So let's talk about some of what's involved and what to expect in meditation.

Why Do People Meditate?

People meditate for many reasons. Some meditate to combat stress. Others meditate to prepare for competition in a sport. Still others meditate to grow spiritually and psychologically, to cure illness and relieve pain or to develop intuition and creativity.

Often meditators will tell you their practice gives them the extra strength to achieve whatever growth and change they're after. Some of them believe they tap this source of strength and energy through meditative work with Kundalini forces. Others believe they're synchronizing brain waves, stepping into the flow or listening to their inner voice.

Some see meditation as a form of prayer that opens their hearts to receive the strength of God's love. Others see it as opening their awareness to a force of life within all of us, the healing energy that the Chinese call "chi" and the Hawaiians call "mana."

If you're interested, then, you'll find a great deal more to learn about meditation than what we'll be talking about here. This is a book of bottom lines and we are limiting our concern to several practical skills or abilities known to come with the practice of meditation.

What Meditation Skills?

We're suggesting you practice a meditation routine at least 20 minutes every day and twice a day if you can arrange it.

The more you practice, the more quickly you'll develop: 1.) relaxation skills for stress management, 2.) concentration-attention skills for changing habits and 3.) commitment skills for achieving goals.

Relaxation Skills for Stress Management

Do you remember the "fight-or-flight" body response and the importance of relaxation for managing the stress of modern life?

Basically we react to danger by instantly mobilizing our body to either confront it or retreat from it. The tension we feel is a necessary part of our preparation to respond.

Unfortunately we are aroused as much by "paper tigers" as real ones. Even when the tigers *are* real, we tend to stay aroused long after they have passed. Our blood pressure, heart rate, respiration and blood lactate levels remain higher than normal.

This leads to a build-up of stress which can make an otherwise ordinary circumstance feel like a major crisis.

With our "valves turned up" all the time, we keep adding a strong dose of tension to every incident of the day. Our judgment is impaired and we have a hard time sorting those situations that are genuinely threatening from those that aren't. How can we help but overreact?

Practicing meditation teaches us to relax, we are able to drain off feelings of fear and uneasiness. We are able to relieve our tension and distress after an unpleasant incident. We learn to calm and collect ourselves in five to ten minutes after a family argument or difficult meeting at work.

We learn to elicit what Herbert Benson calls the "Relaxation Response." This is a capacity of our bodies to enter a state that has lower heart, blood pressure, metabolic and breathing rates. Our brain waves slow to alpha levels. Our blood-lactate levels drop.

Learning to relax when we want gives us a tool that helps us counteract the many harmful physical, social and psychological effects of stress build-up and chronic anxiety. It also increases our sense of personal power and choice.

When something happens in the world around us that we have little or no control over, we are at least able to choose how much we'll let it bother us. We can decide to relax and let it go. We can go into our office, bedroom or wherever and within minutes using our meditative training bring the world back into a less frenzied perspective.

Concentration-Attention Skills for Changing Habits

In Chapter 20 we considered the importance of meditation for changing habits. You have to pay a lot of attention to what you're doing or they'll just take over and do it the old way. Meditation increases your ability to focus and concentrate your attention.

Now, paying attention is related to the ability to relax we were just talking about. Typically we associate relaxation with sleep. When you're very comfortable and relaxed, your mind begins to wander and you drop off into snoozeland.

Meditative relaxation is different. Your muscles and body are relaxed in the same way, but your awareness is very *awake*. That's why you meditate sitting upright. You *want* to remain awake.

Relaxing in meditation is actually freeing your attention from distractions. You want to direct *less* attention to body messages and the continual flux of plans, memories and feelings that fill your usual awareness so that you have *more* attention available for meditating.

Meditating develops a special *alertness*. It is daily practice in sitting quietly and "listening" to your silent inner world with all the attention you can muster.

You're not anxiously awaiting some big event, but remain calm and alert. You are in a state of relaxed attention.

With this practice you obviously learn how to concentrate. You practice not being distracted by the thoughts that come to you. You let them go without being aroused by them. You remain calm and continue to focus attention on your meditation.

Meditators learn not to be as upset by troubling situations; they are able to focus their thoughts and emotions.

This is why meditators change habits more easily. They are able to concentrate, learn faster and establish the habits of thinking and behaving that they *want* to automate (whether driving a car or eating healthier foods).

With meditation you find it easier to pay *more* attention to what you *are* doing (trying a new low-fat soup and sandwich for lunch) and *less* attention to what you're *not* doing (eating another high-fat hamburger and fries for lunch).

You'll also find more to taste in that soup than you would have before. Able to focus your attention, you *notice* more of the delicate flavors.

Being less affected by distractions, you're also less anxious and worrisome, less easily angered. You have more energy available for what you want to do. You're more able to direct your attention, stay on task and get things done.

In conversations you're more able to keep attention on the person you are with. Your mind wanders less and you pick up subtle cues more easily.

Commitment Skills for Achieving Goals

All your life you've been practicing the way you think and behave. Your habits of living, healthy and otherwise, are set deeply in place.

Increasing your abilities to relax and concentrate your attention will help you make important changes, but something else is also needed.

Every kind of self-help book talks about it sooner or later. It's one of those ultimate bottom lines and you've heard it said a million times before.

If you really want to change something in your life, you have to make up your mind to do it. You have to *make a commitment*. Big changes take firm commitments and so on and so forth.

But *how* do we make commitments firm enough to move us to action?

Somehow making commitments is an ability we're just supposed to have. It's a matter of whether or not we have enough "backbone" or strength of character to do what needs doing.

When you think about it, relaxing, paying attention and committing to something are *all* treated that way. If we can't seem to relax, if we're easily distracted or unable to commit ourselves to a certain course of action, the implication is we're simply not trying hard enough.

Yet these are more than matters of trying hard enough. They are mental abilities we can develop by meditating with what we call a *creative* meditation routine.

Why "Creative" Meditation?

Many meditation systems emphasize the passive, *receiving* side of meditation without linking it to action. They have you relax, focus your attention and clear your mind of distractions by counting breaths or repeating a focus word or "mantra" as it is called in the Eastern tradition.

It is expected that you will continue this relaxed, passive and receptive state of mind throughout the meditation period. You practice emptying your mind and *remaining* a "vessel to be filled" for your entire meditation.

In a creative meditation routine we emphasize meditation as a practical tool for *actively* creating change in our lives. In the first part of our meditation routine, we also relax and count breaths to focus our attention. But we later *direct* that attention to the life changes we are making. We state our intentions and mobilize ourselves to take action.

Decades of experimentation with methods such as visualization, guided fantasy and biofeedback training support this approach. Ample research on the healing potentials of the mind supports it.

We've all heard, for example, of the "placebo effect" where an inert substance such as a sugar pill or injection of plain water is designed to look like a real medicine and affects the *believing* patient as if it *were*.

Thousands of studies demonstrate the powers of belief in health and healing. In *Mind and Immunity*, for example, the

Institute for the Advancement of Health reviews over 1300 scientific studies on the effects of mind on the immune system.

We are simply making practical use of this knowledge by incorporating commitments into our daily meditation routine.

By calming and relaxing ourselves, we are asking every cell, tissue, organ in our bodies...every microbe community...every habit...every personality style within us to quiet down and pay attention to what we are about to say.

We then stop counting breaths and begin repeating a word or phrase of commitment.

Say, for example, you're concerned with your health and want to be more fit. Your commitment words might be something like, "getting stronger and healthier."

By repeating these words in daily meditation, you are continually reminding yourself of what you have committed yourself to doing. You *want* to get stronger and healthier.

At the same time you're stating you have already *begun* getting stronger and healthier. You're committing yourself to "work in progress," to something you and your "inner crew" are *already* achieving.

You're *building* your commitment, making it *firm* by repeating it to yourself everyday while in a state of relaxed attention.

And with the last step in a creative meditation routine, you do something that really puts an exclamation point on your words of commitment. You do something that puts your commitment into action. You "ground" your words in concrete experience.

After meditating with "getting stronger and healthier," for example, you might take a *healthy* morning walk. Or, you might instead eat a *healthy*, multi-grain, hot-cereal breakfast.

Either way, you'd be *exercising* your commitment to make it *firm!*

At the same time, you'd be sure to *concentrate* on what you were doing. You'd remind yourself that your brisk walk or nutritious breakfast is helping you "get stronger and healthier."

What Commitment Words?

Some individuals would find the "getting stronger and healthier" phrase works fine for them. Others would mean the same thing by repeating the single word "stronger." Still others would prefer the depth of meaning evoked by words such as "vitality" or "exuberance."

The best words for you are those you favor in your ordinary daily life. If you support the achievements of others or yourself with triumphant exclamations of "ALL RIGHT!" or "YES!" these are the kinds of commitment words you should be using.

Say, for example, a change in appearance was a top priority for you. For a long time you'd wanted to get rid of some fat and develop a fit and trim body.

If you succeeded in this, do you think you might smile and say something like "All right, kid, you're looking good!" to that person in the mirror?

If you would, then "looking good" should serve you well as a commitment phrase. It clearly indicates your goal and supports your efforts in a friendly, down-to-earth way.

Preferring the "looking good" style of language, it would also be likely you'd rather say "feeling good" than "getting stronger and healthier."

The point is to choose words that reflect the way you'd like to be with yourself. They are the ones that will work best for you. Your inner crew is used to you. They laugh at your jokes, love your strengths and understand your weaknesses. If the word "exuberance" tingles you, it will tingle them. If it doesn't—it won't!

The Key to Success

Now and then, beginning meditators get sidetracked with expectations that something sudden and dramatic is going to happen while meditating. The key to developing the meditation skills we've been talking about is to remember: *meditation is exercise.*

Like physical abilities, mental abilities are developed with *exercise.* We train our abilities to relax, concentrate and make commitments by *exercising* them, by practicing them every day.

The basic idea of meditation is similar to other forms of exercise. Walking every day exercises our bodies and gradually benefits our health. Stop walking and these benefits gradually disappear.

The same goes for meditation. Meditating every day exercises our minds and gradually benefits our health. Stop meditating and these benefits gradually disappear.

Counting breaths or repeating a word over and over in meditation is exercise just like doing push-ups, pull-ups and sit-ups over and over is exercise. We do these things to develop our skills and abilities.

Practicing a meditation routine sets the conditions for encouraging mental growth in the same way that a weight-training routine sets conditions for muscle growth.

This growth is *gradual.* Benefits come over time with daily *practice.* Don't expect a sudden earth-shaking mental enlightenment any more than you'd expect giant muscles to suddenly appear with physical exercise.

The Challenge in Meditation

The essential challenge in meditating is to deal effectively with *distractions*.

Your meditations will change as you develop your skill. In initial meditations you'll be more easily distracted by external sounds. A refrigerator, furnace fan, car on the street or dog barking in the distance might seem impossible challenges. That's why it's so important to meditate at times and places that help you minimize outside distractions as much as possible.

In the same way it will take you longer to relax in beginning meditations. You'll notice more itching, twitching and other distracting body messages than you ever thought possible in such a short period of time.

Again, a little advance planning will help minimize this. If you meditate first thing in the morning, go to the bathroom, brush your teeth and take care of other chores that might pester you while meditating. Skip the food and drink until after meditation, unless you *want* to spend it listening to your stomach crew doing its work.

With practice, relaxing will become much easier. At first it will require relaxation phrases, but in time you won't need them. Counting your breaths will relax you just fine. Be patient; it'll come.

Patience is the rule-of-thumb in all of this. If counting breaths is helping you with distractions, hold off on adding commitment words for a while.

There's no time schedule on learning here. You might even want to emphasize counting breaths for several months and just gradually increase your work with commitment words.

Again, meditation is exercise. A meditation can be as hard a "workout" as any other exercise.

When you first begin something like weight-training, you expect a few aches and pains from those out-of-shape muscles. Well, the mental exercise of meditation has its own kind of aches and pains.

You'll be surprised at the power of *distractions,* at your initial inability to quiet down unruly thoughts. Worries, memories, images and sensations will continually jump onto the stage of your awareness. Like a bunch of excited kids they refuse to stop hollering and interrupting. As soon as you get them to settle down a little, they get sleepy, bored and begin to whine—"Are we done yet? Why is this taking so long?"

Don't be disheartened. This is what meditation is all about. You're training your mind by learning to set those distractions aside and turn your attention back to your breathing or commitment words.

Distractions are the *weights* you are lifting to build the mental muscle you need for choosing where you'll aim your attention.

You're meditating for the same basic reason you do other exercises. You want to take care of yourself as best you can. You want to give yourself every possible advantage for living a good and healthy life.

Exercise your mind with regular meditation and you'll feel better, be less anxious, more in control of your temper and more able to stay on task.

Meditation will increase the energy you have available for getting things done by plugging some of the leaks of unwanted distractions and worries. It will help you to remember what you want to remember and forget what you don't.

Instructions

Meditation is practice in relaxing, not being distracted and paying attention, so arrange a time and place least likely to give you outside interference during your routine.

Many like to do it first thing after they get out of bed in the morning and/or last thing before they go to bed at night.

Start with a 10 or so minute meditation and work up to 20 or 30 minutes. Set a timer or sit so that you are able to see the time without changing your position.

Sit in a comfortable, upright position on a straight-backed chair. Don't cross your legs, fold your arms, or clasp your hands. Keep your feet flat on the floor and let your hands rest in your lap or on the chair arms.

Keep your head up. Find the point where it balances with the least muscle effort. If you find your chin resting on your chest you're sleeping, not meditating.

1. Relax Yourself

At first you'll have to take more time with this first step to make sure your muscles are completely relaxed and free of tension.

Shut your eyes, take several deep breaths and begin to relax your entire body. Direct your attention to the different parts of your body and encourage them to relax with relaxation phrases.

I'm relaxing now...I feel my toes relaxing...my feet relaxing...my legs are feeling heavy and relaxed...my hips and stomach are comfortable and relaxing...I feel warm relaxation flowing up over my chest now...my hands are relaxing...my arms are heavy and warm and relaxed...I feel the relaxation in my neck now...my jaw is relaxing...my facial muscles are relaxing...my forehead is relaxed now...my whole body is very heavy, comfortable, quiet and relaxed now.

2. Count Your Breaths

Pay attention to the air moving through your nostrils as you breathe in and out. To help focus your attention you might say to yourself "in" and "out" as you inhale and exhale a few times.

Let your breathing become regular and smooth. Then begin counting as you exhale. Count to four and then repeat. You may find it helpful to say "and" on the inhale: "one...*and*...two... *and*...three...*and*...four... *and*...one... *and*...two...*and*..."

When your mind wanders, don't fret. Gently bring it back to counting with an attitude of "come on now, let's get back to counting breaths." Don't get upset with distractions. Be patient and understanding with yourself and calmly return to counting.

3. Say Your Commitment Words

Keep your attention on your breathing. Without changing rhythm, stop counting your breaths and begin mentally repeating your commitment word or phrase on each exhale. For example, if your goal is weight loss, you might repeat "fit and trim...fit and trim...fit and trim..." Imagine yourself as having achieved this goal and feel your commitment to it.

Now, this will undoubtedly stir up other thoughts to distract you. Don't become upset with them. Let the thoughts and images fade as you bring yourself back to repeating your commitment words. Do this with gentle encouragement—"Come on, better get back to the commitment words."

Continue repeating your commitment words until your meditation is over. If at some point you'd rather, you could return to counting breaths and finish out that way.

4. Demonstrate Your Commitment

After meditating do something that demonstrates the commitment you've stated. Extend your words into action.

We suggested, for example, a commitment to strength and health could be demonstrated in a morning walk or breakfast. It could also be demonstrated in planning a meal or shopping for one or planting seeds in a windowsill lettuce tray or reading a health newsletter or going to bed for a healthy nights sleep.

Any activity that supports your intentions would be all right as long as you focus attention on the fact that you are *doing* what you *say*.

Checklist: Meditation Routines.

☐   Arrange a quiet time and place to practice daily meditating.

☐   Don't expect the dramatic—meditation is exercise to help you learn to relax, concentrate and achieve goals.

☐   Don't let struggles with distractions get you down—they are the "weights" that will build mental muscle.

☐   Try different commitment words and choose those that work best for you.

26

Fat Loss Routines

You're reading this because you have some fat to get rid of. If you've tried to get rid of it before, you know all about dieting, counting calories, exercise and short-lived results.

Now, what we have to tell you may *sound* the same, but listen closely. This time around everything has a different twist to it. There's something *new* about how we get fat and how we get rid of it.

- It still takes gumption to lose fat, but it's easier than before.

- It still takes time and practice, but now we get results.

- It still means counting calories, but not forever.

- It still means watching what we eat, but we no longer starve ourselves.

- It still means exercising, but we no longer beat our brains out.

A Program of Routines

Low-fat for Life is a program that trains healthy habits with eating, exercise and meditation routines. Here, these routines are adapted to meet the specific challenges of fat loss.

Once you've managed to get rid of the fat, you'll keep it off because you'll continue doing your routines (now as new healthy habits)—with one exception. You won't have to keep watching your calories.

Research tells us *losing* fat is something much different than *not gaining* fat. It's fat that makes you fat. You'll need to count calories to lose fat, but once it's gone you can increase low-fat/high-carbohydrate calories without gaining it back.[1]

In a nutshell, then, you *aim* your eating, exercising and meditating toward a *target* weight. This is the approximate weight you estimate you should be.

All of this involves following various rules-of-thumb that will help you:

1. Estimate your target weight and calories.

2. Eat for your target weight.

3. Exercise for your target weight.

4. Meditate for your target weight.

Estimating Your Target Weight and Calories

Our hunch is most of us know quite well what we should weigh and don't have to estimate a target weight to aim for in a fat-loss campaign.

How many times have we checked what we think we should weigh against those charts and tables we find in every magazine article and book on losing weight?

If we want the exact figures and percentages we talk to the health professionals. It takes special tests, measures and equipment (e.g., underwater weighing) to be precise about it.

Many encourage the professional route. If you have a lot of fat pounds to shed, it would make sense.

On the other hand, many have followed general guidelines and lost fat safely on their own—and they learned a great deal about taking better care of themselves in the process.

For example, if you want to know how the weight you're aiming for stacks up with a generally accepted rule-of-thumb guideline, try the following calculation:

a. Take the number of inches in your height that are over five feet.

b. If you are female multiply that number by 5 and add 100. If you are male multiply that number by 6 and add 106.

c. If your wrist measures over six inches as a female or seven inches as a male, you're considered "large boned" and should add 10% to your ideal weight figure.

With this formula a reasonable target weight for John Dough, a 5' 9" male, would be: 9 (number of inches over five feet) x 6 = 54 + 106 = *160 pounds*. If John's wrist measured more than seven inches the 160 figure would be increased 10% to 176 pounds.

What about calories? The *Low-fat for Life* approach to fat loss is to eat the daily food calories necessary to sustain the target weight you're aiming for.

Again, a precise determination of your calorie needs is beyond the scope of our book. Your rate of metabolism or the size of your muscles, for example, are important when considering the calories you need each day. But another rule-of-thumb calculation will head you in the right direction.

Estimate your calorie needs by simply multiplying your target weight by 10. In other words, John Dough would need roughly 1600 calories a day for his target weight of 160 pounds.

Multiplication by 10 should give you a calorie amount low enough to shed fat pounds without sacrificing nutrition, goofing up your metabolism or throwing your body into a starvation response.

Now, if John already weighed 160 pounds he might need anywhere from 1500 to more than 3000 calories a day to sustain that weight, depending upon how fit and active he was. The 1600 calorie figure would help him *get* to his target weight. Keeping it there is a different story.

Later on, when your excess baggage is just a memory, you'll be able to keep the fat off with low-fat eating. You won't have to pay much attention to calories anymore as long as the ones you get are the low-fat kind.

But here we're talking about getting *rid* of some fat. We're estimating the safe amount of calories you should get each day while gradually burning off your stores of fat with aerobic exercise.

How do you allocate your daily calories? Diet and nutrition authorities have convincing arguments for going about this in very different ways. It all sounds very scientific, but in our experience the best pattern of daily eating will be the one you find most satisfying and the easiest to live with.

The basic rules remain pretty much the same. You already know you're supposed to have three healthy main meals every day (yes, eat a breakfast).

If you ordinarily don't eat breakfast, think of it as one of the new fat loss routines you're practicing. Research and our experience tells us in a short time your body will *want* the breakfast you've been practicing. Your body will turn up your appetite valves for it.

The power of habit is amazing. If every night you'd set your alarm clock for 3:00 A.M., get up and eat a large carrot and then return to bed, you'd soon wake up just before 3:00 A.M. without the alarm, dreaming of that damn carrot. Your night-shift inner crew would be waking you up for their carrot snack.

To tap this kind of habit power and simplify the chore of monitoring calories, balance the regularity and variability of your meals. Adapt the *no-think, some-think* and *adventure eating* we talked about in the "Eating Routines" chapter.

Let's get our friend John out here again to see how this might work.

John needs about 1600 calories a day for his 160-pound target weight. He starts the day with a some-think breakfast of hot cereal, bran, fruit and coffee/tea (250 calories). Usually it's oatmeal, but sometimes he has farina or a multi-grain concoction. He does the cereal routine every day except Sunday when he sometimes lounges around with the morning paper and then whips up some of our Banana Blueberry Pancakes for a special brunch.

John likes fruit or a muffin (apple muffins are his favorite) for a mid-morning snack of 100 calories. His lunch is another some-think soup and sandwich (350 calories).

Of course, he *does* choose from a lot of different homemade soups, stews and chowders and likes to try different whole-wheat, rye, and sourdough breads with his garbanzo spread or chicken.

A snack of fruit (100 calories) gets John through to his big eating adventure of the day, dinner. Here he enjoys plenty of choosing and experimenting with foods to come up with a 600–700 calorie meal. He's really getting creative with his wok and knows how to roll a mean enchilada.

Later, John finishes out his 1600-calorie day with an evening snack of 100–200 calories of popcorn, fruit, cereal or one of our great bagels.

Actually, John's eating routine is quite familiar to us. Though Mike is a little taller than he is and has slightly different calorie needs, he followed roughly the same routine seven years ago. It helped him get rid of 35 pounds of fat.

And if you're wondering, no, he hasn't gained them back. This isn't low-calorie, starvation dieting with its yo-yo effect on weight. In fact, if you start losing pounds at too high a rate you may even have to increase your calories a bit to keep the loss gradual enough.

The right way to get rid of fat is a slow but sure process now recommended by many health and fitness authorities.

For example, the 1985 federal government's "Dietary Guidelines for Americans" recommended we not lose more than one to two pounds per week. By its 1990 guidelines, they had cut that range back to one-half to one pound per week.[2] Compare this to some of the dieting lunacy you see advertised.

Do your best to keep your rate of fat loss at the pound-a-week level no matter how eager you may be.

At the same time don't panic if your rate of loss seems to wobble around a bit with nothing happening and then suddenly dropping two or three pounds.

The pound-a-week is, after all, a guideline. You and your body are unique and will work this out together your own way.

Just monitor yourself and make adjustments as best you can to work within guidelines. If you seem to be losing more than a pound a week add a muffin each day and see if that takes care of it.

That's what this is all about: taking care of yourself for the long haul, giving your crew of habits a chance to change over to healthier living. You're training for your target weight. When you get there, keeping it will be easier because you'll already have the *habit* of weighing that amount.

Eating for Your Target Weight

Okay, you've figured about how many calories you're working with and roughly how you'll allocate them to meals and snacks each day. Now, make sure that of those daily calories less than 20% are fat, 10–15% are protein and more than 65% are carbohydrates.

It seems strange considering how protein-crazy we've been for so many years, but authorities are now saying getting enough protein isn't that big a deal. Protein deficiencies are extremely rare and it's now generally believed if you're getting enough calories you should be getting enough protein.[3]

No, protein won't be difficult. Your big job in this high-fat world of ours will be switching from high-fat/low-carbohydrate to low-fat/high-carbohydrate eating.

Box 30: A Reminder

In fat loss we want *complex* carbohydrates. Be careful with the sugars. They interfere with body chemistry and may increase fat storage. Experts tell us to keep sugar calories under 10% of total calories.

The same goes for alcohol. Alcohol interferes with metabolism. And metabolism means fat burning. A recent study found six drinks in a day slowed fat-burning by a third.

New England Journal of Medicine, 1992, Vol. 326, p. 983.

Reducing or avoiding fat foods (meats, whole-milk products, processed baked goods) and working with recipes like ours can keep you under the 20% fat limit, but your basic management approach for practicing this limit needs to be thought out.

More and more nutrition experts are agreeing that the 20% fat level should be the standard for healthy living. Yet, as explained earlier, quite a few suggest working with this dietary standard in a way that seems self-defeating to us. They say you should figure the *total* amount of fat you can have each day and then *budget* that amount into your meals.

Let's call our friend John over here for a minute and we'll show you what we mean. John eats 1600 calories in food each day. He could therefore have 320 fat calories and make the 20% limit.

If he budgets his meals according to his daily fat allotment as these folks suggest, he *could* have a breakfast or lunch high in fat (say a cheeseburger of 300 fat calories) and still make the 20% limit by cutting way back on the fat calories of dinner (20 calories).

To us this doesn't make sense.

If you blow your day's fat budget with a cheeseburger and fries lunch, you'll be forcing yourself into a slim-pickins, no-fat dinner. You won't like it. You'll hedge. You'll cheat and you'll disappoint yourself.

Don't do it!

Our approach may at first *seem* tougher because it won't let you fudge on fat at *any* meal. We're saying you should stick to the calorie needs for your target weight and make sure *all* your meals are under the 20% level of fat calories.

At dinner you won't be trying to remember the fat you had at breakfast or lunch. You'll always *know* it was under 20% of the calories you ate at the time.

Think about it. Do you still want to be budgeting fat ten years down the road? Or maybe you'd rather keep eating cheeseburger lunches, get your fat liposuctioned off every year or so and pray you don't soon die from sausage arteries.

If you *want* a look good and feel good life, *train yourself* to a look good and feel good life. Keep eating under the 20% limit. It's the fastest, most direct way to *genuine* appetite and habit change.

Don't spend the rest of your life grumbling about not getting enough of the unhealthy high-fat foods you used to eat. Train yourself to continually watch for new and great-tasting foods under that 20% limit. You'll find them, *many* of them.

To make lifelong changes, you need to *increase* the foods that genuinely tempt your tastebuds, yet are "legal."

Keep exploring new low-fat tastes and increase the fruit, vegetable, and grain side of your low-fat/high carbohydrate eating. Experiment with recipes from other cultures that already eat this way.

For example, we found delicious new tastes in Chinese and Japanese cuisine. We also learned to modify our old family favorites to create low-fat versions of previously high-fat foods such as enchiladas and pizza. Continually we hunt for and are *finding* new low-fat taste treats.

Remember, you won't suddenly dislike the taste of high-fat foods. That's what everyone will ask you. "Do you mean to tell me you don't like cheeseburgers anymore?"

Look, if the cheeseburger taste has been one of your favorites, it will likely always taste good to you.

But you won't lose sleep over cheeseburgers after you've discovered many low-fat alternatives that you enjoy just as much or more.

Besides, our collective searching for low-fat food alternatives is serving another very important purpose. The increasing number of us out there looking is encouraging the appearance of more and more low-fat and fat-free alternatives in our markets and restaurants. When *we* change, our profit-minded food industry follows. Aim your pocketbook where you want things to go, right?

So, stay with the 20% standard at every meal rather than trying to average it out between higher and lower-fat meals. Every time you stick something into your mouth you'll be telling yourself, the food industry and the rest of the world you're eating *Low-fat for Life!*

Exercising for Your Target Weight

The idea that you could exercise to get rid of fat has been around a long time. But before we understood the effects of different kinds of exercise, the results were disappointing.

Of course, the fast-buck artists have made it difficult to sort fact from fiction. We've payed a lot of money for a lot of baloney. How many boxcars of gimmicks did we buy believing the fantasy of *spot reducing*. We've jiggled, shook, rubbed, pulled, kneaded and sweated with vibrating belts, rollers, stretchers and plastic work-out suits...but the fat remained.

It seemed reasonable that you could shrink your waist with sit-ups and a special sauna belt to "melt" the fat. It also seemed you should be able to "break down" the fat on your hips with leg-lifts and a special roller-massager. It's even likely such exercises toned the muscle underneath...but the fat remained.

No matter how it seems, the fat over a muscle doesn't *belong* to that muscle. As Covert Bailey often remarks, if spot reducing exercise worked, gum-chewers would all have skinny faces.

Whatever its specific location, body fat is stored energy available to the entire muscle system of the body. It will be used when required to fuel any of the body muscles. The muscles moving your swim fins might draw energy from the fat under your chin.

The aerobic activity of *any* muscles will burn body fat. The more muscles involved the more fat burned.

Now, there's nothing very complicated about aerobic exercises. They tend to be things we already know how to do. Some people love certain aerobic exercises and hate others. For example, they might enjoy cross-country skiing or swimming, but not running.

Many books are available that suggest different aerobic exercises for you to consider. Perhaps you'll find one exercise particularly enjoyable. If you do—great!

But we wrote this book from a bottom line perspective. We want you to get the *habit* of exercise. We want aerobic activity to be an ordinary part of your everyday life.

Any of the various kinds of aerobic exercise will do the job, but (as we explained in earlier chapters) when it comes to bottom lines, you can't beat *walking*.

We all began walking as soon as we could stand up and will likely walk until we no longer can. We have done it so long we can easily make it our exercise habit. We are so used to it we exert more energy with less perceived effort than in an exercise of similar intensity.

Let's call our friend John out here for one more brief explanation.

John's target weight is 160 pounds and he now weighs 190. He's eating approximately 1600 low-fat/high-carbohydrate calories and walking an hour a day.

This should work pretty well for him. If he walks four miles in that hour, he'll burn roughly 360 calories. A pound of fat is 3500 calories, so he'll walk off a pound every 9 or 10 days. Actually he'll lose about a pound a week because of the "afterburn" metabolism we told you about in earlier chapters.

And John's no dummy. He makes sure he drinks at least three quarts of water a day to support the fat-burning process. He knows his liver needs this much water to get fat ready for burning in his muscles and then to flush away wastes after it's burned.

To keep his fat-burning furnace (muscles) in top condition, John also works out with weights for 20 minutes, three times a week. He says our strength routine (in "Exercise Routines") is perfect for his needs.

Yes, John is excited about the changes he's made in his life. Know how he helped get those healthy habits in place? That's right, John *meditates*.

Meditating for Your Target Weight

Twenty minutes or so of meditation once or twice a day is time well spent when you are trying to get rid of fat.

In Chapter 20 we explained that eating, exercise and meditation routines reinforce each other. Same goes in a fat-loss program.

Eating, exercise and meditation are synergistic activities—they have a lot more effect *together* than if you added up what they could do *alone*.

For example, research tells us exercise increases our appetite for healthy food, healthy food increases our appetite for exercise and both have a positive effect on our emotions.

Research also tells us meditating helps us form the habits we want, such as eating healthy foods and engaging healthy exercise. Meditation helps us cut through distractions (e.g., unhealthy foods) and pay attention to what we want (e.g., healthy foods). It helps us stick with practicing healthy routines long enough for them to become habits.

Here's a chance to aim that creative meditation routine we told you about in the last chapter. *Relax yourself, focus your attention* and *commit yourself* to the fat-loss goals you want to achieve.

Checklist: Fat Loss Routines.

- ❑ Target weight estimated.
- ❑ Daily calories for fat loss estimated.
- ❑ Extra-filling meals and snacks identified.
- ❑ Water jug marked.
- ❑ Eating routine checklist applied.
- ❑ Exercise routine checklist applied.
- ❑ Meditation routine checklist applied.

Part Four:

Recipes for Training Healthy Appetites

In this last part of the book you'll find the kind of eating that encourages new taste preferences. Over 150 simple and delicious recipes will head you in the right direction and every one is below 20% fat.

About the Recipes

Our recipes are simple and basic. They are intended to help you *make health convenient* and *train healthy appetites*. These are two key strategies to keep in mind whenever you're cooking and baking.

For example, we enjoy breadmaking and recommend it as a rewarding household chore. But if circumstances limit your opportunity to use the "old-fashioned" procedures we describe, by all means consider purchasing a bread-making machine. Like a crock-pot or microwave it's another appliance that will help make health convenient.

Toppings, sauces, soups and stews help you "lead" appetites in healthy directions. With them you establish the conditions which "draw out" new taste preferences.

Finicky appetites can be led to vegetable enjoyment with stir-fry sauces, soups and stews. A trail of strawberry freezer jam leads an appetite from white bread to light-wheat to whole-wheat.

Experiment and discover. Try a half-meat and half-meatless pizza, for example. The comparison might surprise you.

This is the spirit of change you want to encourage. Openness, patience and experimentation will get you where you want to go.

Noticing appetite change in others or yourself is worthy of celebration. For those who never really accepted the idea that they'd actually come to *prefer* healthy foods, the experience of genuine appetite change and newly found taste treats is exhilarating.

Nutrient Analysis

Each recipe is followed by a nutritional analysis listing the percent of calories that are fat, total calories, grams of fat, carbohydrate, protein and dietary fiber and the milligrams of cholesterol and sodium.

The nutrient values were obtained from the following sources:

- Human Information Service. *Composition of Foods, Raw, Processed, Prepared.* Agriculture Handbook No. 8, 8-1, 8-4, 8-5, 8-9 to 8-13, 8-15 to 8-20. Washington, D.C.: U.S. Department of Agriculture.

- Product labels

- Anderson, J. *Plant Fiber in Foods.* Lexington, Kentucky: HCF Nutrition Research Foundation, Inc., 1986.

- Souci, Fachmann, Kraut. *Food Composition and Nutrition Tables 1981/82.* Stuttgart: Wissenschaftliche Verlagsgesellschaft mbH, 1981.

- Information provided by the manufacturers.

- Pennington, J. *Food Values of Portions Commonly Used.* New York: Harper and Row, 1989.

Carefully calculated, the values should be considered a close approximate. For the sake of clarity, we rounded the figures to the nearest whole numbers—so there may be a small discrepancy between an analysis and the sum of its parts. For example, the fat percent may seem low because the fat grams have been rounded up (2.7g $\times$ 9 $\div$ 150 = 16% fat, while 3 $\times$ 9 $\div$ 150 = 18% fat). Our calculations used the more accurate data.

Secondly, nutritional data differs slightly from source to source. Even specific foods may vary in nutrient content (e.g., a Washington-grown Macintosh apple may have more or less carbohydrates than a Wisconsin-grown Yellow Delicious). In addition, certain nutrient information is simply not available. Therefore, people with a *highly* specific, medically-prescribed diet should consult their physician.

When a choice of ingredients is given, we have analyzed the recipe based on the first one in the list.

Serving Size

Each nutrient analysis is for one serving, the size of which is usually indicated. We tried to make them as convenient as possible (e.g., 1 cup of soup), but in some cases (as in casseroles and stir-fries), the serving analysis is for one-fourth of the total (serves 4). Divide them into four parts when serving.

Most recipes list the quantity of legumes, pasta and grains in cooked amounts. See Appendix C for conversion of dry to cooked.

Most vegetable and fruit recipes list quantity in cups. See Appendix C for weight conversions.

Nutrient Levels

Every recipe in this book meets our 20% or less fat guideline, but some may wish to reduce their fat intake even further. Where possible, we suggest alternatives for modification. For example, some recipes were analyzed with a low-fat cheese containing four grams of fat per ounce. Reduce the fat percentage with non-fat cheese in its place. Other fat-reducing methods you may wish to experiment with are: 2 egg whites instead of 1 whole egg, non-fat rather than low-fat dairy products, less oil, leaner types or smaller portions of meat (see Appendix A).

You may also notice that the protein content in some recipes is higher than the recommended 15% of total calories. They were intended to be only one part of a meal with other, higher-carbohydrate foods included to balance them out.

Seasonings and Oil

Herbs and spices indicated in the recipes are dried unless it says "fresh." Reduce or increase the amounts according to personal preference. The rule-of-thumb when using fresh is to use double the amount than if they were dried. Salt is usually listed as optional.

Use the oils you believe are best (e.g., canola or olive). The goal in our recipes is to use as little as possible of *any* type.

27

Soups

Soup is more than winter-time fare—make it part of your weekly menu plan. It's a delicious way to get a wide variety of vegetables, grains and legumes into your diet. Make your own broth and you have the control over salt, fat and nutrient content (see cooking directions below). Soup recipes can easily be doubled, stored in freezer containers and reheated when you need a quick meal.

A crock-pot is a very convenient way to prepare soup. The 4- or 5-quart size works well for many of the recipes. Simply combine all the soup ingredients in the crock-pot, set on low (or follow specific directions for your appliance), let it slow-cook all day. Add extra herbs the last half-hour to highlight their flavor. If indicated, add pasta the last 15–20 minutes before serving.

See Appendix C for vegetable, pasta and legume yield conversions. See Chapter 31 for bean cooking directions.

Chicken Broth Cooking Directions

1   stewing chicken, fryer or 3 pounds parts (necks, backs, etc.)
3   stalks celery including leaves, cut into 2–3" lengths
1   large onion, quartered
5   sprigs fresh parsley
2   cloves garlic, crushed
1   teaspoon thyme (or other preferred herb)
1   bay leaf
    some peppercorns

Wash chicken in cold water. Put in large pot and cover with 10 cups cold water. Bring to a boil. If water has scum, pour off, start again with fresh water. Bring to a boil and now add rest of ingredients. Turn down heat, simmer uncovered for 2–3 hours.

Remove chicken, discard skin and bones, cut pieces of meat to size desired for casseroles, sandwiches, soups, etc. Strain broth, discard vegetables; refrigerate. When hardened, remove the fat which has settled on the top and discard. The broth is now ready to use or store in freezer. Makes 5–6 cups.

Vegetable Broth Cooking Directions

5   cups water
2   onions, quartered
2   carrots, chunks
3   stalks celery, including leaves
8   mushrooms, sliced in half
2   cloves garlic, crushed
2   bay leaves
4   sprigs fresh parsley
    salt and pepper to taste

Place all in soup pot; bring to boil. Reduce heat, partially cover; simmer 1 hour. Strain; refrigerate or use immediately. Makes approximately 1 quart.

Beef Broth Cooking Directions

    2–3 pounds beef soup bones
      4 stalks celery, including leaves, cut into 2–3" lengths
      2 large onions, quartered
      6 sprigs fresh parsley
      2 cloves garlic, crushed
      2 teaspoons thyme
      2 bay leaves
        some peppercorns

Brown beef bones before combining with remaining ingredients in a large soup pot. Add 10 cups of water, bring to a boil, turn down heat, simmer about 2 hours. Strain broth, refrigerate. Remove the fat which has hardened on top. The broth is now ready to use or store in the freezer. Makes 5–6 cups.

Vegetable Chowder

2 cups carrots, diced
3 cups potatoes, diced
½ cup onion, diced
1 cup fresh broccoli florets
1 cup fresh cauliflower florets
2 cups frozen corn
1 cup fresh mushrooms, sliced
4 cups skim milk
   salt and black pepper, optional
   fresh parsley, chopped, sprinkled on top

Place a steamer basket in a 4-quart soup pot with 1 inch of water. Layer the prepared vegetables in the basket in the order given above. Cover and steam until tender, about 20 minutes. Drain off any extra liquid. Slide vegetables off basket into pot.

In blender place 1 cup of the milk and 1 cup of the steamed mixed vegetables; puree, return to pot. Add remaining milk; heat, but do not boil.

Makes 8 cups

1 cup serving:
   151 calories
   0.5g fat
   31g carbohydrates
   8g protein
   2mg cholesterol
   4g fiber
   85mg sodium

Split Pea Soup

2 cups dried green split peas
6 cups water
2 cups chicken broth (homemade or canned)
1 clove garlic, minced
1 tablespoon dried parsley
1 teaspoon thyme
1/2 teaspoon salt, optional
1/4 teaspoon black pepper
2 cups potatoes, diced small
1 cup carrots, diced small
1 cup onion, diced small
1/2 cup celery, diced small

In a 4-quart soup pot combine split peas and water; bring to boil and cook 2 minutes; cover and let stand 1 hour.

Add the rest of the ingredients, bring to a boil, turn down to a simmer and cook for 1 hour until vegetables are tender. Stir occasionally to prevent scorching. Add extra water or broth if soup seems too thick.

*Note: See crock-pot directions in chapter introduction.

Makes 8 cups

1 cup serving:
220 calories
1g fat
40g carbohydrates
14g protein
0mg cholesterol
6g fiber
357mg sodium

Potato Dumpling Soup

8 cups potatoes, diced
1 cup celery, chopped
1 cup onion, chopped
4 cups chicken broth (homemade or canned)
½ teaspoon salt, optional
2 tablespoons dried parsley
¼ teaspoon white pepper
3 cups skim milk, warmed
Dumplings:
1 cup unbleached flour
1½ teaspoons baking powder
½ teaspoon salt
2 teaspoons dillweed
1 egg white
1 cup skim milk

In 5-quart soup pot combine potatoes, celery, onion, chicken broth, salt, parsley and pepper; simmer until tender, about 20 minutes.

In medium bowl combine flour, baking powder, salt and dillweed. In small bowl combine egg white and milk. Combine wet and dry ingredients just until moistened. Drop by tablespoon (8 mounds) on top of soup. Cover pot, simmer gently 20 minutes.

Add warm milk, stir, heat through, serve.

Makes 12 cups soup and 8 dumplings

1½ cups soup with 1 dumpling:

263 calories   2g fat   50g carbohydrates   13g protein
3mg cholesterol   4g fiber   850mg sodium

Lentil-Barley Soup

1 cup carrots, sliced
1 cup onion, chopped
1 cup celery, chopped
1 clove garlic, minced
4 cups canned, peeled tomatoes
1 cup dry lentils
1 cup pearl barley
1 cup chicken broth (homemade or canned)
1 cup tomato juice, unsalted
5 cups water
½ teaspoon rosemary, crushed
½ teaspoon oregano
¼ teaspoon pepper

Combine all ingredients in 5-quart soup pot; bring to a boil, reduce heat, simmer 1 hour or until vegetables are tender. Add extra liquid as needed for consistency you prefer.

*Note: See crock-pot directions in chapter introduction.

Makes 10 cups.

1 cup serving:
  170 calories
  0.8g fat
  34g carbohydrates
  8g protein
  0mg cholesterol
  7g fiber
  355mg sodium

Tarragon Chicken Soup

2 cups carrots, sliced
4 cups potatoes, diced
1 cup onion, chopped
4 cups chicken broth (homemade or canned)
8 ounces cooked chicken cut into small pieces, no skin
2 teaspoons dried tarragon
1/4 teaspoon pepper

In 4-quart soup pot simmer carrots, potatoes, and onion in broth until tender, about 20 minutes. Add chicken pieces and seasonings; continue to simmer about 1/2 hour longer.

Makes 7 cups

1 cup serving:
189 calories
4g fat
24g carbohydrates
15g protein
30mg cholesterol
3g fiber
493mg sodium

Cioppino-Style Soup

1 pound frozen haddock fillets
1 cup green pepper, chopped small
1/2 cup onion, chopped small
1 clove garlic, minced
2 cups canned, peeled tomatoes, undrained
1/4 cup fresh parsley, chopped
1/2 teaspoon dried oregano
1/2 teaspoon dried basil
1/8 teaspoon black pepper
1 6 1/2–ounce can minced clams, drained
1/2 cup dry red wine

Thaw fish and cut into small pieces; set aside.

In 4-quart soup pot combine green pepper, onion and garlic in a small amount of water; cook until vegetables are tender. Add undrained tomatoes and seasonings; cover and simmer 15 minutes. Add fish and simmer another 5–7 minutes, or until fish flakes easily with fork. Add clams and wine; heat through and serve immediately.

Makes 6 cups

1 cup serving:
173 calories
1g fat
10g carbohydrates
23g protein
64mg cholesterol
1g fiber
307mg sodium

Hardy Legume Soup

¼ cup dried split peas
¼ cup dried lentils
¼ cup pearl barley
4 cups chicken broth (homemade or canned)
1 tablespoon dried parsley
1 teaspoon thyme
½ teaspoon salt, optional
¼ teaspoon pepper
1 cup onion, chopped
1 cup carrots, chopped
1 cup pinto beans, cooked (or canned, drained)
1 cup navy beans, cooked (or canned, drained)

In 5-quart soup pot combine split peas, lentils, barley and broth; bring to a boil, turn down heat and simmer ½ hour. Add the seasonings and vegetables; continue to simmer until tender, about ½ hour. Add beans and extra broth or water for thinner consistency if desired, let simmer another ½ hour.

*Note: See crock-pot directions in chapter introduction.

Makes 7 cups

1 cup serving:
177 calories
1g fat
30g carbohydrates
12g protein
1mg cholesterol
7g fiber
620mg sodium

Navy Bean Soup

1 cup carrots, diced
1 cup celery, diced
1 cup onion, diced
2 cups potatoes, diced
1 cup water
6 cups cooked navy beans (or canned, drained)
3 cups tomato juice, unsalted
1 bay leaf
½ teaspoon salt
¼ teaspoon pepper

In 5-quart soup pot combine carrots, celery, onion and potatoes; add water; simmer until vegetables are tender. Add remaining ingredients; simmer about 1 hour longer. Add more water if soup is too thick. Remove bay leaf before serving.

*Note: See crock-pot directions in chapter introduction.

Makes 12 cups

1 cup serving:
    174 calories
    0.6g fat
    34g carbohydrates
    9g protein
    0mg cholesterol
    8g fiber
115mg sodium

Chicken Noodle Soup

2 cups carrots, sliced
1 cup celery, sliced
½ cup onion, chopped
7 cups chicken broth (homemade or canned)
½ teaspoon salt, optional
¼ teaspoon pepper
1 cup peas, fresh or frozen
8 ounces cooked chicken, no skin, cut into small pieces
3 cups cooked whole-wheat flat noodles

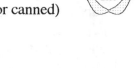

In 4-quart soup pot combine carrots, celery, onion, broth and seasonings; simmer until vegetables are tender, about 45 minutes. Add peas, chicken and noodles; heat through another 15–20 minutes.

Makes 10 cups

1 cup serving:
  152 calories
   3g fat
  18g carbohydrates
  14g protein
  21mg cholesterol
   2g fiber
 710mg sodium

Vegetable Bean Soup

1 cup vegetable broth
4 cups canned, peeled tomatoes, undrained
1 cup onion, chopped
1 cup celery, chopped
1 cup cabbage, chopped
1/4 cup parsley, chopped
1 clove garlic, minced
1 cup great northern beans, cooked (or canned, drained)
1 cup lima beans, cooked (or canned, drained)
1 cup adzuki beans, cooked (or canned, drained)
1 cup black beans, cooked (or canned, drained)
1/2 cup garbanzo beans, cooked (or canned, drained)

In 4-quart soup pot combine vegetable broth, tomatoes, vegetables and seasonings; cook until vegetables are tender, about 1/2 hour. Add beans; continue to simmer another 1/2–1 hour.

*Note: See crock-pot directions in chapter introduction.

Makes 10 cups

1 cup serving:

   145 calories
     2g fat
   28g carbohydrates
    8g protein
   0mg cholesterol
    5g fiber
273mg sodium

Oriental Chicken Soup

1 cup carrots, diagonally sliced
¼ cup green onions, sliced, tops included
4 cups chicken broth (homemade or canned)
1 cup fresh snow pea pods, strings removed,
  cut in 1" pieces
1 cup fresh mushrooms, sliced
½ cup fresh spinach, cut into thin strips
6 ounces cooked chicken, cut into small pieces, no skin
3 ounces Japanese somen noodles (found in ethnic section of supermarket). If not available, vermicelli can
  be used.

19% fat

In 4-quart soup pot combine carrots, onion and broth; simmer until tender-crisp, about 20 minutes. Add pea pods and
mushrooms; simmer another 10 minutes. Add spinach and
chicken, heat through 5 minutes. Break somen noodles in
half, drop in soup, simmer 3–4 minutes. Serve immediately.

Makes 7 cups

1 cup serving:
  134 calories
   3g fat
  14g carbohydrates
  12g protein
  22mg cholesterol
   2g fiber
  702mg sodium

Potato and Broccoli Soup

6 cups potatoes, diced
1 cup onions, diced
4 cups vegetable or chicken broth
2 cups skim milk
2 cups broccoli, chopped, fresh or frozen
½ teaspoon salt, optional
¼ teaspoon pepper

In 4-quart soup pot cook potatoes and onions in vegetable broth until tender, about 15–20 minutes. Pour part of the mixture into a blender with part of the milk and puree. Do not overprocess or potatoes will be gummy. Pour into another container; continue to puree small amounts of potato mixture and milk. Then return all to the soup pot with the seasonings.

In medium, covered saucepan steam or cook broccoli in a small amount of water until tender. Drain and add to the soup; heat soup slowly to prevent scorching; do not boil.

Makes 11 cups

1 cup serving:
   113 calories
   0.8g fat
   21g carbohydrates
   6g protein
   1mg cholesterol
   2g fiber
420mg sodium

Minestrone

1 cup carrots, sliced
1 cup celery, sliced
1/2 cup green pepper, diced
1 cup onion, chopped
1 cup cabbage, sliced
1 cup green beans, fresh or canned
1 cup yellow or green zucchini, sliced
1 1/2 cups kidney beans, cooked (or canned, drained)
4 cups canned, peeled tomatoes
3 cups chicken broth (homemade or canned)
1 teaspoon basil
1/4 teaspoon oregano
1/4 teaspoon black pepper
1 clove garlic, minced
1 1/2 cups cooked whole-wheat elbow macaroni

In 5-quart soup pot combine all ingredients except macaroni, bring to a boil, turn down to a simmer; cook until vegetables are tender, about 1 1/2 hours. Add macaroni last 15 minutes before serving.

*Note: See crock-pot directions in chapter introduction.

Makes 13 cups

1 cup serving:
93 calories
0.8g fat
18g carbohydrates
5g protein
0mg cholesterol
3g fiber
392mg sodium

Chili

1 pound lean ground round
1 cup onion, diced
½ cup green pepper, diced
2 cups kidney beans, cooked (or canned)
6 cups tomato juice, unsalted
4 cups canned, peeled tomatoes, undrained
3 cups cooked whole-wheat elbow macaroni
1 tablespoon chili powder
1 teaspoon cumin
1 clove garlic, minced
dash cayenne or red pepper

In nonstick fry pan brown meat; drain off any fat. Add onion and green pepper; cook until softened. In 5-quart soup pot combine meat mixture, kidney beans, tomato juice, canned tomatoes and seasonings; simmer 1 hour. Add macaroni last 15 minutes before serving.

Makes 11 cups

1 cup serving:
   225 calories
    3g fat
   31g carbohydrates
   20g protein
 35mg cholesterol
    4g fiber
285mg sodium

Split Pea and Barley Soup

  5 cups chicken broth (homemade or canned)
  4 cups water
1½ cups dried split peas
  ½ cup pearl barley
  1 cup carrots, diced
  ½ cup onion, diced
  ½ cup celery, diced
  1 clove garlic, minced
  ½ teaspoon thyme
  ⅛ teaspoon white pepper

In 4-quart soup pot combine all ingredients; bring to a boil, reduce heat and simmer until done, about 1 hour. Stir occasionally to prevent scorching. Add more liquid to get consistency desired.

*Note: See crock-pot directions in chapter introduction.

Makes 6½ cups

1 cup serving:
    245 calories
      2g fat
     42g carbohydrates
     16g protein
      1mg cholesterol
      7g fiber
    620mg sodium

Fish Chowder

4 cups potatoes, cubed
2 cups corn, fresh or frozen
1 cup onion, diced
1 cup fresh mushrooms, sliced
12 ounces cod, fresh or frozen (thawed), cut
   into 1" pieces
1 12-ounce can evaporated skim milk
½ teaspoon salt, optional
¼ teaspoon pepper

In 4-quart soup pot place metal steamer basket and 2 cups of water, bring to boil. Layer potatoes, corn, onion and mushrooms in basket; cover and steam until vegetables are tender, about 15 minutes.

Slide vegetables off steamer into the bottom of pot, leaving the small amount of cooking water.

Place fish on top of vegetables, cover, simmer about 10 minutes. Add evaporated skim milk and seasonings, heat until milk is hot, but do not allow to boil. Serve immediately.

Makes 8 cups

1 cup serving:
183 calories
0.7g fat
31g carbohydrates
15g protein
20mg cholesterol
3g fiber
230mg sodium

Cornmeal Vegetable Soup

½ cup dry lentils
1½ cups water
2 cups chicken broth (homemade or canned)
1 cup lima beans, cooked (or canned)
1 cup frozen corn
1 cup fresh or frozen green beans
1 cup zucchini, sliced
1 cup celery, sliced
1 cup carrots, sliced
½ cup onion, chopped
½ cup green pepper, chopped
4 cups canned, peeled tomatoes, undrained
1 clove garlic, minced
1 teaspoon chili powder
¼ teaspoon ground cumin
⅛ teaspoon black pepper

Topping:
¾ cup yellow cornmeal
1¼ cup skim milk
1 egg, beaten or 2 egg whites
2 ounces low-fat cheese (4 grams or less per ounce)

In 5-quart soup pot combine lentils and water; bring to boil, reduce heat, cover and simmer for 20 minutes, drain. Add broth, lima beans, corn, green beans, zucchini, celery, carrots, onion, green pepper, tomatoes and seasonings. Return to boiling, reduce heat, cover and simmer about 20 minutes or until vegetables are tender.

Cornmeal Topping: In small saucepan gradually stir milk into the cornmeal. Cook and stir until thickened. Remove from heat; stir in beaten egg. Drop 7 mounds onto hot soup.

Cover and simmer about 20 minutes. Sprinkle with cheese and serve.

Makes 7 cups and 7 dumplings

1 cup with 1 dumpling:

   260 calories
     6g fat
    45g carbohydrates
    15g protein
  44mg cholesterol
     8g fiber
 665mg sodium

Garbanzo Goodness

3 cups chicken broth (homemade or canned)
2 cups vegetable broth
4 cups tomatoes, canned, peeled, undrained
2 cups potatoes, diced
1 cup carrots, diced
1 cup onion, chopped
1 cup celery, sliced
1 cup corn, fresh or frozen
1 cup peas, fresh or frozen
1 cup mushrooms, fresh, sliced
1 cup kidney beans, cooked (or canned, drained)
2 cups garbanzo beans, cooked (or canned, drained)
2 cloves garlic, minced
1 teaspoon oregano
1 teaspoon cumin
2 bay leaves
¼ teaspoon crushed red pepper
¼ cup fresh parsley, minced (add last 10 minutes)

In 5-quart soup pot combine all ingredients except parsley; bring to a boil, reduce heat, simmer for 1½–2 hours. Add parsley, remove bay leaves.

*Note: See crock-pot directions in chapter introduction.

Makes 11 cups

1 cup serving:
169 calories   2g fat   32g carbohydrates   9g protein
    0mg cholesterol   6g fiber   478mg sodium

28

Muffins and Quick Breads

Muffins and quick breads are simple, fast and habit-forming. They *make health convenient* and *train appetites to healthy snacks*. Quick breads don't even require kneading or extra time to rise.

Cooking Tips

- Baking powder and baking soda begin "action" when combined with liquid. Preheat your oven and prepare the pans before mixing the batter. To make sure muffins and quick breads rise well, mix batters gently but quickly and bake immediately.

- Ovens vary in temperature conditions, so adjust baking times and temperatures to suit your own. Use a toothpick to test for doneness. It should come out clean when inserted in the center. Watch closely the last couple of minutes, or you'll overbake and dry out the muffins or quick bread.

- Salt was eliminated from most recipes because there's enough sodium in baking powder. If you want even lower amounts, low-sodium baking powder is available.

- Use nonstick muffin tins or bread pans—they don't need to be oiled.

- Remember to refrigerate any leftovers after the first day of baking. No preservatives are used so they might mold or spoil.

Banana Muffins

¼ cup wheat germ
¾ cup wheat bran
1 cup whole-wheat flour
1 tablespoon baking powder
¼ teaspoon baking soda
1 cup mashed ripe banana (2–3 bananas)
⅓ cup honey
¼ cup non-fat yogurt
1 egg, lightly beaten, or 2 egg whites

Preheat oven to 350°.

In medium bowl combine wheat germ, wheat bran, flour, baking powder and baking soda.

In medium bowl combine mashed bananas, honey, non-fat yogurt and egg.

Combine wet and dry ingredients just until moistened. Spoon into lightly oiled muffin tins. Bake about 15 minutes. Serve warm.

Makes 12

1 muffin:
    117 calories
    1g fat
    25g carbohydrates
    4g protein
    23mg cholesterol
    4g fiber
116mg sodium

Apple Muffins

1¼ cups whole-wheat flour
1 cup rolled oats
2 teaspoons baking powder
1 teaspoon cinnamon
2 eggs, or 4 egg whites
1 tablespoon oil
⅓ cup honey
½ cup skim milk
2 cups apples, peeled, diced small (about 2 medium)

Preheat oven to 350°.

In medium bowl combine flour, rolled oats, baking powder and cinnamon.

In small bowl beat eggs; add oil, honey and skim milk.

Combine wet and dry ingredients just until moistened; gently fold in apple pieces. Spoon into lightly oiled muffin tins. Bake 15–20 minutes. Serve warm.

Makes 12

1 muffin:
138 calories
3g fat
25g carbohydrates
4g protein
46mg cholesterol
3g fiber
89mg sodium

Blueberry Bran Muffins

1 cup wheat bran
1⅓ cups whole-wheat flour
1 teaspoon baking soda
1 egg, or 2 egg whites
1 tablespoon oil
⅓ cup honey
1¼ cups buttermilk, ½% lowfat (non-fat, if available)
1 cup blueberries, fresh or frozen

Preheat oven to 400°.

In medium bowl combine wheat bran, flour and baking soda.

In small bowl beat egg; add oil, honey and buttermilk.

Combine wet and dry ingredients just until moistened; gently fold in blueberries. Spoon into lightly oiled muffin tins. Bake about 15 minutes. Serve warm.

Makes 12

1 muffin:

    121 calories
    2g fat
    23g carbohydrates
    4g protein
    23mg cholesterol
    4g fiber
    35mg sodium

Pumpkin Muffins

1½ cups whole-wheat flour
½ cup rolled oats
2 teaspoons baking powder
¼ teaspoon baking soda
1 teaspoon cinnamon
½ teaspoon ginger
½ teaspoon mace
⅛ teaspoon cloves
2 egg whites
1 cup canned pumpkin
½ cup light molasses
½ cup orange juice
2 tablespoons oil

Preheat oven to 375°.

In medium bowl combine flour, oats, baking powder, baking soda, cinnamon, ginger, mace and cloves.

In medium bowl beat egg whites until frothy; add pumpkin, molasses, orange juice and oil; mix well.

Combine wet and dry ingredients just until moistened. Spoon into lightly oiled muffin tins. Bake 15–20 minutes. Serve warm.

Makes 12

1 muffin:

134 calories
3g fat
25g carbohydrates
4g protein
0mg cholesterol
3g fiber
83mg sodium

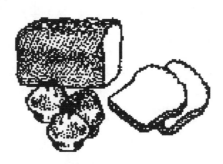

Pineapple Muffins

2½ cups oat bran
1 tablespoon baking powder
4 egg whites
1 cup pineapple juice frozen concentrate
1 cup crushed pineapple, drained
½ cup blueberries, fresh or frozen

12%
fat

Preheat oven to 350°.

In medium bowl combine oat bran, baking powder.

In medium bowl combine egg whites, concentrate, pineapple and blueberries.

Combine wet and dry ingredients just until moistened. Spoon into lightly oiled muffin tins. Bake about 15 minutes.

Makes 12 muffins

1 muffin:

131 calories
2g fat
24g carbohydrates
5g protein
0mg cholesterol
12g fiber
125mg sodium

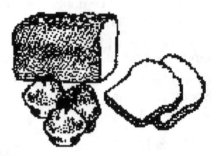

Oatbran Raisin Muffins*

2¼ cups oat bran
1 tablespoon baking powder
¼ cup brown sugar
½ cup raisins
1¼ cup skim milk
2 egg whites
2 tablespoons corn syrup

Preheat oven to 425°.

In large bowl combine oat bran, baking powder, brown sugar and raisins.

In medium bowl combine milk, egg whites and corn syrup.

Combine wet and dry ingredients. Spoon into lightly oiled muffin tins.

Bake 13–15 minutes. Oat bran may not brown like a flour-base muffin so be careful not to overbake.

* Adapted from Robert Kowalski

Makes 12

1 muffin:

114 calories
2g fat
21g carbohydrates
5g protein
0mg cholesterol
11g fiber
133mg sodium

Cranberry Quick Bread

  1 cup whole-wheat flour
  1 cup unbleached flour
  ³/₄ cup sugar
  1 teaspoon baking soda
  2 egg whites, lightly beaten
  ¹/₃ cup orange juice
  ¹/₄ cup applesauce
  2 tablespoons white vinegar plus water to make ²/₃ cup
  1 cup cranberries, coarsely chopped

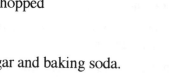

Preheat oven to 350°.

In large bowl combine flour, sugar and baking soda.

In medium bowl combine egg whites, orange juice, apple-sauce, vinegar water and cranberries.

Combine wet and dry ingredients just until moistened. Spoon into lightly oiled 9" x 5" loaf pan. Bake 1 hour or until a toothpick comes out clean. Remove from pan and cool on wire rack.

Makes one 9" x 5" loaf

One ¹/₂" slice (1.5 oz):
    85 calories
  0.3g fat
    19g carbohydrates
    2g protein
  0mg cholesterol
    1g fiber
  6mg sodium

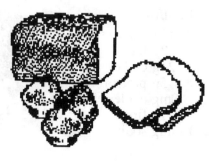

Applesauce-Raisin Quick Bread

1 cup whole-wheat flour
1 cup unbleached flour
³/₄ cup sugar
3 teaspoons baking powder
¹/₂ teaspoon baking soda
1 teaspoon cinnamon
2 egg whites, lightly beaten
1¹/₂ cups applesauce
¹/₂ cup raisins

3% fat

Preheat oven to 350°.

In medium bowl combine flour, sugar, baking powder, baking soda and cinnamon.

In small bowl combine egg whites, applesauce and raisins.

Combine wet and dry ingredients just until moistened. Spoon into lightly oiled 9" x 5" loaf pan. Bake 1 hour or until toothpick comes out clean. Remove from pan and cool on wire rack.

Makes one 9" x 5" loaf

One ¹/₂" slice (1.75 oz.):

101 calories
0.3g fat
24g carbohydrates
2g protein
0mg cholesterol
2g fiber
78mg sodium

Carrot Quick Bread

1 cup whole-wheat flour
1 cup unbleached flour
³/₄ cup sugar
1 teaspoon baking soda
1 teaspoon cinnamon
¹/₂ teaspoon nutmeg
¹/₄ teaspoon cloves
2 egg whites, lightly beaten
1 cup grated carrots, packed
¹/₄ cup molasses
¹/₂ cup applesauce

Preheat oven to 350°.

In medium bowl combine flour, sugar, baking soda and spices.

In small bowl combine egg whites, carrots, molasses and applesauce; mix well.

Combine wet and dry ingredients just until moistened.

Spoon into lightly oiled 9" x 5" loaf pan. Bake 50–60 minutes or until a toothpick comes out clean. Remove from pan and cool on wire rack.

Makes one 9" x 5" loaf

One ¹/₂" slice (1.5 oz.):
    97 calories
    0.3g fat
    22g carbohydrates
    2g protein
    0mg cholesterol
    1g fiber
    10mg sodium

Banana Quick Bread

1½ cups unbleached flour
1 cup whole-wheat flour
½ cup sugar
2 teaspoons baking powder
1 teaspoon baking soda
1 teaspoon cinnamon
2 cups mashed bananas (4–6 bananas)
½ cup applesauce
3 egg whites, lightly beaten
1 teaspoon vanilla

Preheat oven to 350°.

In large bowl combine flour, sugar, baking powder, baking soda and cinnamon.

In medium bowl combine mashed banana, applesauce, egg whites and vanilla.

Combine wet and dry ingredients just until moistened. Spoon into lightly oiled 9" x 5" loaf pan.

Bake 1 hour or until a toothpick comes out clean. Remove from pan and cool on wire rack.

Makes one 9" x 5" loaf

One ½" slice (1.75 oz.):

118 calories
0.5g fat
27g carbohydrates
3g protein
0mg cholesterol
2g fiber
56mg sodium

Pumpkin Quick Bread

1 cup unbleached flour
½ cup whole-wheat flour
½ cup sugar
1 teaspoon baking powder
1 teaspoon baking soda
1 teaspoon cinnamon
½ cup raisins
½ cup applesauce
1 cup canned pumpkin
4 egg whites

Preheat oven to 350°.

In large bowl combine flour, sugar, baking powder, baking soda, cinnamon and raisins.

In medium bowl combine applesauce, pumpkin and egg whites.

Combine wet and dry ingredients just until moistened.

Spoon batter into lightly oiled 9" x 5" loaf pan. Bake 1 hour or until toothpick comes out clean. Remove from pan and cool on wire rack.

Makes one 9" x 5" loaf

One ½" slice (1.5 oz):
    79 calories
    0.3g fat
    18g carbohydrates
    2g protein
    0mg cholesterol
    1g fiber
    36mg sodium

Light Wheat Quick Bread

3 cups whole-wheat flour
3 cups unbleached flour
2 packages active dry yeast
1 teaspoon sugar
$^1/_2$ teaspoon salt
$^1/_4$ teaspoon baking soda
2 cups skim milk
$^1/_2$ cup water

Preheat oven to 400°.

In large bowl combine whole-wheat flour, yeast, sugar, salt and baking soda.

Heat milk and water to 120°; add to dry mix and beat well.

Stir in unbleached flour, a cup at a time, to make a stiff batter.

Lightly oil two 8½" x 4½" bread pans. Divide batter into the 2 pans. Cover with a towel; let rise in warm place, about 1 hour.

Bake 25 minutes at 400°. Remove from pans and cool on wire rack.

*Note: Differs from other quick breads in that it uses yeast, but it is still quick to put together and bake.

Makes 2 small loaves

One $^1/_2$" slice (1.3 oz.):

    77 calories
  0.4g fat
   16g carbohydrates
    3g protein
  0mg cholesterol
    2g fiber
42mg sodium

29

Pancakes, Waffles and Cereals

We especially enjoy the *variety* of grains we are able to include in our diet with the recipes in this chapter. Even shopping for whole grains is an eye-opener. Check out food co-ops and natural foods stores. You'll be surprised at the wide selection available and the economy offered with bulk packaging.

Don't limit these recipes to breakfasts. A heaping bowl of Fiber 20 Oatmeal, for example, tastes great for lunch. At our house we sometimes enjoy a lunch or even dinner of pancakes or waffles. Low-fat granola is one of our all-purpose snack foods.

Double Grain Pancakes

Pancake mix:

   1 cup rolled oats
   1 cup whole-wheat flour
   1 cup wheat bran
   6 tablespoons wheat germ
   1 tablespoon baking powder

Pancake batter:
   1 egg, beaten, or 2 egg whites
   1 cup skim milk
   1 cup pancake mix

Pancake mix:
Combine all ingredients, store in covered container in refrigerator.

Batter:
In medium bowl mix egg and milk; add pancake mix and stir just until moistened. Drop by spoonful onto hot griddle or nonstick fry pan, using nonstick cooking spray as needed. Serve hot with one of our fruit syrups (see Chapter 38).

Makes ten 4" pancakes

1 pancake:
    52 calories
    1g fat
    8g carbohydrates
    3g protein
  28mg cholesterol
    2g fiber
  62mg sodium

Banana-Blueberry Pancakes

1 ripe medium banana, mashed
2 eggs, or 4 egg whites
1¾ cups skim milk
1⅓ cups whole-wheat flour
⅓ cup yellow cornmeal
½ teaspoon nutmeg
1 teaspoon baking powder
1 cup blueberries, fresh or frozen

14% fat

In small bowl combine mashed banana, eggs and skim milk.

In medium bowl combine flour, cornmeal, nutmeg and baking powder.

Combine wet and dry ingredients just until moistened; gently fold in blueberries.

Drop batter by spoonfuls onto hot griddle or nonstick fry pan, using nonstick cooking spray as needed. Serve hot with one of our fruit syrups (see Chapter 38).

Makes twenty 3½" pancakes

1 pancake:

    60 calories
    0.9g fat
    11g carbohydrates
    3g protein
    28mg cholesterol
    2g fiber
    40mg sodium

French Toast

4 egg whites
¼ cup skim milk
4 slices Light Wheat Bread (see Chapter 30),
   approx. ½" thick

In medium bowl beat egg whites until frothy; add milk and stir to combine. Pour into shallow bowl or pie plate. Soak bread slices about 1 minute on each side.

Heat large nonstick fry pan using nonstick cooking spray; brown bread on both sides. Serve hot with one of our fruit syrups (see Chapter 38).

*Note: If using packaged bread soaking time will be shorter.

Makes 4 slices

1 slice:

    103 calories
      1g fat
     17g carbohydrates
      7g protein
    0mg cholesterol
      2g fiber
   65mg sodium

Wilma's Waffles

1½ cups unbleached flour
½ cup whole-wheat flour
2 teaspoons baking powder
1½ teaspoons baking soda
½ teaspoon cinnamon
1⅓ cups buttermilk, ½% lowfat (non-fat, if available)
1⅓ cups apple juice
1 tablespoon honey
4 egg whites

In large bowl combine flour, baking powder, baking soda and cinnamon; set aside.

In medium bowl combine buttermilk, apple juice and honey; set aside.

In medium bowl, beat egg whites until stiff peaks form.

Combine flour mixture and buttermilk mixture in large bowl just until moistened. Gently fold in beaten egg whites. Spoon onto heated waffle iron, using nonstick cooking spray as needed. Serve warm with one of our fruit syrups (see Chapter 38).

Makes four 7" x 7" waffles

1 waffle:

273 calories
2g fat
52g carbohydrates
13g protein
0mg cholesterol
3g fiber
352mg sodium

Granola

3 cups rolled oats
½ cup wheat germ
½ cup wheat bran
½ teaspoon cinnamon
⅔ cup raisins
¼ cup apple juice frozen concentrate
2 tablespoons honey
1 tablespoon oil
½ teaspoon vanilla

Combine dry ingredients in large bowl and mix well.

In small saucepan heat concentrate, honey and oil until warm. Add vanilla. Pour over dry ingredients and mix very well.

Spread on nonstick baking sheet. Bake 20–30 minutes at 300°, stirring occasionally, until mixture is crunchy. Cool. Store in a covered container.

*Note: If desired, add extra dried fruits to granola after it has been baked.

Makes 5 cups

1 cup:
    390 calories
      8g fat
     70g carbohydrates
     13g protein
     0mg cholesterol
      9g fiber
     9mg sodium

Fiber 20 Oatmeal

½ cup rolled oats
1 cup plus 2 tablespoons water (or skim milk)
1 teaspoon sugar or honey
2 tablespoons oat bran
2 tablespoons wheat bran
1 banana, sliced (or raisins)

Stove-top method: Combine oats and water in a 1-quart pot. Bring to a boil, reduce heat; simmer 5–6 minutes or until reaches desired consistency. Mix in rest of ingredients and serve.

Microwave: Place oats and water in bowl that holds 2 cups and cook 4 minutes according to your microwave's proper setting (e.g., high). Mix in rest of ingredients and serve.

*Note: Provides minimum amount of recommended daily fiber intake—20 grams.

Serves 1

1 serving:
346 calories
5g fat
68g carbohydrates
11g protein
0mg cholesterol
21g fiber
2mg sodium

Farina

1 cup water
3 tablespoons farina

2%
fat

In small saucepan bring water to boil, add farina
slowly while stirring continuously, turn heat to
low, simmer 2–3 minutes or until reaches desired consistency.

*Note: Farina is the same as the commercial Cream of
Wheat, but much more economical when purchased in bulk
from a natural food store.

Makes about 1 cup cooked

1 cup cooked:
    121 calories
    0.2g fat
    26g carbohydrates
    4g protein
    0mg cholesterol
    0g fiber
    1mg sodium

Corn-ucopia

1 cup cracked wheat
1 cup rolled oats
1 cup polenta or corn grits
½ cup wheat bran
½ cup brown rice
½ cup sunflower seeds

Combine ingredients and store in an airtight container.

To cook: In 2-quart pot bring 3 cups of water to a boil. Add 1 cup of dry mix, stir well, cover; simmer 30 minutes, stirring occasionally.

*Note: If desired, serve with fresh or dried fruits, sweetener and/or a dash of cinnamon.

Makes 3 cups cooked

1 cup cooked:
    173 calories
      4g fat
     30g carbohydrates
      6g protein
    0mg cholesterol
      2g fiber
    1mg sodium

Super Six

1½ cups brown rice
1½ cups rolled wheat
1½ cups rolled rye
1½ cups oat groats
 1 cup pearl barley
 1 cup millet

Combine ingredients and store in airtight container.

To cook: In 2-quart pot bring 3 cups of water to a boil. Add 1 cup of dry mix, stir well, cover; simmer for 30 minutes, stirring occasionally.

*Note: If desired, serve with fresh or dried fruits, sweetener and/or a dash of cinnamon.

Makes 3 cups cooked

1 cup cooked:

168 calories
1g fat
36g carbohydrates
5g protein
0mg cholesterol
2g fiber
1mg sodium

Buckwheat Special

½ cup rolled oats
½ cup millet
½ cup buckwheat groats
½ cup raisins

Combine all in 2-quart pot, cover with about 2 cups water; let soak overnight.

To cook: Bring to a boil, turn down to medium heat, cook about 15 minutes, stirring frequently. Add extra water if needed to gain consistency desired.

*Note: If desired, serve with fresh or dried fruits, sweetener and/or a dash of cinnamon.

Makes 3 cups cooked

1 cup cooked:
   349 calories
     3g fat
   77g carbohydrates
   10g protein
  0mg cholesterol
     3g fiber
   7mg sodium

Get-Yer-Grits

1 cup soy grits
1 cup millet
1 cup rolled oats
1 cup pearl barley

9% fat

Combine ingredients in an airtight container, store in refrigerator. Place 1 cup dry mix and 2 cups water in 2-quart pot; soak overnight.

Cook over medium heat, stirring frequently, adding extra water if needed to gain consistency desired. Cook about 15 minutes.

*Note: If desired, serve with fresh or dried fruits, sweetener and/or a dash of cinnamon.

Makes 2 cups cooked

1 cup cooked:
    280 calories
      3g fat
     52g carbohydrates
     17g protein
      0mg cholesterol
      5g fiber
     3mg sodium

30

Breads, Bagels and Rolls

Homemade bread—smells wonderful, tastes great and is an excellent source of complex carbohydrates, fiber and nutrients. Most of the recipes in this chapter follow the same basic process described below.

1. Dissolve the yeast

Yeast consists of millions of fast-growing plant cells. When provided with moisture, warmth and carbohydrates, yeast becomes active, will reproduce rapidly and give off carbon dioxide which makes dough rise. The water temperature (95°–115°) for dissolving yeast is important; if its too hot it will kill the yeast, if too cool it will slow down the action. A thermometer is very helpful. It takes about 10 minutes for the yeast to become active and bubbly. If it doesn't bubble, start over with fresh yeast and check water temperature carefully.

2. Mix the dough.

When the ingredients are mixed together, the liquid enables the protein in the flour to start bonding together and form gluten. The gluten forms an elastic network which traps the gas released by the yeast enabling the bread to rise and hold its shape. Cool heated liquids to lukewarm so as not to destroy the yeast. Some salt is added to control the action of the yeast and thus the rate at which the dough rises.

Add the flour gradually to the liquids, stirring or beating well until it becomes a more compact mass. Leave about ¼ cup of the flour for kneading.

3. Knead the dough.

The kneading process stretches or develops the gluten evenly throughout the bread. Turn dough from bowl out onto floured surface, fold in half towards you, push it down and away from you with the palms of your hands, rotate dough a quarter of a turn. Develop a rhythm of folding toward you, pushing away and turning the dough. Knead in the reserved flour if the dough feels sticky. It will take about 10 minutes of vigorous kneading to make the dough feel smooth and elastic.

4. Let the dough rise.

The kneaded dough is placed in a lightly oiled bowl, turned once to oil the top, covered with a dish towel, set in a warm (75°–85°), draft-free place to rise. It takes about 1 hour for the dough to reach a volume almost double its original size. To test, stick 2 fingers one inch into the dough. Dents will remain if dough has doubled. If hole slowly springs back, let dough rise longer.

5. Punch the dough down.

Punch down firmly with your fist into the center of the dough. This lets the gas escape and mixes the yeast cells more evenly throughout the dough. Fold edges of dough from sides of bowl inward and turn out onto floured surface.

If indicated in recipe knead a few times, invert bowl over dough, let stand 5–10 minutes before proceeding.

6. Shape the dough into loaves.

Divide dough into pieces called for in recipe. For round loaves shape with your hands to make a smooth, slightly flattened ball. Place on baking sheet far enough apart so loaves won't touch as they rise and spread. If shaping to fit pans, roll to flatten into a rectangle about the length of the pan. Then roll up into a log shape, pinch seams together, tuck ends under, place in lightly oiled pans.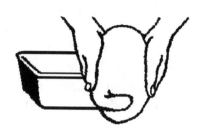

7. Let the loaves rise.

A second rise results in a more evenly textured bread and a lighter loaf. Cover loaves with dish towel, set in warm, draft-free place, let rise until almost double in size, usually 30 minutes. In a pan the sides of the loaf will come up to the top of the pan while the center of the top of the loaf will be an inch or two above the pan.

8. Bake the bread.

Bread is usually baked in a 350° pre-heated oven for 35–45 minutes. Remove from pans and cool on a rack. When done it will be golden brown and should sound hollow when thumped on the bottom.

9. Store the bread.

Cool completely, wrap in plastic bag, store in refrigerator after 1 or 2 days. Shelf life is shorter than it is for store bread as there are no preservatives in homemade. Slicing the loaf before freezing lets you take out one slice at a time if desired.

Light Wheat Bread

1 package active dry yeast
½ cup warm water (95°–115°)
1 cup apple juice
2 tablespoons honey
2 tablespoons oil
½ teaspoon salt
¾ cup buttermilk, ½% lowfat (non-fat, if available), at
   room temperature
½ cup rye flour
2 cups unbleached flour
3 cups whole-wheat flour

14% fat

In small bowl dissolve yeast in warm water; let sit until bubbly, about 10 minutes.

In small pan heat apple juice, honey, oil and salt until warm.

In large bowl combine yeast mixture and all liquids. Add rye flour; add rest of flour, one cup at a time, stirring well after each addition.

Turn out onto floured surface and knead until smooth and elastic, about 10 minutes. Place in lightly oiled bowl, cover with towel; let rise in warm place until double in size, about 1 hour.

Punch dough down. Divide into 2 loaves. Place in lightly oiled 8½" x 4½" x 2½" bread pans, cover with towel; let rise in warm place until double in size, about 1 hour.

Preheat oven to 350°, bake 30–35 minutes. Remove from pans and cool on wire rack.

Makes 2 loaves

One ½" slice (1.66 oz):

| 81 calories | 1g fat | 16g carbohydrates | 3g protein |
| 0mg cholesterol | | 2g fiber | 7mg sodium |

Whole-Wheat Bread

2 packages active dry yeast
1 cup warm water (95°–115°)
⅓ cup honey
2 cups skim milk
4 tablespoons unsalted margarine
½ teaspoon salt
8 cups whole-wheat flour

In small bowl sprinkle yeast into warm water, add 1 teaspoon of the honey, stir until yeast is dissolved; let sit until bubbly, about 10 minutes.

In medium saucepan combine remaining honey, milk, margarine and salt; heat until margarine melts. Pour into large bowl and cool to lukewarm.

Stir yeast mixture into milk mixture. Add flour, a cup at a time, stirring well after each addition.

Turn out onto floured surface; knead until smooth and elastic, about 10 minutes. Place dough in large, lightly oiled bowl, cover with towel; let rise in warm place until double in size, about 1 hour.

Punch dough down, turn out onto floured surface, knead a few times, invert bowl over dough; let rest 10 minutes.

Divide into 2 loaves and place in lightly oiled 8½" x 4½" x 2½" bread pans, cover with a towel; let rise in warm place until double in size, about 45 minutes.

Preheat oven to 350°. Bake 35–40 minutes. Remove from pans and cool on wire racks.

Makes 2 loaves

One ½" slice (2.5 oz):

122 calories   2g fat   24g carbohydrates   5g protein
     0mg cholesterol   4g fiber   43mg sodium

Rye Bread

2 packages active dry yeast
2½ cups warm water (95°–115°)
¼ cup light molasses
2 tablespoons unsalted margarine, melted
1 tablespoon caraway seeds
1 teaspoon salt
2½ cups rye flour
2½ cups whole-wheat flour
3 cups unbleached flour
   cornmeal to sprinkle on baking sheet

In small bowl sprinkle yeast into ½ cup of the warm water. Stir in 1 teaspoon of the molasses until the yeast dissolves; let sit until bubbly, about 10 minutes.

In large bowl combine remaining water, molasses, margarine, caraway seeds and salt. Add yeast mixture, rye flour and rest of flour, a cup at a time, stirring well after each addition.

Turn out onto lightly floured surface and knead until smooth and elastic, about 10 minutes. The dough will be more on the sticky side; adding too much extra flour will make the loaf heavy. Place in lightly oiled bowl, cover; let rise in warm place until double in size, about 1 hour.

Punch dough down, turn out onto lightly floured surface, knead a few times, invert bowl over dough; let rest 10 minutes.

Divide and shape into 2 round loaves. Place 4" apart on lightly oiled baking sheet that has been sprinkled with a little cornmeal. Cover with a towel; let rise in warm place until double in size, about 45 minutes.

Preheat oven to 375°; bake 35 minutes. Remove from baking sheet and cool on wire rack.

Makes 2 round loaves

1 oz:

    62 calories
    0.7g fat
    12g carbohydrates
    2g protein
    0mg cholesterol
    1g fiber
    1mg sodium

Oatmeal-Raisin Bread

```
  1  cup raisins
 ½  cup apple juice
  1  tablespoon cinnamon
  2  cups skim milk, scalded*
  2  cups rolled oats
 ½  cup honey
  2  tablespoons unsalted margarine
 ½  teaspoon salt
  1  package active dry yeast
 ¼  cup warm water (95°–115°)
2½  cups whole-wheat flour
2½  cups unbeached flour
```

In small saucepan bring to boil raisins, apple juice and cinnamon. Turn off heat, cover; set aside for 15 minutes.

In large bowl combine hot milk, oats, honey, margarine and salt.

In small bowl dissolve yeast in warm water; let sit until bubbly, about 10 minutes.

When oats mixture has cooled to lukewarm, add yeast mixture and raisin liquid. Stir in flour, a cup at a time, stirring well after each addition.

Turn out onto lightly floured surface and knead until dough is smooth and elastic, about 10 minutes. Place in lightly oiled bowl, cover with a towel; let rise in a warm place until double in size, about 1 hour.

Punch dough down, invert bowl over dough; let rest 10 minutes. Divide into 2 loaves. Place in lightly oiled 8½" x 4½" x 2½" bread pans, cover with a towel; let rise in a warm place until double in size, about 35–45 minutes.

Preheat oven to 375°; bake 40–45 minutes. Remove from pans and cool on wire racks.

*Scalded: To scald milk, heat in saucepan until small bubbles start to form around the edge of the pan. Do not boil.

Makes 2 loaves

One ¹/₂" slice (1.75 oz):

   120 calories
    1g fat
   25g carbohydrates
    4g protein
  0mg cholesterol
    2g fiber
43mg sodium

Dilly Casserole Bread

  1 package active dry yeast
½ cup warm water (95°–115°)
  1 cup non-fat cottage cheese
  1 teaspoon sugar
  1 tablespoon dried minced onion flakes
  2 teaspoons dill seeds
  1 tablespoon oil
  1 egg, or 2 egg whites
¼ teaspoon baking soda
2½ cups whole-wheat flour

In small bowl dissolve yeast in warm water; let sit until bubbly, about 10 minutes.

In small sauce pan heat cottage cheese to lukewarm, stirring constantly. Combine with yeast mixture, sugar, onion flakes, dill seeds, oil, egg and baking soda in a large bowl. Add flour, a cup at a time, stirring well after each addition. Cover with a towel; let rise until double in size, about 1 hour.

Turn out onto lightly floured surface and knead about 5 minutes, adding flour as needed for stickiness. Place in oiled round 1½-quart casserole. Cover, let rise in warm place until double in size, about 30 minutes.

Preheat oven to 350°; bake 40–50 minutes. Remove from casserole and cool on wire rack.

  Makes 1 round loaf

1 oz:

     47 calories
   0.7g fat
     8g carbohydrates
     3g protein
  0mg cholesterol
    1g fiber
39mg sodium

Cinnamon Swirl Bread

  1 package active dry yeast
  1/4 cup warm water (95°–115°)
  2 cups skim milk, scalded*
  1/3 cup sugar
  1/2 teaspoon salt
  4 tablespoons unsalted margarine
  3 cups whole-wheat flour
2 3/4 cups unbleached flour
  1/3 cup sugar
  1 tablespoon cinnamon

In small bowl dissolve yeast in warm water; let sit until bubbly, about 10 minutes.

In large bowl combine the hot mik, sugar, salt and margarine. Cool to lukewarm.

Stir in 2 cups of the flour and beat well. Add softened yeast, mix. Add rest of flour, a cup at a time, stirring well after each addition.

Turn out onto lightly floured surface and knead until dough is smooth and elastic, about 10 minutes. Place in lightly oiled bowl, cover with a towel; let rise in warm place until double in size, about 1 hour.

Punch dough down, invert bowl over dough, let rest 10 minutes. Cut dough into 2 pieces. Roll each to a 15" x 7" rectangle on a lightly floured surface.

Combine 1/3 cup sugar with 1 tablespoon cinnamon. Spread half over each rectangle. Sprinkle each with 1 1/2 teaspoons water. Roll dough into loaves. Place in 8 1/2" x 4 1/2" x 2 1/2" lightly oiled bread pans. Cover, let rise in warm place until double in size, about 30 minutes.

Preheat oven to 350°; bake 30–35 minutes. Remove from pans and cool on wire rack.

*To Scald: Heat milk in saucepan until small bubbles start to form around edge of pan. Do not boil.

Makes 2 loaves

One $1/2$" slice (1.5 oz):

    101 calories
      2g fat
     19g carbohydrates
      3g protein
    0mg cholesterol
      2g fiber
   42mg sodium

Sourdough Bread and Rolls

The starter: Make 3–4 days before you plan to bake the bread for the first time. The starter is then refrigerated for future baking and will keep indefinitely as long as it is occasionally replenished.

5% fat

  1 package active dry yeast
  1 cup whole-wheat flour
  1 cup unbleached flour
  1 tablespoon non-fat dry milk
2¼ cups warm water (95°–115°)

Combine all ingredients in large bowl, stir well, cover with towel; let stand at room temperature for 3–4 days until it smells slightly sour. Mixture will be bubbly. It should now be stored in refrigerator (2-quart glass jar with lid works well) until you are ready to bake.

The starter should be used once a week to keep it alive (active). To replenish the starter after using part of it in the recipe, simply return equal amounts of flour and water that has been taken (e.g., if you take out 1 cup of starter for the bread recipe, add back to the jar of remaining starter 1 cup flour and 1 cup warm water). Again cover with towel, let stand at room temperature until bubbly (usually 1 day), return to refrigerator.

The bread: The night before baking:

  1 cup starter
  1 cup warm water (95°–115°)
  1 cup unbleached flour

Combine in large bowl, cover with towel, let stand overnight (Replenish starter).

The next day:

    1 package active dry yeast
    2 tablespoons unbleached flour
    ½ cup apple juice
    ½ cup water
    1 tablespoon honey
    ½ teaspoon salt
    1 cup unbleached flour
    4 cups whole-wheat flour

In small bowl combine yeast and 2 tablespoons flour. In small saucepan heat apple juice, water, honey and salt to 105°–115°. Pour half the liquid over the yeast/flour, stir; let stand 7–10 minutes or until bubbly.

Now take the large bowl with the "night before" starter mixture, stir down, add balance of warm liquid and the bubbly yeast mixture; stir well.

Add the flour, a cup at a time, stirring well after each addition. Turn out onto floured surface and knead 10 minutes. Dough will be slightly sticky when done.

Place dough in lightly oiled bowl, cover with towel; let rise in warm place until double in size, about 1 hour.

Punch dough down. Divide and shape into 2 round loaves, place on lightly oiled baking sheet, cover with towel; let rise in warm place until almost double in size, about ½ hour.

Preheat oven to 350°; bake 35 minutes. Remove from sheet and cool on rack.

For sandwich buns:

Follow same procedure as bread. Instead of shaping into loaves, roll out dough to approximately ½" thickness. Cut to size desired. A 4½" jar lid works well to make 14 buns. Place on lightly oiled baking sheets, let rise about 20 minutes. Bake 10–15 minutes at 350°. Remove and cool on rack.

*Note: Remember to put the "starter jar" back in refrigerator after it has bubbled.

*Note: Refrigerate or freeze the bread or rolls after the first day or they may develop a strong fermented odor and taste.

*Note: This recipe may seem too time-consuming and difficult for beginners, but once you've tried it you'll be surprised at how easy it is to make.

Makes 2 round loaves or 14 buns

1 oz:

    55 calories
  0.3g fat
  12g carbohydrates
    2g protein
 0mg cholesterol
    1g fiber
23mg sodium

Cornmeal Rolls

1 package active dry yeast
3/4 cup warm water (95°–115°)
1 teaspoon sugar
2 egg whites
1 tablespoon oil
1/2 teaspoon salt, optional
1/3 cup cornmeal
1 cup unbleached flour
1 1/2 cups whole-wheat flour

14% fat

In small bowl sprinkle yeast into water, stir until dissolved, let sit until bubbly, about 10 minutes.

In medium bowl combine sugar, egg whites, oil, salt and yeast mixture. Stir in cornmeal. Add flour, a cup at a time, stirring well after each addition. Turn out onto floured surface, knead about 8 minutes.

Place dough in lightly oiled bowl, cover with towel; let rise in warm place until double in size, about 1 hour.

Punch dough down, roll out to 1/2" thickness. Cut out rolls with 2 1/2" round cutter. Place on nonstick baking sheet, cover with a towel; let rise until double in size, about 1/2 hour. Preheat oven to 400°; bake 15–20 minutes. Remove from baking sheet, serve warm.

Makes 12 rolls

1 roll:

111 calories
2g fat
21g carbohydrates
4g protein
0mg cholesterol
3g fiber
106mg sodium

Light Wheat Rolls

2 teaspoons active dry yeast
¼ cup warm water (95°–115°)
1 cup warm skim milk
1 egg white, lightly beaten
1 tablespoon sugar
1 tablespoon oil
½ teaspoon salt
1½ cups whole-wheat flour
2 cups unbleached flour

In small bowl sprinkle yeast into warm water, add a bit of sugar, stir to dissolve; let sit until bubbly, about 10 minutes.

In medium bowl combine milk, egg white, sugar, oil and salt. Add yeast mixture. Add flour, a cup at a time, stirring well after each addition.

Turn out into floured surface, knead until soft and pliable, about 8 minutes. Place in lightly oiled bowl, cover with towel; let rise in warm place until double in size, about 1 hour.

Punch dough down, knead a few times, invert bowl over dough; let rest 5 minutes.

Spray a muffin tin with nonstick cooking spray. Pull off pieces of dough about the size of a walnut, shape into balls, place 3 balls to a muffin cup to form a 3-leaf clover. Cover with a towel, let rise in warm place until double in size, about 30 minutes.

Preheat oven to 375°; bake about 20 minutes or until nicely browned on tops. Remove from tin and serve warm.

Makes 12 rolls
1 roll:
141 calories   2g fat   27g carbohydrates   5g protein
  0mg cholesterol   2g fiber   112mg sodium

Cranberry Bread

1 package active dry yeast
3 cups warm water (95°–115°)
½ cup sugar
3 tablespoons honey
3 tablespoons dry milk
2 tablespoons unsalted margarine, melted
1 teaspoon salt
4 cups whole-wheat flour
4 cups unbleached flour
2 cups cranberries, coarsely chopped

In large bowl stir yeast into warm water, let sit until bubbly, about 10 minutes. Stir in sugar, honey, dry milk, margarine and salt. Add flour, a cup at a time, stirring well after each addition. Add chopped cranberries.

Turn out onto floured surface, knead 10 minutes, until smooth and elastic, adding extra flour if dough feels too sticky.

Divide into 2 loaves. Place in lightly oiled 8½" x 4½" bread pans, cover with towel; let rise in warm place until double in size, about 1 hour.

Bake 35 minutes at 350°. Remove from pan and cool on wire rack.

Makes 2 loaves

One ½" slice (2.25 oz):
    123 calories
     1g fat
    25g carbohydrates
    4g protein
    2mg cholesterol
    2g fiber
    73mg sodium

Cinnamon Rolls

½ cup skim milk, scalded*
2 tablespoons oil
3 tablespoons honey
1 egg white
1 teaspoon salt
1 package active dry yeast
½ cup warm water (95°–115°)
2 cups unbleached flour
1¼ cups whole-wheat flour
3 tablespoons sugar
2 teaspoons cinnamon
  Powdered sugar and milk for frosting, if desired

Scald milk (*heat in saucepan until small bubbles start to form around the edge of the pan, but do not boil), let cool to lukewarm. Add oil, honey, egg white and salt; set aside.

In medium bowl dissolve yeast in water; add the milk mixture. Add flour a cup at a time, stirring well after each addition.

Turn out onto floured surface, knead until soft and pliable, about 5 minutes. Place in lightly oiled bowl, cover with towel, let rise in warm place until double in size, about 1 hour.

Punch dough down. Roll out to 12" x 15" rectangle.

Mix together sugar and cinnamon, sprinkle over the dough, and then sprinkle a little water (less than a teaspoon) on top of all. Roll the dough along its length jelly-roll style.

With sharp knife cut pieces off the roll about 1" thick. Place in 2 lightly oiled round baking pans, cover with towel, let rise in warm place until double in size, about 30 minutes.

Preheat oven to 350°; bake 20 minutes. Take out of pans and cool on wire rack.

Frosting: ¹/₂ cup powdered sugar mixed with very small amount of milk to gain consistency desired. Drizzle on rolls with spoon or frost with knife.

Makes 12 rolls

1 roll with 2 teaspoons frosting:

183 calories
3g fat
36g carbohydrates
5g protein
0mg cholesterol
2g fiber
12mg sodium

Bagels

2 packets active dry yeast
3 cups warm water (105°–115°)
3 tablespoons honey
1 teaspoon salt
3 cups unbleached flour
5 cups whole-wheat flour

Toppings:
   1 egg white, lightly beaten
   poppy seeds or sesame seeds or dried onion flakes

In large bowl dissolve yeast and 1 tablespoon of the honey in the water. When it's bubbly, add rest of the honey, salt and 4 cups of the flour; stir vigorously. Add rest of flour, a cup at a time, stirring well after each addition.

Turn out onto a floured surface, knead for 10 minutes. Place dough in lightly oiled bowl, cover with towel; let rise 1 hour.

Bring large (3–4 quart) pot of water to a boil. I use a stainless steel pan that holds 1 gallon of water and has a 12" diameter surface, which holds 6 bagels at a time. A smaller pot that holds 3 or 4 bagels will also work.

While the water is heating, punch dough down and divide into 20 equal parts (approximately 4 ounces on a scale).

Roll each piece of dough into a strand about 8–9" long. Connect each end by wrapping them around each other to form a doughnut shape.

When the water comes to a boil, carefully drop in a few bagels (depending on size of pot), allowing room to expand.

When water returns to a boil, set a timer for 2 minutes. Using a slotted spoon, turn the bagels over and boil 2 minutes on the other side. Place on a rack with a paper towel underneath to drain. Continue until all 20 are done.

Preheat oven to 350°. Place bagels on nonstick baking sheets. Brush on egg whites and sprinkle on topping of your choice.

Bake 20 minutes. Cool on racks.

Makes 20 bagels, 1 bagel:
172 calories   1g fat   37g carbohydrates   7g protein
0mg cholesterol   6g fiber   120mg sodium

Cinnamon Raisin Bagels

1 tablespoon cinnamon
3/4 cup raisins
1/2 cup honey (in place of 3 tablespoons honey)

4% fat

The same procedure as bagels except add cinnamon, raisins and more honey with the flour mixture.

Makes 20 bagels, 1 bagel:
206 calories   1g fat   46g carbohydrates   7g protein
0mg cholesterol   6g fiber   121mg sodium

Rye Bagels

1 cup rye flour (in place of 1 cup whole-
    wheat flour)
3 tablespoons molasses (in place of 3 table-
    spoons honey)
2 teaspoons caraway seed

5% fat

The same procedure as bagels except add rye flour, molasses and caraway with the flour mixture.

Makes 20 bagels, 1 bagel:
169 calories   0.9g fat   36g carbohydrates   7g protein
0mg cholesterol   5g fiber   120mg sodium

Corn Bread

2 cups cornmeal
½ cup whole-wheat flour
1 tablespoon brown sugar
1 teaspoon baking powder
½ teaspoon baking soda
2 cups buttermilk, ½ % fat (non-fat, if available)
1 tablespoon oil
1 egg white, lightly beaten

Preheat oven to 425°.

In large bowl combine cornmeal, flour, brown sugar, baking powder and baking soda.

In medium bowl combine buttermilk, oil and egg white.

Add wet ingredients to dry ingredients, stirring just until moistened.

Pour into lightly oiled 8" x 8" pan. Bake 20–25 minutes or until toothpick comes out clean.

Makes 8 pieces

1 piece:
    180 calories
    4g fat
    32g carbohydrates
    7g protein
    0mg cholesterol
    4g fiber
125mg sodium

Pita Bread

1   package active, dry yeast
1½ cups warm water (95°–115°)
1   teaspoon salt, optional
2   cups whole-wheat flour
1½ –2 cups unbleached flour

In medium bowl stir yeast, water, salt and 1½ cups of the whole-wheat flour for 100 strokes; let rest for 15 minutes.

Add rest of flour, stirring well. Turn out onto floured surface, knead 7–10 minutes. Place in lightly oiled bowl, cover with a towel; let rise in warm place for 45 minutes.

Divide into 8 equal balls; roll out into circles 7" in diameter. Place on floured counter, cover with a towel; let rise for 30 minutes.

Preheat oven and baking sheets to 475°*. Using a spatula, gently lift pita circles to heated sheets (2 to a sheet). Bake 4–6 minutes or until puffed up and lightly browned.

To keep pitas soft, immediately remove from sheets, stack 4 high, wrap in a towel and place in a paper bag for 10–15 minutes. Serve warm.

* The high temperature causes the pita to puff up, leaving the hollow center or pocket for making sandwiches.

Makes 8 pitas

1 pita:
    178 calories
    1g fat
    38g carbohydrates
    7g protein
    0mg cholesterol
    7g fiber
    291mg sodium

Breadsticks

  1 package active dry yeast
  1 teaspoon sugar
  1 cup warm water (90°–105°)
1½ cups whole-wheat flour
1½ cups unbleached flour
  1 egg white, lightly beaten, for topping
     poppy seed, sesame seed, fennel seed, coarse salt, or
     parmesan cheese

5% fat

Preheat oven to 425°.

In large bowl dissolve yeast and sugar in warm water; add flour, stirring well.

Turn out onto floured surface, knead until dough is easy to handle, about 5 minutes.

Divide dough into 14 equal pieces. Shape into sticks about 6"–7" long. Place on baking sheet sprayed with nonstick cooking spray. Brush with egg white. Sprinkle on seed of your choice, salt or parmesan cheese.

Bake until brown, about 15 minutes.

  Makes 14 sticks

  1 breadstick:

      90 calories
    0.5g fat
     19g carbohydrates
      4g protein
    0mg cholesterol
      2g fiber
     5mg sodium

Flour Tortillas

1½ cups unbleached flour
1½ cups whole-wheat flour
  1 cup water

5%
fat

In medium bowl combine flour and water. Add a
little extra water if dough feels too stiff or extra flour if too
sticky.

Turn out onto floured surface, knead 4–5 minutes. Divide
dough into 12 equal balls.

On a floured surface roll out each ball to a circle approximately 7" in diameter.

Heat a nonstick fry pan to medium heat; do not use any oil
or spray. Place 1 tortilla at a time in pan. Heat on one side
until bubbles form in dough, about 30 seconds. Flip over to
heat other side, about 15 seconds. Place on a towel without
stacking.

The tortillas will be soft, pliable and lightly browned.

  Makes 12 tortillas

  1 tortilla:

      100 calories
      0.6g fat
      21g carbohydrates
       4g protein
      0mg cholesterol
       2g fiber
      1mg sodium

31

Legumes

If you're looking for a complex carbohydrate food that's low in fat, high in fiber, contains no cholesterol, offers complete protein when combined with a grain and comes with a supply of vitamins and minerals—you've found it.

Legumes—dried beans, lentils and peas—are a bargain economically and nutritionally. You'll find canned versions of some varieties, but you'll want to cook your own in order to sample the many types available in dried form.

See Chapters 27, 34 and 36 for additional legume recipes.

Basic Cooking Directions

1.) Sort through dry beans and pick out any stones or dirt.

2.) Wash or rinse in a colander under cold water.

3.) Place measured beans in a large cooking pot and cover with cold water (6–8 cups of water for 2 cups of dried beans).

4.) Soak for 8–10 hours at room temperature.*

5.) Discard the soak water and add fresh water to cover the beans.**

6.) Bring pot of beans to a boil, reduce heat, skim off any foam that comes to the top.

7.) Simmer gently for 1–1½ hours, stirring occasionally. †
Add extra hot water if needed to keep beans covered.

8.) The beans are done when the skins begin to break open and they are tender enough to bite through. They are now ready for use in a recipe or can be cooled, refrigerated and/or frozen for later use.

If you forgot to soak the beans, there is a quick method that will work for most varieties.††

1.) Sort for stones. Wash beans.

2.) In a large pot, cover beans with cold water.

3.) Bring to a boil and boil for 2 minutes.

4.) Remove pot from heat, cover, let sit for 1 hour.

5.) Discard water, add fresh, proceed with cooking as in step 6 of basic cooking directions.

* Soaking softens the bean and cuts down on the length of cooking time needed to achieve tenderness. Split peas and lentils don't need to be soaked and take approximately 45 minutes to cook.

** Discarding the soaking water will remove some of the water-soluble chemical compounds that cause gas. But be aware that it takes time for your body to adapt to changes in eating. As you regularly include beans in your diet, your digestive system will develop the enzymes necessary for breaking down the complex sugars in beans.

† The cooking time may vary due to the dryness of the legume, type of legume and the hardness of the water. Begin checking them 1/2 hour before the minimum recommended time.

†† You can also cook beans quickly in a pressure cooker. Check appliance booklet for instructions.

BBQ Pintos

3 cups pinto beans, cooked (or canned, drained)
½ cup onion, chopped
½ cup green pepper, chopped
2 cups tomato sauce
1 clove garlic, minced
1 tablespoon chili powder
½ teaspoon cumin
½ teaspoon salt, optional
⅛ teaspoon cayenne pepper

5%
fat

Combine all in 3-quart casserole or bean pot. Cover and bake 1 hour at 350°. Stir occasionally and add extra liquid if mixture gets too dry.

Makes 4 cups

1 cup:
    231 calories
      1g fat
     45g carbohydrates
     13g protein
    0mg cholesterol
     11g fiber
  328mg sodium

Triple Baked Bean

2 cups pinto beans, cooked (or canned,
  drained)
2 cups kidney beans, cooked (or canned,
  drained)
2 cups navy beans, cooked (or canned,
  drained)
1 cup tomato juice
½ cup onion, chopped
2 tablespoons brown sugar
2 tablespoons molasses
2 tablespoons cider vinegar
½ teaspoon salt, optional
⅛ teaspoon cayenne pepper

3% fat

Combine all ingredients in 3-quart casserole or bean pot.
Cover and bake 1 hour at 350°; stir occasionally. If mixture
is too dry, add extra tomato juice. Consistency when done
will be moist but not soupy.

Makes 6 cups

1 cup:
    280 calories
      1g fat
    54g carbohydrates
    16g protein
    0mg cholesterol
    14g fiber
  201mg sodium

Cajun Kidney Beans

4 cups kidney beans, cooked (or canned, drained)
1 cup vegetable stock (homemade)
1 cup onion, chopped
1 cup celery, chopped
1/2 cup green pepper, chopped
2 cloves garlic, minced
2 bay leaves
1 tablespoon cajun seasoning

In large saucepan combine beans, stock, onion, celery, green pepper, garlic, bay leaves and cajun seasoning. Bring to a boil, reduce heat, cover; simmer 1/2 hour. Stir occasionally, add water as necessary to prevent scorching. Remove bay leaves before serving.

Makes 4 cups

1 cup:

    252 calories
    1g fat
    46g carbohydrates
    16g protein
    0mg cholesterol
    15g fiber
    24mg sodium

Mexican Beans

¹/₂ cup onion, chopped
1 clove garlic, minced

8% fat

2¹/₂ cups kidney beans, cooked (or canned, drained)
2 cups garbanzo beans, cooked (or canned, drained)
2 cups canned, peeled tomatoes, drained
1 4–ounce can chopped green chilies (ethnic section of supermarket)
1 teaspoon chili powder
1 tablespoon cornstarch in 2 teaspoons water
Topping:
³/₄ cup yellow cornmeal
2 cups water

In large nonstick fry pan, sauté onion and garlic, using non-stick cooking spray as needed. Add kidney beans, garbanzo beans, stewed tomatoes, green chilies and chili powder; bring to boil, reduce heat, simmer about 5 minutes. Thicken with cornstarch if too much liquid.

In medium saucepan combine cornmeal and water. Cook and stir until thick.

Spoon hot bean mixture into 11³/₄" x 7¹/₂" x 1³/₄" baking dish; spoon cornmeal mixture over bean mixture. Bake 25 minutes at 375° or until cornmeal topping is light brown.

Serves 8

1 serving:
167 calories   2g fat   31g carbohydrates   9g protein
    0mg cholesterol   7g fiber   170mg sodium

Baked Beans

6 cups navy beans, cooked (or canned), save
    liquid
½ cup onion, chopped
½ cup catsup, low sodium, lite
¼ cup light molasses
⅓ cup brown sugar
1 teaspoon dry mustard
1 teaspoon salt

Place beans, 2 cups of the bean liquid and rest of ingredients
in 3-quart casserole or bean pot.. Mix well; cover and bake
3–4 hours at 250°–300°, stirring occasionally and add extra
liquid if needed for consistency.

Serves 6

1 serving:
    340 calories
      1g fat
     68g carbohydrates
     16g protein
      0mg cholesterol
     14g fiber
    537mg sodium

Pineapple Pintos

½ cup pineapple juice
2 tablespoons brown sugar
2 tablespoons cider vinegar
1 tablespoon low-sodium soy sauce
½ cup green pepper, cut in thin strips
½ cup onion, chopped
½ cup mushrooms, sliced
4 cups pinto beans, cooked (or canned, drained)
1 tablespoon cornstarch in 1 tablespoon water
¾ cup pineapple chunks

In small bowl combine pineapple juice, brown sugar, cider vinegar and soy sauce; set aside.

In nonstick fry pan sauté green pepper, onion and mushrooms until tender-crisp. Add beans and sauce mixture; heat through. Thicken with cornstarch. Add pineapple, heat a few more minutes. Serve on hot rice.

Makes 5 cups

1 cup:
   245 calories
    1g fat
   49g carbohydrates
   12g protein
   0mg cholesterol
   10g fiber
 102mg sodium

Refried Beans

3 cups pinto beans, cooked (or canned) save
   liquid
2 cloves garlic, minced
¼ cup onion, chopped
¼ cup green pepper, chopped
¼ teaspoon cumin
¼ teaspoon salt, optional
¼ –½ cup bean liquid

Place all ingredients in nonstick fry pan. Mash beans with a fork. Cook mixture on low heat 15–20 minutes, adding liquid as needed to get consistency desired (thicker, lumpy or thinner, smooth).

Alternate to hand mashing: process beans in blender (puree setting) or food processor. Then place in fry pan with other ingredients and cook.

Makes 3 cups

1 cup:
   245 calories
     1g fat
    46g carbohydrates
    14g protein
    0mg cholesterol
    12g fiber
 196mg sodium

15 Bean Salad

2 cups dry beans, purchased variety package
  or bulk from natural foods store
¼ cup onion, diced
¼ cup green pepper, diced
¼ cup celery, diced
2 tablespoons parsley, finely chopped
2 cloves garlic, minced
6 tablespoons dressing (recipe below)
  fresh ground Five Pepper Blend or black pepper

6%
fat

Dressing:
⅓ cup pineapple juice
¼ cup rice vinegar
1 tablespoon low-sodium soy-sauce
2 teaspoons sugar
1 teaspoon olive oil

Soak beans overnight in 4-quart pot. Drain, add fresh water
to cover, cook gently for 45 minutes, drain. The beans
should be more firm in texture, not too soft or mushy—thus
the shorter cooking time.

In large serving bowl combine beans, onion, green pepper,
celery, parsley, garlic and dressing; mix well, chill. Serve as
is or on a plate of greens with cucumber and tomato slices.
Add extra dressing if desired.

Makes 6 cups

1 cup with 1 tablespoon dressing:
230 calories   2g fat   41g carbohydrates   14g protein
  0mg cholesterol   9g fiber   92mg sodium

32

Fruits and Vegetables

We wish that everyone could harvest fresh fruits and vegetables from their own gardens and yards. But other good choices are pick-your-owns, roadside stands, farmer's markets and food co-ops. Many supermarkets now offer organic produce in addition to commercial varieties.

If you're not certain of the source, be sure to wash produce in cold water. If it has a wax coating (often found on apples and cucumbers) you'll have to peel. This is unfortunate. Fruits and vegetables are most nutritious when eaten raw with the peelings. The vitamins and minerals are just underneath the skin.

When preparing vegetables for mealtime, chop or slice just before you are ready to cook. Then cook them quickly just before you are ready to serve. This retains maximum color, flavor and nutrients.

The best cooking methods are steaming, baking, microwaving and stir-frying. See Chapters 27, 34 and 35 for more vegetable recipes.

Microwave Tips

- To prevent from bursting in the microwave (or oven), pierce the skin of whole potatoes, sweet potatoes or yams, winter squash and eggplant to allow excess steam to escape.

- Cook fresh vegetables in a covered glass casserole. For one pound of vegetables add 2–4 tablespoons of water.

- Stir and check for doneness often. Over-cooked vegetables are not very appealing.

- Frozen vegetables may be microwaved in their container. Check directions on carton.

- Microwaves vary in power levels so check cooking times appropriate for yours.

Stir-fry Vegetable Cooking Directions

Select 3 or 4 vegetables for color and texture. See list of possibilities. Prepare by cutting into shapes desired (diagonal slices, chunks, florets, match-stick strips, wedges, thin slice, etc.) and to uniform size.

Heat wok. Add minimum amount of oil (nonstick cooking spray works), broth or water.

Add longest-cooking vegetable first and end with those which cook fastest. Quickly stir and toss the vegetables to cook all sides evenly until crisp/tender.

Add sauce if desired (see recipes in Chapter 38), heat through and serve immediately.

Longest cooking, 3–4 minutes

Broccoli, carrots, cauliflower, green beans

Medium cooking, 2–3 minutes

Asparagus, bamboo shoots, canned, celery, Chinese cabbage, green or sweet red pepper, kohlrabi, onions, snow pea pods, zucchini

Shortest cooking, 1 minute

Bean sprouts, mushrooms, tomatoes, waterchestnuts

Our Daily Fruit Bowl

1 apple, cut into bite-size pieces
1 banana, sliced
1 cup grapes
1 cup peaches, canned slices, juice packed
1 cup pears, cut into bite-size pieces
1 cup pineapple, canned chunks, juice packed
1 cup raspberries, fresh or frozen
1 cup strawberries, fresh or frozen
1 cup juice from canned fruit

Combine all in serving bowl and refrigerate. Very simple to prepare and easy to keep on hand. Add or substitute other fresh fruits when in season. If using all fresh fruit, add apple or orange juice for the liquid.

Makes about 8 cups

1 cup:
106 calories
0.5g fat
27g carbohydrates
1g protein
0mg cholesterol
3g fiber
3mg sodium

Apple Salad

3 medium-size apples, peeled if desired, cut
  into bite-size pieces
²/₃ cup crushed pineapple, drained, save juice
¹/₃ cup celery, diced small
2 tablespoons raisins

Dressing:
  3 tablespoons non-fat yogurt
  2 teaspoons non-fat mayonnaise
  1 tablespoon pineapple juice
  ¹/₈ teaspoon cinnamon

Combine apple pieces, pineapple, celery and raisins in serving bowl. In small bowl combine dressing ingredients; pour
over apple mixture, mix well, refrigerate. Serve chilled on
lettuce leaves.

Makes 3 cups
1 cup:
    122 calories
    0.6g fat
    31g carbohydrates
    1g protein
    0mg cholesterol
    4g fiber
    43mg sodium

Poppy Seed Fruit Salad

1 cup pineapple chunks, fresh or canned (drained)
1 cup grapes, green or red
½ cup strawberries, fresh or frozen
½ cup blueberries, fresh or frozen
1 kiwi, peeled and sliced
1 apple, cut into bite-size pieces

Dressing:
½ cup non-fat yogurt
1 tablespoon honey
½ teaspoon vanilla
½ teaspoon poppy seed

Prepare fruit; place in serving bowl. Combine dressing ingredients and gently fold into fruit. Serve chilled.

Makes 4 cups
1 cup:
    119 calories
    0.8g fat
    28g carbohydrates
    3g protein
    1mg cholesterol
    4g fiber
    22mg sodium

Baked Apples and Prunes

  4 medium-size baking apples
 12 prunes
  2 teaspoons honey
    dash cinnamon
 ¼ cup apple juice

With small knife cut a hole around apple stem and remove.
Place apples and prunes in microwave dish (or baking dish
if using oven). Put ½ teaspoon honey and dash cinnamon in
each apple stem hole. Add apple juice to dish; microwave
15 minutes (or bake 40–60 minutes at 350°), basting several
times during cooking time. Serve warm.

Serves 4

1 baked apple:
   159 calories
   0.6g fat
   42g carbohydrates
   1g protein
   0mg cholesterol
   5g fiber
   3mg sodium

Microwave Applesauce

4 cups cooking apples, peeled, cored, cut into
   small chunks
¼ cup apple juice
¼ cup honey*

Place apples and juice in 2-quart microwave dish, cover, microwave on high for 4 minutes; stir; microwave 3–4 minutes longer or until you gain consistency desired. Stir in honey. Refrigerate.

*Note: For a smoother applesauce process in a blender after microwaving.

*Note: Add honey to taste according to tartness of apples.

Makes 2¼ cups

½ cup:
    159 calories
    0.6g fat
    45g carbohydrates
    0g protein
    0mg cholesterol
    4g fiber
    1mg sodium

Sweet Potatoes and Apples

4 medium sweet potatoes, peeled
3 cooking apples, peeled if desired
¼ cup unsweetened apple juice

2%
fat

Cut sweet potatoes and apples into slices.

Arrange in alternate layers in a casserole. Pour apple juice over the top. Cover and bake 45–60 minutes at 350° or until tender.

Serves 4

1 serving:
    179 calories
    0.4g fat
    44g carbohydrates
    2g protein
    0mg cholesterol
    4g fiber
    12mg sodium

Oven-"fried" Zucchini and Tomatoes

1 medium-size zucchini, ¹/₄" slices
2 medium-size firm tomatoes, ¹/₂" slices
1 egg white, beaten until frothy
16 squares non-fat soda crackers, rolled into
   crumbs

Dip slices into egg white; coat with crumbs (shaking in a paper bag work well). Place on nonstick baking sheets sprayed with nonstick cooking spray.

Preheat oven to 400°. Bake 10 minutes, turn to other side, bake 10 more minutes.

Makes about 25 slices

Whole batch:
   191 calories
   0.2g fat
   42g carbohydrates
   8g protein
   0mg cholesterol
   1g fiber
   422mg sodium

Sugar Snap Peas and Carrots

2 cups sugar snap peas or snow pea pods,
   strings removed
1 cup carrots, thinly sliced
1 tablespoon parsley, finely chopped

Layer peas and carrots in 1-quart microwave dish. Add
small amount of water, cover, microwave on high for 5 minutes. Uncover, microwave on high for 3 more minutes or until tender. Sprinkle on chopped parsley, serve.

*Note: When in season, substitute fresh asparagus for peas.

Makes 3 cups
1 cup:
    61 calories
   0.2g fat
    12g carbohydrates
    3g protein
   0mg cholesterol
    4g fiber
21mg sodium

Broccoli

1 pound broccoli
   lemon juice

15% fat

Prepare broccoli: separate into bite-size florets, pare and slice stalk into pieces.

Bring 1" water to boil in 3-quart saucepan. Place broccoli on steamer rack, cover pan, steam until just tender and still bright green, 5–7 minutes. Drain. Sprinkle with lemon juice. Serve hot.

Serves 4

1 serving:

     31 calories
    0.5g fat
     6g carbohydrates
     3g protein
    0mg cholesterol
     3g fiber
    31mg sodium

Winter Squash

fresh winter squash (e.g., butternut, acorn)
Toppings:
    brown sugar
    non-fat margarine
    Butter Buds

Wash dirt off skin, do not peel. Cut squash into desired serving sizes, remove seeds and stringy portion.

Baking: Place in roasting pan with small amount of water on bottom. Cover and bake 1 hour at 350° or until tender.

Steam: Place in metal steamer basket and 1" of water in bottom of 3-quart kettle. Arrange squash pieces on rack. Cover and cook on medium heat until squash is tender, about 20–30 minutes. Add extra hot water to bottom of kettle if needed during steaming time.

Serve with 1 or more toppings.

½ squash serves 1 person

½ squash:

    78 calories
    1g fat
    18g carbohydrates
    2g protein
    0mg cholesterol
    6g fiber
    2mg sodium

Braised Cabbage

1 1½–2 pound head of green cabbage
½ cup chicken broth, homemade or canned
   salt and pepper, optional
1 tablespoon fresh parsley, finely chopped
½ teaspoon caraway seeds, optional

Slice head into 6 wedges.

Coat nonstick fry pan with nonstick cooking spray. Add cabbage, cook a few minutes on each side. Add broth, seasonings and parsley, cover; cook 15 minutes, basting several times with the liquid. Add caraway seeds just before serving.

Makes 6 wedges

1 wedge:

    30 calories
   0.5g fat
     6g carbohydrates
     2g protein
   0mg cholesterol
     2g fiber
  84mg sodium

Stuffed Green Peppers

4 large green peppers
1 cup refried beans, homemade (or canned, no lard)
1 cup cooked brown rice
4 ounces low-fat cheese (4 g fat or less per ounce)
   tomato sauce, salsa or hot sauce, optional

Cut off tops and remove core and seeds of peppers. Place on steamer rack in 4-quart pot with 1" of boiling water. Cover and steam 15 minutes until peppers are soft, not limp.

Turn down heat, fill each pepper with ¼ cup beans and ¼ cup rice, add a little sauce, cover and heat through, about 10 minutes. Put 1 ounce of cheese on top, let melt, serve.

Serves 4

1 stuffed pepper:
   183 calories
   1g fat
   30g carbohydrates
   15g protein
   5mg cholesterol
   6g fiber
   253mg sodium

Home-fries

4 large cooked potatoes, peeled (left-over
   boiled or baked potatoes work well)
   salt and pepper, optional

Cut potatoes into cubes. Coat nonstick fry pan
with nonstick cooking spray. Add potato cubes and cook on
medium heat, turning several times with spatula, until
browned with crispy edges, 20–30 minutes.

Serves 4

1 serving:
   145 calories
   0.2g fat
   34g carbohydrates
   3g protein
   0mg cholesterol
   2g fiber
   8mg sodium

Hash-browns

4 large potatoes
   minced onion, optional
   salt and pepper, optional

1% fat

Peel potatoes; grate or shred. Coat nonstick fry pan with
nonstick cooking spray. Place raw potato shreds in heated
pan, brown on one side, turn with spatula, brown on other
side, using extra cooking spray if needed. Takes 30–45 minutes on medium heat.

Serves 4

1 serving:
   145 calories
   0.2g fat
   34g carbohydrates
   3g protein
   0mg cholesterol
   2g fiber
   8mg sodium

Oven-fries

4 large potatoes, unpeeled
  nonstick cooking spray
  salt, optional

1%
fat

Scrub potatoes. Place in large kettle, cover with
cold water, bring to boil, turn down heat, cook 15–20 minutes or until almost tender. Don't cook completely. Drain
and cool.

Peel if desired. Slice into French-fry or thicker wedge shape.

Coat nonstick baking sheet with nonstick cooking spray.
Sprinkle sheet with salt if desired. Place fries in single layer
on sheet. Spray and salt top side of fries. Bake about 45 minutes at 350°, turning once when top side browns.

Serves 4

1 serving:
  145 calories
  0.2g fat
  34g carbohydrates
  3g protein
  0mg cholesterol
  2g fiber
  8mg sodium

Vegetable-Pasta Salad

3 cups cooked pasta, spiral or shell
1/2 cup peas, fresh or frozen (thawed)
1/2 cup celery, sliced
1/2 cup green or sweet red pepper, thinly sliced
   strips
1/2 cup carrot, thinly sliced
1/2 cup zucchini or yellow summer squash, sliced
1/4 cup red onion, thinly sliced
2 tablespoons fresh parsley, chopped
1/2 cup non-fat mayonnaise
   fresh ground black pepper
   cherry tomatoes for garnish

4% fat

Prepare pasta and vegetables. combine with mayonnaise and parsley in large serving bowl. top with pepper and tomatoes. Refrigerate until ready to serve.

Makes about 6 cups

1 cup:
   129 calories
   0.5g fat
   29g carbohydrates
   5g protein
   0mg cholesterol
   1g fiber
   178mg sodium

Vegetable-Legume Salad

6% fat

½ cup onion, chopped
½ cup green pepper, chopped
2 cloves garlic, minced
1 cup canned, peeled tomatoes, undrained
1 teaspoon chili powder
½ teaspoon thyme
½ teaspoon oregano
½ cup cooked kidney beans
½ cup cooked lentils
½ cup cooked brown rice
2 tablespoons fresh parsley, chopped
4 cups lettuce, shredded
1 cup carrot, grated
1 cup zucchini, chopped
1 cup fresh tomato, chopped
1 cup sprouts, alfalfa or your choice
4 tablespoon non-fat sour cream

In a nonstick fry pan, sauté onion, green pepper and garlic. Add tomatoes and seasonings; heat through. Add beans, lentils and rice just to warm. Sprinkle on parsley.

Assemble on individual plates:

- 1 cup shredded lettuce

- ½ cup legume and rice mixture

- ¼ cup each of carrots, zucchini, tomato and sprouts

- 1 tablespoon non-fat sour cream

Serves 4

1 serving:
155 calories   1g fat   31g carbohydrates   8g protein
   0mg cholesterol   7g fiber   197mg sodium

Cole Slaw

3 cups green cabbage, shredded
1 tablespoon onion, minced
¼ cup sugar
¼ cup non-fat mayonnaise
¼ cup lemon juice

Combine all ingredients, mix well, refrigerate until ready to serve.

Makes 3 cups

1 cup:

 106 calories
 0.2g fat
 28g carbohydrates
 1g protein
 0mg cholesterol
 2g fiber
166mg sodium

Onion Rings

1 large onion to make 5 ounces of rings
¼ cup skim milk
¼ cup unbleached flour plus 1–2 extra tablespoons
3 egg whites, beaten until frothy
1 slice whole-wheat bread, whirled quickly in blender
   until crumb size is reached

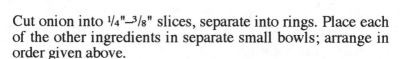

Cut onion into ¼"–³/₈" slices, separate into rings. Place each of the other ingredients in separate small bowls; arrange in order given above.

With one hand, dip each ring first into the milk, then the flour and then the egg white. For the crumbs, hold the ring above the dish and with your other hand sprinkle the crumbs over the onion ring (If you place the ring in the dish, the bread crumbs will get wet and won't stick to the onion).

Place on nonstick baking sheets sprayed wiht nonstick cooking spray. Bake about 10 minutes at 350°. Serve immediately.

Serves 2

1 serving:
   178 calories
      1g fat
     31g carbohydrates
     11g protein
     1mg cholesterol
      3g fiber
   97mg sodium

Lettuce Super Salad

6 cups mixed lettuce leaves (green and red loose leaf, buttercrunch, bibb, romaine, etc.), torn into bite-size pieces

2 cups fresh spinach, torn into bite-size pieces

1 cup broccoli florets

1 cup cauliflower florets

½ cup carrot, thinly sliced

½ cup radish, sliced

1 tomato, sliced

1 cup alfalfa sprouts

Rinse lettuce and spinach under cold, running water. Spinach may have to be rinsed several times to get rid of sand. Drain well by whirling in a salad basket, blotting with paper towel or wrapping in a cotton towel. Chill until ready to serve.

For crisp-tender texture, blanch broccoli and cauliflower by placing in boiling water. When water returns to boiling again, drain immediately and plunge vegetables in icy cold water to prevent further cooking. Drain well.

Combine all ingredients in serving bowl. Serve with choice of no-oil salad dressing or toss with dressing on page 330.

Serves 4

1 serving:

52 calories   0.8g fat   11g carbohydrates   4g protein

0mg cholesterol   2g fiber   59mg sodium

33
Poultry and Fish

Just a few pointers:

- Recipes calling for skinned chicken parts were analyzed using 3 ounces of mixed (light and dark) cooked chicken, which represents an average yield from a single part (e.g., leg, wing or breast).

- To be assured of low-fat ground chicken or turkey, have a skinless breast portion freshly ground.

- Fresh fish should have a pleasant aroma, not a "fishy" smell.

- Be sure to thaw frozen poultry and fish in the refrigerator. Thawing at room temperature encourages bacterial growth.

- Think of all meat and fish as just one part of the meal and not the main course.

Sweet and Sour Meatballs

1 slice whole-wheat bread, dried for crumbs*
1 pound ground chicken or turkey
1 can water chestnuts, drained, diced small
½ cup onion, chopped
⅛ teaspoon garlic powder
1 cup green pepper, chopped
1½ cup carrots, diagonally sliced
2 cups pineapple juice
1 teaspoon dry mustard
1 teaspoon grated fresh gingerroot (produce section of supermarket)
2 tablespoons brown sugar
1 tablespoon lemon juice
1 tablespoon cornstarch in 2 teaspoons water
½ cup pineapple chunks
4 cups hot cooked brown rice

In large bowl mix bread crumbs, ground chicken, water chestnuts, onion and garlic powder. Form 16 balls; brown in large nonstick fry pan using nonstick cooking spray as needed.

Add green pepper, carrots, pineapple juice, dry mustard, gingerroot, brown sugar and lemon juice; simmer ½ hour. Add extra juice if needed for consistency. Thicken juice with cornstarch mixture. Add pineapple chunks, heat through. Serve on hot rice.

*To make bread crumbs: Dry slices of whole-wheat bread by leaving out on counter on a wire rack (or do it quickly in microwave, but watch carefully). Break the bread into pieces, drop in a blender, blend on appropriate setting for fine flour-like crumbs. Add seasonings and store in a sealed plastic bag in the refrigerator. Keep a supply on hand for other recipes that call for crumb toppings.

Serves 4

1 serving:
>   632 calories
>   11g fat
>   93g carbohydrates
>   41g protein
> 102mg cholesterol
>   0g fiber
> 364mg sodium

Chickpeas and Chicken Cacciatore

1 cup onion, chopped
1 cup green pepper, chopped
1 cup fresh mushrooms, sliced
4 cups canned, peeled tomatoes, undrained
2 cloves garlic, minced
1 teaspoon basil
1 teaspoon oregano
2 cups cooked chickpeas (or canned, drained)
4 chicken parts, skinned (see chapter introduction)
  fresh parsley, chopped, for garnish
4 cups cooked whole-wheat elbow macaroni (or brown
  rice, if you prefer)

16% fat

In large nonstick fry pan, sauté onions, green pepper and
mushrooms. Add tomatoes, seasonings, and chickpeas; stir
well. Simmer 20 minutes.

Add chicken, spooning sauce mixture on top. Cover pan and
continue to simmer another 30–40 minutes, until chicken is
cooked.

Serve hot over cooked macaroni or brown rice.

Serves 4

1 serving:
    568 calories
    10g fat
    82g carbohydrates
    43g protein
    76mg cholesterol
    7g fiber
    736mg sodium

Broiled Marinated Fish

¼ cup fresh lime juice (about 1 lime)
1 tablespoon low-sodium soy sauce
2 garlic cloves, minced
2 teaspoons chicken broth (homemade or canned)
1 teaspoon onion, minced
¼ teaspoon crushed red pepper
4 5-ounce haddock fillets (marinated 1 hour before cooking)

Combine first 6 ingredients; pour over haddock fillets in baking dish. Refrigerate 1 hour. Broil, grill or microwave, basting with marinade.

A ½" fillet cooks in about 5 minutes. Measure fish at thickest point to determine cooking time. Fish cooks fast—be careful not to overcook as it will dry out and get tough. When fish is done, it becomes opaque and flakes with a fork.

Serves 4

1 fillet:

   132 calories
     1g fat
     2g carbohydrates
   27g protein
  82mg cholesterol
     0g fiber
226mg sodium

7% fat

Sweet and Savory Chicken

4 chicken parts, skinned (see chapter introduction), marinated 1 hour before cooking
2 tablespoons low-sodium soy sauce
½ teaspoon ground ginger
½ teaspoon garlic powder
2 cups apple juice, no sugar added
1 cup fresh mushrooms, sliced
1 cup green pepper, chopped
1 cup peas, frozen
½ cup green onions, sliced
1 tablespoon cornstarch in 2 teaspoons water
4 cups hot cooked brown rice

Marinate chicken in soy sauce, ginger and garlic mixture for
1 hour (refrigerate).

Brown chicken in nonstick fry pan. Add apple juice, mushrooms, green pepper, peas and green onions; bring to a boil,
reduce heat, cover pan and simmer 1 hour. Thicken juice
with cornstarch mixture. Serve over hot rice.

*Note: When in season add 1 cup sliced fresh asparagus.

Serves 4

1 serving:
   509 calories
   8g fat
   75g carbohydrates
   33g protein
   76mg cholesterol
   6g fiber
   361mg sodium

Chicken Paprikash

1 cup onion, chopped
1 cup green pepper, chopped
4 cups canned, peeled tomatoes, save liquid
1 tablespoon paprika
4 chicken parts, skinned (see chapter introduction)
1/4 cup non-fat yogurt
1/4 cup non-fat sour cream
4 cups hot cooked whole-wheat elbow macaroni

16% fat

In large nonstick fry pan, combine onion, green pepper, tomatoes and paprika; place chicken on top. Cover and simmer 1 hour, adding juice from tomatoes as needed to keep some liquid in pan bottom.

Combine yogurt and sour cream. Stir into the vegetable mix after moving chicken to the side. Warm through, but don't boil. Serve chicken and vegetable sauce over macaroni.

Serves 4

1 chicken piece and 1/2 cup sauce:
    463 calories
      8g fat
    64g carbohydrates
    39g protein
  77mg cholesterol
     3g fiber
783mg sodium

Curried Fish

2 pounds frozen haddock fillets
½ cup green pepper, chopped
½ cup onion, chopped
½ cup celery, chopped
2 tablespoons unsalted margarine
2 tablespoons whole-wheat flour
2 teaspoons curry powder
2 cups liquid from fish stock
4 cups hot cooked brown rice

16% fat

In covered saucepan cook frozen fillets in water just until it flakes, about 8 minutes. Save liquid.

In medium nonstick fry pan sauté green pepper, onion and celery in margarine; stir in flour and curry powder. Add the fish liquid and simmer until thickens. Flake fish into small pieces, add to the vegetable mix; heat through. Serve on rice.

Serves 4

1 serving:

    506 calories
      9g fat
     56g carbohydrates
     49g protein
    131mg cholesterol
      4g fiber
    165mg sodium

"Kentucky-fried" Chicken

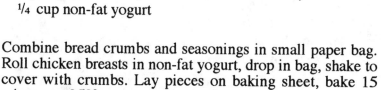

2 slices whole-wheat bread, dried, made into crumbs*

¹/₈ teaspoon onion powder

¹/₈ teaspoon garlic powder

¹/₈ teaspoon ground ginger

¹/₈ teaspoon cayenne pepper

4 chicken breasts (3 ounces of meat for each)

¹/₄ cup non-fat yogurt

18% fat

Combine bread crumbs and seasonings in small paper bag. Roll chicken breasts in non-fat yogurt, drop in bag, shake to cover with crumbs. Lay pieces on baking sheet, bake 15 minutes at 350°; turn once at 10 minutes.

*To make bread crumbs: Dry slices of whole-wheat bread by leaving out on counter on a wire rack (or do it quickly in microwave, but watch carefully). Break the bread into pieces, drop in a blender, blend on appropriate setting for fine flour-like crumbs. Add seasonings and store in a sealed plastic bag in the refrigerator. Keep a supply on hand for other recipes that call for crumb toppings.

Serves 4

1 serving:

190 calories

4g fat

9g carbohydrates

29g protein

73mg cholesterol

1g fiber

75mg sodium

Burrito Burgers

1 pound ground chicken or turkey
1 cup refried beans (homemade or canned, no lard)
8 1-ounce slices of non-fat cheese
8 flour tortillas, homemade (recipe in chapter 30) or packaged
1 can chopped green chilies
½ cup onion, chopped
2 tomatoes, chopped
   lettuce, chopped
   hot sauce or salsa

Combine meat and refried beans; shape into 8 patties. Place 1 piece of cheese on each pattie. Fold pattie over to form a semi-circle.

Grill patties or cook in nonstick fry pan using nonstick cooking spray as needed.

Warm tortillas in microwave or on grill. Fill with burger and top with chilies, onion, tomatoes, lettuce and hot sauce.

Makes 8 burgers

1 burger:
   288 calories
     5g fat
    30g carbohydrates
    31g protein
    56mg cholesterol
     4g fiber
   275mg sodium

Grilled Fish

1 pound fish fillets (haddock, perch or sole),
   fresh or frozen, thawed
1 lemon
   minced garlic, paprika, salt, pepper

Prepare coals (or gas grill). Arrange fillets on sheet of foil.
Squeeze half of the lemon over the fish. Sprinkle with sea-
sonings. Grill about 8 minutes or until fish flakes easily.
Serve with lemon wedges cut from other half.

Serves 4

1 serving:
    95 calories
   0.8g fat
     1g carbohydrates
    20g protein
   49mg cholesterol
     0g fiber
   61mg sodium

Chicken 'n' Spice

2 tablespoons chicken or vegetable broth
2 tablespoons low-sodium soy sauce
2 tablespoons honey
1 tablespoon white cooking wine
½ teaspoon thyme
½ teaspoon paprika
½ teaspoon allspice
¼ teaspoon cayenne pepper
¼ teaspoon black pepper
4 chicken breasts (3 ounces of meat for each)

16%
fat

Combine the marinade ingredients. Place in casserole with chicken breasts. Bake 20 minutes at 350°, basting meat occasionally.

* Note: We frequently substitute rabbit meat in this recipe.

Serves 4

1 serving:
   186 calories
   3g fat
   10g carbohydrates
   27g protein
   73mg cholesterol
   0g fiber
   330mg sodium

OJ Baked Chicken

½ cup orange juice
¼ cup low-sodium soy sauce
2 tablespoons honey
1 teaspoon dry mustard
1 teaspoon ground ginger
1 teaspoon thyme
1 clove garlic, minced
4 chicken breasts (3 ounces of meat for each)

Combine all in casserole or small roasting pan. Bake 20 minutes at 350°, basting meat occasionally with the marinade.

Serves 4

1 serving:
  202 calories
  3g fat
  14g carbohydrates
  28g protein
  73mg cholesterol
  0g fiber
  547mg sodium

BBQ Chicken

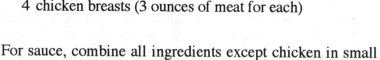

½ cup catsup, low-sodium, lite
¼ cup brown sugar
¼ cup orange juice
½ cup onion, chopped small
1 clove garlic, minced
1 tablespoon cider vinegar
½ teaspoon prepared mustard
½ teaspoon worcestershire
¼ teaspoon black pepper
4 chicken breasts (3 ounces of meat for each)

For sauce, combine all ingredients except chicken in small saucepan. Bring to a boil, turn down heat, simmer 5 minutes.

Bake chicken breasts in covered pan 20 minutes at 350°, basting occasionally with barbeque sauce (about half of the batch). Uncover pan the last 15 minutes.

For grill, cook chicken breasts basting with barbeque sauce.

Serves 4

1 breast:
    175 calories
      3g fat
      8g carbohydrates
    27g protein
  73mg cholesterol
      0g fiber
184mg sodium

Fish Sandwich

1 5-ounce fish fillet (perch, cod, etc.) fresh or frozen, thawed
1 slice whole-wheat bread, dried, crushed into crumbs

1/8 teaspoon onion powder
1/8 teaspoon garlic powder
1/8 teaspoon paprika
  dash cayenne pepper
1 sourdough bun (see recipe in chapter 30), or purchased whole-wheat bun
2 tablespoons tartar sauce (see recipe in chapter 38), or non-fat bottled

Combine crumbs and seasonings in small paper bag. Drop in fish fillet and shake to coat. Cook on each side in fry pan sprayed with nonstick cooking spray until fish flakes easily. It cooks quickly. Serve on bun with tartar sauce.

Makes 1 sandwich

1 fish sandwich:
    400 calories
      5g fat
     56g carbohydrates
     35g protein
    82mg cholesterol
      5g fiber
    348mg sodium

34

Stews and Casseroles

Stews and casseroles are easy to prepare, one-dish meals. Put together a stew in a crock-pot before you leave for work and it will be ready to serve for dinner. Casseroles prepared ahead can be frozen and then conveniently reheated when you need a quick meal.

It's an economical and nutritious way of cooking. By using less meat and including more grains, legumes, vegetables and fruit, you'll be adding the fiber and complex carbohydrates that are so important to your health.

Crock-pot Method

If a recipe calls for meat, brown it first in a fry pan. Then add it to the crock-pot along with the rest of the ingredients. Turn the setting to low and let it slow-cook all day (or night). Add extra herbs the last half-hour to highlight their flavor. Add pasta last 15–20 minutes. The thickening of the liquid or gravy may be done right in the crock-pot just before the stew is ready to serve.

Confetti Casserole

1 pound ground round, lean
½ cup onion, chopped
½ cup celery, chopped
1 cup carrots, grated
5 ounces frozen chopped spinach (½ box)
4 cups canned, peeled tomatoes, undrained
1 15-ounce can tomato puree, no salt added
1 teaspoon oregano
½ teaspoon garlic powder
¼ teaspoon black pepper
2 cups hot cooked whole-wheat flat noodles

Brown meat in nonstick fry pan; drain off any fat. Add onion, celery and carrot; continue to cook. Add tomatoes, tomato puree, seasonings and frozen spinach; simmer 20–30 minutes. Combine with noodles in 3-quart casserole. Bake 30 minutes at 350°.

Serves 4

1 serving:
    455 calories
      8g fat
    54g carbohydrates
    46g protein
  96mg cholesterol
     6g fiber
793mg sodium

B & B's English Stew

1 pound top round steak, visible fat removed,
  cut into cubes
1 cup green pepper, coarsely chopped
1 cup fresh mushrooms, sliced
1 cup carrots, coarsely chopped
1 cup onion, coarsely chopped
4 cups canned, peeled tomatoes, undrained
$\frac{1}{2}$ teaspoon thyme
$\frac{1}{4}$ teaspoon black pepper
3 cups potatoes, sliced
1 tablespoon cornstarch in 2 teaspoons water

17% fat

Brown round steak cubes in nonstick fry pan. Transfer to 3-quart casserole. Add green pepper, mushrooms, carrots, onion, tomatoes and seasonings. Push vegetables to one side and stir in cornstarch mixture to liquid in bottom of casserole. Layer the sliced potatoes on top of vegetables. Cover casserole; bake 1½–2 hours at 300°.

Serves 4

1 serving:
    428 calories
      8g fat
     49g carbohydrates
     43g protein
    96mg cholesterol
      7g fiber
    743mg sodium

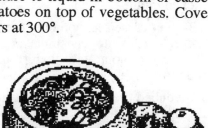

Chestnut and Chicken Casserole

¹/₂ cup onion, chopped
5 ounces chopped, frozen spinach (¹/₂ box)
1 can cream of mushroom soup, Campbell's
   Healthy Request
¹/₂ cup chicken broth (homemade or canned)
8 ounces cooked chicken, skinned, cut into small pieces
1 can water chestnuts, drained, sliced
4 cups hot cooked brown rice
2 tablespoons non-fat yogurt
1 slice whole-wheat bread, cubed for topping

15% fat

In small nonstick fry pan, sauté onion using nonstick cooking spray if needed. Cook and drain spinach according to package directions.

Combine ³/₄ of condensed cream of mushroom soup with chicken broth.

In 3-quart casserole, combine the onion, spinach, soup/broth mix, chicken, water chestnuts and rice. Combine the remaining ¹/₄ can of soup with yogurt and spread on top of ingredients.

Sauté cubed bread in small nonstick fry pan, using nonstick cooking spray if needed. Put on top of casserole ingredients. Cover and bake 45 minutes at 350°. Serve hot.

Makes 7 cups

1 cup:
   253 calories
   4g fat
   39g carbohydrates
   15g protein
   29mg cholesterol
   4g fiber
   293mg sodium

Mrs. Miller's Baked Dish

1 pound ground round, lean
1 cup green pepper, chopped
1/2 cup onion, chopped
4 cups hot cooked whole-wheat flat noodles
1/8 teaspoon black pepper
1 can condensed tomato soup, low sodium

In nonstick fry pan, brown meat; drain fat. Add green pepper and onion, continue to cook.

In 2- or 3-quart casserole combine the meat mixture, noodles, pepper and tomato soup mixed with 1 can of water. Bake 1 hour at 350°.

Makes 6 cups

1 cup:
    310 calories
      6g fat
    34g carbohydrates
    30g protein
    64mg cholesterol
     1g fiber
   234mg sodium

Mexican Pinto Stew

4 cups canned, peeled tomatoes, undrained
2 cups cooked pinto beans (or canned, drained)
1 4-ounce can diced green chilies (ethnic section of supermarket)
1/4 cup onion, chopped
1/4 teaspoon garlic powder
1/4 teaspoon ground cumin
8 ounces cooked chicken, skinned, cut into small pieces

15% fat

In large saucepan combine tomatoes, beans, green chilies, onion and seasonings; bring to a boil, reduce heat, simmer for 15 minutes.

Add chicken and heat through. Serve hot.

* Note: Tastes good over rice.

Makes 6 cups

1 cup:
   204 calories
     4g fat
    28g carbohydrates
    18g protein
    34mg cholesterol
     5g fiber
   468mg sodium

Layered Tortilla Casserole

1 cup onion, chopped
1/2 cup green pepper, chopped
1 clove garlic, minced
1 tablespoon chili powder
1 cup tomato sauce
2 cups cooked pinto beans (or canned, drained)
1/2 cup non-fat plain yogurt
1/2 cup non-fat cottage cheese
6 corn tortillas
3 ounces lowfat cheese (4 grams fat or less per ounce)

15% fat

In large nonstick fry pan sauté onion, green pepper and garlic. Add chili powder, tomato sauce and cooked pintos; heat through.

In small bowl combine yogurt and cottage cheese; set aside.

Quickly heat corn tortillas just to soften and warm, using either a nonstick fry pan (no oil) or microwave (watch closely).

Layer in 11 3/4" x 7 1/2" glassware pan:

3 tortillas

1/2 pinto mixture

1/2 yogurt mixture

Repeat layers a second time.

Sprinkle cheese on top. Bake 20–30 minutes at 350°.

Serves 4
1 serving:
342 calories   6g fat   53g carbohydrates   21g protein
   12mg cholesterol   10g fiber   275mg sodium

Eggplant Casserole

  1 eggplant (20 ounces of slices)
  2 egg whites, beaten frothy
 12 non-fat soda crackers, rolled into crumbs
  1 cup onion, chopped
  1 cup green pepper, 1" cubes
  2 cups mushrooms, sliced
  2 cups zucchini or yellow summer squash, sliced
1½ cups tomato sauce
  1 teaspoon basil
 ½ teaspoon thyme
 ½ teaspoon oregano
 ¼ teaspoon garlic powder
  1 large fresh tomato, sliced in wedges
  4 ounces non-fat cheese, shredded

Peel eggplant, cut into ½" slices. Dip each slice in egg white and coat with crumbs (shaking in a paper bag works well). Place slices on nonstick baking sheet that has been sprayed with nonstick cooking spray. Bake 15 minutes on each side.

In nonstick fry pan sauté remaining vegetables until softened.

In 3-quart casserole layer eggplant slices, vegetable mixture, tomato sauce and seasonings. Top with tomato wedges. Bake 45 minutes at 350°. Add cheese. Bake 5–10 minutes longer or until it melts.

Makes 7 cups

1 cup:

106 calories   0.4g fat   19g carbohydrates   10g protein

3mg cholesterol   4g fiber   181mg sodium

Lentil-Bean-Vegetable Stew

2 cups potatoes, sliced
1 cup onion, chopped
1 cup green or sweet red pepper, chopped
1 cup carrots, sliced
5 ounces frozen chopped spinach (½ box)
½ cup dry lentils
1 cup kidney beans, cooked (or canned, drained)
1 cup garbanzo beans, cooked (or canned, drained)
4 cups canned, peeled tomatoes, undrained
2 tablespoons dried parsley
1 tablespoon chili powder
2 teaspoons basil
1 teaspoon ground cumin
2 cloves garlic, minced

7% fat

Combine all ingredients in large casserole. Bake 2 hours at 350°. Stir occasionally and add extra liquid if needed for consistency.

* Note: For crock-pot method see chapter introduction.

Makes 10 cups

1 cup:
    154 calories
    1g fat
    31g carbohydrates
    8g protein
    0mg cholesterol
    6g fiber
    292mg sodium

Wild Rice Casserole

½ cup wild rice (needs pre-soaking time of 1–
   2 hours)
½ cup long-grain white rice
2½ cups whole-wheat bread cubes
1 cup apple pieces, diced
1 cup fresh mushrooms, diced
½ teaspoon nutmeg
1 teaspoon sage
1½ cups chicken broth (homemade or canned)

Rinse wild rice in strainer under running water to clean. Place in bowl, cover with water, soak 1–2 hours.

Drain rice and place in 2-quart saucepan. Add 2 cups water, cover, bring to a boil, turn to low heat and simmer for 20 minutes. Add the ½ cup of white rice and continue to cook 15 minutes longer.

Cut bread into cubes. Coat nonstick fry pan with nonstick cooking spray. Sauté bread cubes, apple pieces and mushrooms. Add seasonings.

In casserole combine cooked rice, bread mixture and chicken broth. Bake 20–30 minutes at 350°.

Makes 6 cups

1 cup:
   169 calories
     2g fat
    34g carbohydrates
     6g protein
    0mg cholesterol
     2g fiber
  198mg sodium

Tamale Pie

1 cup onion, diced small
½ cup green pepper, diced small
½ cup carrot, diced small
¼ cup apple juice
½ cup corn, frozen
½ cup peas, frozen
2 cups kidney beans, cooked (or canned, drained)
2 cups canned, peeled tomatoes, drained
¼ cup tomato sauce, no salt added
2 cloves garlic, minced
2 teaspoons ground cumin
2 teaspoons chili powder
2 teaspoons dried parsley
¼ teaspoon coriander

Crust:
1 cup cornmeal
1 tablespoon whole-wheat flour
1½ teaspoon baking powder
1 egg white, lightly beaten
½ cup skim milk
1 tablespoon oil
2 tablespoons canned, chopped green chilies, optional

In large fry pan, cook onion, green pepper and carrots in apple juice. Add rest of ingredients and cook until vegetables are tender, about 25 minutes.

Pour mixture into 11¾" x 7½" bakeware dish.

Prepare topping: In medium bowl combine cornmeal, flour and baking powder. In small bowl combine egg white, milk, oil and chopped green chilies. Pour wet ingredients into dry ingredients, mix just until moistened. Spread on top of vegetable-bean mixture.

Bake 20–25 minutes at 350° or until topping is done.

Serves 4

1 serving:

    390 calories
      6g fat
    72g carbohydrates
    17g protein
    1mg cholesterol
    15g fiber
  563mg sodium

Pasta and Bean Stew

5 cups cooked beans, several varieties (Some
    possibilities: 2 cups kidney, 2 cups pinto, 1
    cup lima, or: 2 cups black beans, 2 cups
    great northern, 1 cup dry split peas)

2 cups tomato juice
½ cup vegetable broth, or water
⅓ cup apple juice
⅓ cup low-sodium soy sauce
1 cup onion, diced
1 cup mushrooms, sliced
½ cup celery, diced
½ cup carrot, diced
2 cloves garlic, minced
1 teaspoon basil
1 teaspoon dried parsley
1 bay leaf
¼ teaspoon black pepper
1½ cups cooked whole-wheat elbow macaroni

Combine all except macaroni in 5-quart soup pot. Bring to
boil, turn down heat, simmer 2 hours, stirring occasionally.
Add macaroni the last 15 minutes before serving. Remove
bay leaf.

* Note: For crock-pot method see chapter introduction.

Makes 9 cups

1 cup:

    188 calories
      2g fat
    37g carbohydrates
    11g protein
    0mg cholesterol
      7g fiber
303mg sodium

Beef Stew

1 pound top round steak, visible fat removed,
   cut into cubes
2 cups carrots, sliced
1 cup celery, sliced
1 cup onion, coarsely chopped
3 cups potatoes, sliced
2 cups fresh mushrooms, sliced
¼ teaspoon black pepper
½ teaspoon salt, optional
   cornstarch and water to thicken gravy

18%
fat

Brown meat in large fry pan. Add 2 cups water, cover pan, simmer 1 hour.

Add carrots, celery, onion and simmer another ½ hour.

Add potatoes, mushrooms and seasonings; continue to simmer ½ hour longer. Add water as needed to make a broth that covers meat and vegetables. When meat and vegetables are tender, add cornstarch and water mixture to thicken broth. Serve hot.

*Note: Venison works well as a replacement for beef.

Serves 4

1 serving:
   377 calories
   8g fat
   36g carbohydrates
   41g protein
   96mg cholesterol
   6g fiber
   410mg sodium

Tuna Twist Casserole

12% fat

1/2 cup onion, diced
1/2 cup carrot, diced
1/4 cup green pepper, diced
1 clove garlic, minced
1 6 1/2-ounce can tuna, white in spring water, drained
1/4 cup fresh parsley, chopped fine
1/4 teaspoon paprika
1 cup non-fat cottage cheese
1/2 cup non-fat yogurt
4 cups cooked vegetable rotini macaroni
1 slice whole-wheat bread, cut into cubes for topping
1/4 cup grated Parmesan cheese

In nonstick fry pan sauté onion, carrot, green pepper and garlic using nonstick cooking spray as needed. Add the tuna, parsley and paprika.

In 3-quart casserole combine cottage cheese and yogurt; stir in the tuna-vegetable mixture and macaroni. Top with bread cubes and Parmesan cheese. Bake 30 minutes at 350°. Serve hot.

Serves 4

1 serving:
256 calories
4g fat
29g carbohydrates
26g protein
26mg cholesterol
2g fiber
560mg sodium

35

Stir-fries

Those unfamiliar with this method of cooking need not worry. The instructions are simple to follow and the task itself is accomplished quickly. The key to success is being well organized before the cooking starts.

The idea is to stir-fry quickly, using small amounts of oil so that the juices are sealed in the meat for tenderness and the vegetables can retain their nutrients, color and crispness. If you would like to eliminate all the oil in the recipes, try substituting small amounts of a liquid such as stock, broth or water.

Though you may get by with a nonstick fry pan, the best utensil for stir-fries is the *wok*. Its high sides are perfect for quickly turning and tossing food pieces with a ladle and spatula.

General Preparation Steps

1.) Gather recipe ingredients.

2.) Start cooking the rice—see next page for directions.

3.) Marinate meat if called for in recipe.

4.) Combine sauce ingredients if called for.

5.) Make cornstarch thickener; set aside.

6.) Prepare the meat. Slice uniform pieces across the

grain for tenderness. Meats are easier to slice if partially frozen.

7.) Cut vegetables according to directions. Uniform size is important so all are cooked to same degree of crisp/tenderness.

8.) Prepare seasonings such as garlic or gingerroot. Both are available in the supermarket produce department.

General Cooking Steps

1.) Heat the wok.

2.) Add oil to wok and heat before you add vegetables.

3.) Stir-fry each vegetable separately and set aside (some cook faster than others).

4.) Stir-fry the meat, leave in wok.

5.) Add the sauce, heat through.

6.) Thicken if called for.

7.) Add vegetables back to wok.

8.) Quickly mix everything together.

9.) Serve immediately.

Cooking Brown Rice

1.) Place 2 cups of dry brown rice in a 3-quart saucepan with lid.

2.) Add 4 cups cold water.

3.) Bring to a boil, immediately reduce heat to lowest possible setting, simmer 45–50 minutes.

4.) Do not stir or lift the cover while cooking.

Makes 7 cups of cooked rice. It is now ready to be used in a recipe or it can be refrigerated or frozen for later use. It reheats in minutes in a microwave or on the stovetop (2 tablespoons hot liquid for each cup of cooked rice).

Mandarin Orange Chicken

2 tablespoons low-sodium soy sauce
2 teaspoons cornstarch
2 tablespoons orange juice
2 tablespoons dry sherry
2 teaspoons oil
1 teaspoon grated fresh gingerroot (produce section of supermarket)
2 cups fresh snow pea pods, strings removed
½ cup onion, sliced
8 ounces chicken breast, skinned, boned, cut into ½" x 2" strips
1 11-ounce can mandarin orange slices, drained
½ ounce (⅛ cup) slivered or sliced almonds
2 cups hot cooked brown rice

13% fat

Combine soy sauce, cornstarch, orange juice and sherry; set aside. Heat part of the oil in wok. Stir-fry gingerroot, pea pods and onions about 2 minutes until crisp-tender. Remove from wok.

Heat remaining oil in wok. Add chicken and stir-fry 3–4 minutes. Add soy sauce mixture; cook and stir until thickened. Return the vegetables to the wok; add oranges and almonds, heat through. Serve at once on hot rice.

Serves 2

1 serving:

641 calories
9g fat
86g carbohydrates
48g protein
97mg cholesterol
8g fiber
585mg sodium

Pineapple Chicken Stir-Fry

1 pound chicken breast, skinned, boned, cut
  in $1/2$ " x 2" strips
1 tablespoon low-sodium soy sauce
1 tablespoon oil
1 cup onion, sliced
1 cup celery, diagonally sliced
1 can water chestnuts, drained, sliced
1 cup pineapple juice (save from canned chunks)
1 tablespoon grated fresh gingerroot
1 tablespoon cornstarch in 2 teaspoons water
$1/2$ cup pineapple chunks, canned, save juice
4 cups hot cooked brown rice

15%
fat

Marinate chicken strips in soy sauce while preparing remaining ingredients.

Heat half the oil in wok. Stir-fry onion, celery and water
chestnuts 2–3 minutes or until tender-crisp. Remove from
wok.

Add remaining oil and stir-fry chicken strips 3–4 minutes or
until almost done. Add pineapple juice and grated gingerroot; heat through until bubbly. Add cornstarch mixture to
thicken sauce.

Return vegetables to wok; heat through. Add pineapple
chunks; heat through. Serve at once on hot rice.

Serves 4

1 serving:

   541 calories
    9g fat
   71g carbohydrates
   42g protein
  97mg cholesterol
    4g fiber
227mg sodium

Vegetable and Noodle Stir-fry

2 teaspoons oil
2 cloves garlic, finely chopped
1 cup celery, diagonally sliced
1 cup fresh snow pea pods, strings removed
1 cup green or sweet red pepper, cut in strips
½ cup green onions, including tops, sliced
1 cup water chestnuts, sliced
2 cups fresh mushrooms, sliced
4 tablespoons oyster sauce
4 ounces dry somen noodles

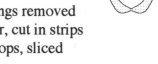

15% fat

Have kettle of boiling water ready to cook noodles.

Heat wok. Heat oil. Stir-fry garlic.

Add celery, stir-fry 1–2 minutes. Add snow pea pods and continue to stir-fry. Then add pepper strips, stir-fry 1 more minute. Next the green onions and finally the mushrooms.

Drop somen noodles into the boiling water. Cook for 2 minutes; drain.

Add oyster sauce to the vegetables; heat through. Add the noodles and mix well. Serve at once.

Serves 4

1 serving:
   181 calories
    3g fat
   34g carbohydrates
    6g protein
   0mg cholesterol
    3g fiber
550mg sodium

Bamboo and Chicken Stir-Fry

1 tablespoon oil
2 cups fresh snow pea pods, strings removed
½ cup green onions, including tops, sliced
2 cups fresh mushrooms, sliced
1 15-ounce can bamboo shoots, drained
1 pound chicken breasts, skinned, boned, cut in ½" x 2"
  strips
1 cup chicken broth (homemade or canned)
2 tablespoons low-sodium soy sauce
2 tablespoons cornstarch in 4 teaspoons water
4 cups hot cooked brown rice

16% fat

Heat part of the oil in wok. Stir-fry snow pea pods, onions and mushrooms 2–3 minutes or until tender-crisp. Remove from wok.

Heat remaining oil. Stir-fry chicken strips 3–4 minutes or until done. Add broth and soy sauce; heat until bubbly. Thicken with cornstarch mixture.

Return vegetables and bamboo shoots to wok; heat through. Serve on hot rice.

Serves 4

1 serving:
    553 calories
    10g fat
    98g carbohydrates
    48g protein
    98mg cholesterol
    9g fiber
    528mg sodium

Beef, Mushroom and Snow Peas

2 tablespoons dry sherry
2 tablespoons low-sodium soy sauce
1 tablespoon cornstarch
1 clove garlic, crushed
½ pound top round steak, visible fat removed,
   sliced in ½" x 2" strips
1 tablespoon oil
1 cup fresh mushrooms, sliced
2 cups fresh snow pea pods, strings removed
1 cup beef broth (homemade or canned)
1 tablespoon cornstarch in 2 teaspoons water
4 cups cooked brown rice

Combine dry sherry, soy sauce, cornstarch and garlic. Add beef strips and marinate 30 minutes.

Heat half the oil in wok. Stir-fry mushrooms and snow pea pods 2–3 minutes until tender-crisp. Remove from wok.

Heat remaining oil. Stir-fry beef strips 3–4 minutes, until done. Add beef broth and heat until bubbly. Thicken sauce with cornstarch mixture. Return vegetables to wok, heat through. Serve at once on hot rice.

Serves 4

1 serving:

    437 calories
      9g fat
    60g carbohydrates
    27g protein
  48mg cholesterol
     6g fiber
477mg sodium

Beef and Broccoli Stir-Fry

marinade:

  1 tablespoon low-sodium soy sauce
  1 tablespoon cornstarch
  1 clove garlic, crushed
  4 slices gingerroot, pared

  ½ pound top round steak, visible fat removed, cut in ½"
    x 2" strips
  4 cups fresh broccoli
  1 cup fresh mushrooms, sliced
  2 tablespoons oyster-flavored sauce
  1 tablespoon cornstarch
  2 tablespoon low-sodium soy sauce
  1 cup water
  1 tablespoon oil
  4 cups hot cooked brown rice

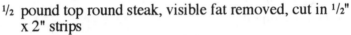

Combine marinade ingredients; add beef strips and marinate for 30 minutes.

Prepare the broccoli: separate into florets and cut stems into strips after paring off tough outer layer of stalks.

Combine remaining oyster-flavored sauce, cornstarch, soy sauce and water; set aside.

Heat half the oil in wok. Add broccoli and stir-fry 2 minutes. Add 2–3 tablespoons of water, cover wok, steam 2 minutes or until broccoli is tender-crisp, remove cover. Add mushrooms, stir-fry 1 minute. Remove vegetables from wok.

Add remaining oil to wok. Remove beef strips from marinade, stir-fry 3–4 minutes or until done. Return vegetables to wok; add oyster sauce mixture. Heat through until thickened. Serve at once on hot rice.

*Note: When in season substitute fresh asparagus for the broccoli.

Serves 4

1 serving:

    417 calories
    9g fat
    59g carbohydrates
    26g protein
    48mg cholesterol
    6g fiber
    301mg sodium

Szechuan Shrimp

½ cup catsup, low sodium, lite
4 tablespoons low-sodium soy sauce
2 tablespoons dry sherry
1 teaspoon sugar
1 teaspoon ground ginger
½ teaspoon crushed red pepper
2 cloves garlic, minced
½ tablespoon oil
½ cup green onions, including tops, sliced
1 cup green pepper, chopped
1 pound shrimp (fresh or frozen), shelled and deveined
4 cups hot cooked brown rice

Combine catsup, soy sauce, dry sherry, sugar, ginger, red pepper and garlic; set aside.

Heat half the oil in wok and stir-fry onions and green pepper 1–2 minutes or until tender-crisp. Remove from wok.

Heat remaining oil. Stir-fry shrimp just until pink and firm, about 2 minutes. Return vegetables to wok. Add catsup mixture; heat until bubbly. Serve at once on hot rice.

Serves 4

1 serving:
    417 calories
    5g fat
    60g carbohydrates
    30g protein
    173mg cholesterol
    4g fiber
    874mg sodium

Chicken, Broccoli and Spinach

16%
fat

12 ounces fresh broccoli (about 4 cups)
 6 ounces fresh snow pea pods, strings removed
 1 cup onion, sliced
¼ pound fresh spinach (about 3 cups), cut in
   strips
 1 cup chicken broth (homemade or canned)
 1 tablespoon low-sodium soy sauce
½ teaspoon sugar
⅛ teaspoon ground ginger
 1 tablespoon oil
 1 pound chicken breast, skinned, boned, cut into ½" x 2"
   strips
 2 tablespoons cornstarch in 4 teaspoons water
 4 cups hot cooked brown rice

Separate broccoli into florets and cut stems into pieces. Prepare rest of vegetables.

Combine chicken broth, soy sauce, sugar and ginger; set
aside.

Heat half the oil in wok. Stir-fry broccoli, pea pods, onion,
and spinach 2–3 minutes or until tender-crisp. Remove from
wok.

Heat remaining oil and stir-fry chicken strips 3–4 minutes or
until done. Add broth mixture; cook until hot and bubbly.
Thicken with cornstarch mixture. Return vegetables to wok;
again cook until hot and bubbly. Serve immediately on hot
rice.

Serves 4

1 serving:
550 calories   10g fat   68g carbohydrates   48g protein
   98mg cholesterol   9g fiber   459mg sodium

5-Spice Stir-Fry

2 cups broccoli, stalks and florets, prepared in
  bite-size pieces

2 cups cauliflower, broken into florets

8 ounces top round steak, visible fat removed,
  sliced in 1/2" x 2" strips

1 cup beef broth (homemade or canned)

2 tablespoons low-sodium soy sauce

1/2 teaspoon 5-spices powder

2 cloves garlic, minced

1 teaspoon ground ginger

1 tablespoon oil
  cornstarch and water

4 cups hot cooked brown rice

19% fat

Prepare vegetables; set aside.

Prepare meat; set aside.

Combine broth, soy sauce and seasonings in small bowl; set aside.

Heat part of the oil in wok. Add broccoli and cauliflower, stir-fry 2 minutes. Add small amount of water (1–2 tablespoons), cover wok and steam for 2 minutes or until vegetables are tender-crisp. Remove from wok.

Add remaining oil to wok. Stir-fry beef strips for 3–4 minutes or until done.

Add the broth mixture and heat until bubbly. Return the vegetables to wok. Thicken with cornstarch and water.

Serve at once on hot rice.

Serves 4

1 serving:

| 408 calories | 9g fat | 48g carbohydrates | 27g protein |
| 48mg cholesterol | 6g fiber | 492mg sodium | |

Sweet and Sour Chicken

⅓ cup sugar
⅓ cup catsup, low sodium, lite
⅓ cup cider vinegar
½ cup pineapple juice
½ teaspoon garlic powder
2 teaspoons oil
8 ounces chicken breast, skinned, boned, cut in ½" x 2" strips
½ cup onion, coarsely chopped
1 cup green pepper, 1" squares
1 tablespoon cornstarch in 2 teaspoons water
1 fresh tomato, wedges
½ cup pineapple chunks, canned, save juice
4 cups hot cooked rice

Combine sugar, catsup, cider vinegar, pineapple juice and garlic powder; set aside.

Heat part of the oil in wok and stir-fry chicken strips 2–3 minutes or until done. Remove from wok. Heat remaining oil and stir-fry onion and green pepper.

Return chicken to wok. Add sauce mixture and heat until bubbly and hot. Thicken with cornstarch mixture. Add tomato and pineapple chunks, heat through. Serve on hot rice.

Serves 4

1 serving:
    484 calories
    6g fat
    85g carbohydrates
    24g protein
    49mg cholesterol
    4g fiber
    192mg sodium

Egg Rolls

1 cup green pepper, finely chopped
1 cup celery, finely chopped
1 cup onion, finely chopped
1 cup mushrooms, finely chopped
1 8-ounce can water chestnuts, finely
  chopped
1 cup cabbage, finely shredded
2 cloves garlic, finely chopped
1 cup mung bean sprouts
1 tablespoon low-sodium soy sauce
1 package egg roll wrappers, approx. 7" x 7" (produce
  ethnic section)
1 egg white, beaten frothy

Prepare vegetables. Heat wok, sauté vegetables and garlic, stirring constantly, about 5 minutes. Turn off heat. Add bean sprouts and soy sauce, stir well. Set aside; let cool to lukewarm.

Take 1 wrapper out of package, position corner down. Place 2 heaping tablespoons of vegetable mixture in middle. Fold 3 corners over filling, roll to fourth corner; seal with a drop of water. Dip in egg white, place on nonstick baking sheet sprayed with nonstick spray. Continue with each wrapper.

Bake 15 minutes at 350° until lightly browned and crispy. Serve hot with the following sauces:

Sweet and Sour

1 cup pineapple juice
½ cup apple cider vinegar
4 tablespoons honey
2 teaspoons low-sodium soy sauce
  cornstarch and water to thicken

Combine in small saucepan, heat to boiling point, turn down heat, thicken with cornstarch, cool to room temperature. Leftover sauce can be frozen.

Hot Mustard

3 tablespoons dry mustard
3–4 tablespoons water

Combine mustard with water in small dish. Serve at room temperature.

Makes 16 egg rolls

1 egg roll (no nutrient information was available for the wrappers):

16 calories
0.1g fat
3g carbohydrates
1g protein
0mg cholesterol
1g fiber
40mg sodium

36
Meat or Meatless

Quite a few people would like to train their appetites to a diet that has less meat. The key is to *lead* appetites with recipes that allow meat *or* a substitute without losing the familiar tastes—pizza, spaghetti, enchiladas and so on.

These "changeover" recipes allow you to go *both* ways in the same meal. You can accomodate both the "eagers" and "reluctants" at your table. Try, for example, a pan of pizza that is divided down the middle with meat on the one side and the meat substitute on the other. A pan of 6 enchiladas can be divided into three meat and three meatless.

Burritos—Meatless

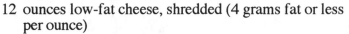

12 flour tortillas, homemade (recipe in chapter
   30), or packaged
 3 cups refried beans, homemade (or canned,
   no lard)
 3 cups cooked brown rice
12 ounces low-fat cheese, shredded (4 grams fat or less
   per ounce)
Toppings:
    shredded lettuce
    cut-up tomatoes
    minced onions
    chopped green chilies
    salsa, hot sauce or non-fat sour cream

Have all ingredients ready to assemble.

 1 tortilla filled with:

     ¼ cup refried beans

     ¼ cup rice

     1 ounce shredded cheese

Eat as is or place in microwave to melt cheese. Add toppings
as desired.

   Makes 12

   1 taco burrito:
      299 calories
        5g fat
       46g carbohydrates
       15g protein
       14mg cholesterol
        6g fiber
      100mg sodium

Burritos—Meat

12 flour tortillas, homemade (recipe in chapter 30), or packaged
 1 pound ground round (or turkey)
½ cup onion, chopped
½ cup green pepper, chopped
 1 clove garlic, minced
½ teaspoon chili powder
½ teaspoon cumin
12 ounces non-fat cheese, shredded
   shredded lettuce
   cut-up tomatoes
   salsa or hot sauce

Prepare tortillas, or warm packaged ones quickly in a microwave just before serving.

In nonstick fry pan brown meat, drain off any fat. Add onion, green pepper and seasonings; cook until vegetables are softened.

Place one part meat mixture in middle of tortilla, add cheese and toppings; fold over and serve.

Makes 12

1 taco burrito:
    199 calories
      2g fat
     23g carbohydrates
     22g protein
     29mg cholesterol
      3g fiber
    220mg sodium

Mexican Pizza—Meat

Crust:

   1 package active dry yeast
  3/4 cup warm water (105°–115°)
  1/2 teaspoon oil
   1 cup unbleached flour
  2/3 cup whole-wheat flour
  1/2 cup cornmeal
  1/4 teaspoon salt

Filling:

   8 ounces ground round (or turkey, chicken)
  1/4 cup onion, chopped
  1/4 cup green pepper, chopped
   2 cloves garlic, minced
   2 cups tomato puree, no salt added
   2 cups refried beans, homemade (or canned, no lard)
  1/4 cup green olives, sliced
   3 ounces low-fat cheese, shredded (4 grams fat or less
     per ounce)

Toppings:

    shredded lettuce
    sliced tomatoes
    chopped green onion
    hot sauce or salsa

Crust:

In medium bowl dissolve yeast in water. Add oil, flour, cornmeal and salt; mix well. Knead 3–4 minutes. Place in bowl, cover with towel, let rise while preparing the filling.

Filling:
In nonstick fry pan, brown meat, pour off any fat. Add on-ion, green pepper and garlic; continue to cook until softened. Add tomato puree; simmer 15 minutes.

Continue with Crust:
Punch dough down; place on floured surface and roll out to 9" x 12" size. Place on nonstick baking sheet. Pre-bake 8–10 minutes at 350°.

Assemble:
Spread refried beans evenly over the pre-baked crust. Spoon meat mixture over the beans; top with sliced olives and shredded cheese. Bake 10–15 minutes at 350° or until cheese melts.

Serve with various toppings.

Serves 4

1 serving:
592 calories   11g fat   85g carbohydrates   41g protein
59mg cholesterol   15g fiber   349mg sodium

Mexican Pizza—Meatless

8 ounces ground round (or turkey, chicken)
—replaced by:
1 cup cooked lentils

12% fat

Serves 4

1 serving:
541 calories   7g fat   95g carbohydrates   27g protein
11mg cholesterol   17g fiber   315mg sodium

Spaghetti—Meat

1 pound lean ground round
2 cups fresh mushrooms, sliced
½ cup onion, chopped
½ cup green pepper, chopped
½ cup zucchini, sliced
4 cups canned, peeled tomatoes, undrained
2 cups tomato puree, no salt added
2 cloves garlic, minced
1 teaspoon basil
½ teaspoon oregano
4 cups cooked whole-wheat spaghetti

In large nonstick fry pan brown meat, drain off any fat. Add mushrooms, onion, green pepper and continue to cook. Add zucchini, tomatoes, puree and seasonings. Simmer 30 minutes. Serve over hot spaghetti.

Makes 7 cups of sauce

1 cup spaghetti with 1 cup sauce:

    381 calories
      5g fat
    57g carbohydrates
    32g protein
   55mg cholesterol
     3g fiber
431mg sodium

Spaghetti—Meatless

2 cups fresh mushrooms, sliced
1 cup onion, diced

½ cup green pepper, diced
2 cloves garlic, minced
5 cups tomato sauce
1 tablespoon basil
½ teaspoon oregano
½ teaspoon thyme
　　salt and pepper, optional
4 cups cooked whole-wheat spaghetti

In nonstick fry pan sauté mushrooms, onion, green pepper and garlic. Add to 3- or 4-quart kettle along with sauce and seasonings. Simmer 1 hour. Serve hot over cooked spaghetti.

Makes 4 ½ cups of sauce

1 cup spaghetti with 1 cup sauce:
　　284 calories
　　　2g fat
　　63g carbohydrates
　　12g protein
　0mg cholesterol
　　　5g fiber
44mg sodium

Green Enchiladas—Meat

12 flour tortillas, homemade (recipe in Chapter
    30), or packaged
12 ounces cooked chicken, cut into small piec-
    es
½ cup onion, diced
 2 cans Campbell's Healthy Request cream of chicken
    soup
 1 cup chicken broth (homemade or canned)
 2 4-ounce cans chopped green chilies (ethnic section of
    supermarket)
 1 10-ounce box frozen chopped spinach, cooked accord-
    ing to package directions, drained
½ cup non-fat sour cream
 3 ounces low-fat cheese, shredded (4 grams fat or less
    per ounce)

Prepare tortillas. If using purchased tortillas, quickly heat to soften in dry fry pan just before you are ready to assemble.

Combine chicken and onion; set aside.

Sauce:
In blender combine soup, broth, green chilies and spinach, using high speed to blend until smooth. Pour sauce into bowl and add sour cream, stirring until blended.

Assemble:
Dip a tortilla into sauce, fill with one part of the chicken and onion, roll up, place in 9" x 12" baking pan. Repeat with rest of tortillas, placing 6 to a pan. Cover with any leftover sauce, sprinkle on cheese, bake 15 minutes at 350°.

Makes 12

1 enchilada:
    228 calories
      5g fat
    30g carbohydrates
    17g protein
    34mg cholesterol
      2g fiber
357mg sodium

Green Enchiladas—Meatless

12 ounces cooked chicken
½ cup onion, chopped
—replaced by:
   3 cups cooked brown rice (¼ cup per enchilada)
  ¾ cup onion, diced (1 tablespoon per enchilada)
   1 4-ounce can chopped green chilies (1 teaspoon per enchilada)

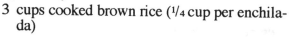

*Note: Sauce stays the same.

Makes 12

1 enchilada:
    236 calories
      3g fat
    43g carbohydrates
    10g protein
    8mg cholesterol
      3g fiber
332mg sodium

Pizza—Meatless

Crust: (needs 1-hour rising time)
   1 teaspoon yeast
   1 cup warm water
   1½ cups whole-wheat flour
   1 –1½ cups unbleached flour

Topping:
   1 cup tomato puree, no salt added
     basil
     thyme
     oregano
     garlic powder
     fennel seeds
   1 cup fresh mushrooms, sliced
   ½ cup onion, diced
   ¼ cup green pepper, diced
   ¼ cup green olives (or ripe olives), sliced
   4 ounces low-fat cheese, shredded (4 grams fat or less
     per ounce)

Crust:
In medium bowl dissolve yeast in warm water; let sit until
bubbly, about 10 minutes. Add flour, a cup at a time, stirring
well after each addition. Place dough on floured surface and
knead for 8–10 minutes. Place in lightly oiled bowl, cover
with towel, let rise until double in size, about 1 hour.

Punch down and turn out onto floured surface. Using rolling
pin roll out to 9" x 12". Place on lightly oiled baking sheet.
Pre-bake 5–8 minutes at 350° or until lightly browned and it
comes "loose" from the pan.

Topping:
While the dough is rising, prepare topping ingredients.

Assemble:
  Pre-baked crust
  Spread tomato puree evenly over crust
  Sprinkle on seasonings according to your taste
  Arrange vegetables and olives
  Sprinkle cheese on top

Bake 10–15 minutes at 350°. Slide pizza off pan onto cutting surface, cut into serving sizes desired.

* Note: We make 2 pizzas for 4 adults.

Makes 1 pizza

½ pizza:
  763 calories   14g fat   126g carbohydrates   36g protein
    28mg cholesterol   18g fiber   144mg sodium

Pizza—Meat

¼ cup green olives (or ripe olives)
—replaced by:
  3 ounces Canadian bacon or ground round, cooked

16% fat

Makes 1 pizza

½ pizza:
  807 calories
  14g fat
  126g carbohydrates
  45g protein
  49mg cholesterol
  17g fiber
  732mg sodium

Pita Pizza—Meat

8 pitas, homemade (see Chapter 30), or pur-
    chased
8 ounces ground round, chicken or turkey
1 cup tomato puree
½ cup onion, diced
½ cup mushrooms, diced
¼ cup green pepper, diced
8 ounces non-fat cheese, shredded
    basil, oregano, thyme, garlic

In nonstick fry pan brown meat, drain off any fat. Prepare rest of ingredients.

Preheat oven to 350°.

Assemble: Place pitas on nonstick baking sheet. Spread each with 2 tablespoons tomato puree. Sprinkle on seasonings desired. Divide up onion, mushrooms, green pepper and meat evenly among the 8 pitas. Top with cheese.

Bake about 10 minutes or until cheese melts.

*Note: If you like a thinnner "crust," cut 4 pitas in half to form 8 circles.

Makes 8 pita pizzas

1 pizza:
    331 calories
      7g fat
    43g carbohydrates
    24g protein
    38mg cholesterol
      8g fiber
    365mg sodium

Pita Pizza—Meatless

8 pitas, homemade (see Chapter 30), or purchased
1 cup tomato puree
2 cups refried beans, homemade (or canned)
½ cup onion, diced
1 4-ounce can green chilies
8 ounces low-fat cheese, shredded (4 grams of fat or less
   per ounce)
   salsa, hot sauce, sliced tomatoes and/or lettuce

20% fat

Prepare ingredients.

Preheat oven to 400°.

Assemble: Place pitas on nonstick baking sheets. Spread
each with 2 tablespoons tomato puree and with ¼ cup refried beans. Divide up onion and green chilies evenly among
the 8 pitas. Top with cheese.

Bake 5–8 minutes or until cheese melts. Add toppings.

Makes 8 pita pizzas

1 pizza:
  287 calories
   6g fat
  43g carbohydrates
  15g protein
  14mg cholesterol
   8g fiber
353mg sodium

Omelet — Meatless

1 egg
5 egg whites
1 tablespoon water
  dash black pepper
1–2 drops Tabasco, optional
¼ cup mushrooms, sliced small
2 tablespoons onion, diced
1 tablespoon green pepper, diced
2 ounces non-fat cheese, shredded

Have vegetables and cheese prepared before you start cooking; place near fry pan.

In small bowl beat egg, egg whites, water and seasonings about 30 seconds with a wisk or table fork.

Coat 10" nonstick fry pan with nonstick cooking spray, bring to medium heat. Pour eggs into pan. When omelet has set on bottom, sprinkle on vegetables and cheese. With a spatula fold the omelet in half, covering the filling. Turn heat down to low and let omelet cook a minute for cheese to melt. Serve with toast.

Makes 1 omelet

1 omelet with 1 slice light wheat bread:

   333 calories
     7g fat
    23g carbohydrates
    44g protein
  284mg cholesterol
     2g fiber
 727mg sodium

Omelet—Meat

—add:

½ ounce Canadian bacon

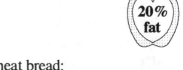

Makes 1 omelet

1 omelet with 1 slice light wheat bread:

     355 calories
       8g fat
      23g carbohydrates
      47g protein
    291mg cholesterol
       2g fiber
    927mg sodium

Red Enchiladas—Meatless

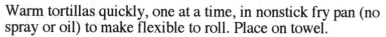

12 flour tortillas, homemade (see recipe in
    chapter 30), or packaged
2 15-ounce cans enchilada sauce
3 cups refried beans, homemade (or canned)
1 cup onion, diced
6 ounces low-fat cheese (4 grams or less per ounce)

Warm tortillas quickly, one at a time, in nonstick fry pan (no
spray or oil) to make flexible to roll. Place on towel.

Place enchilada sauce in shallow bowl in which you can dip
the tortillas.

Assemble:

    Dip tortilla in sauce.

    Fill with ¼ cup refried beans and 1 tablespoon onion.

    Roll up and place seam side down in 9" x 12" baking pan.

    Cover with left-over sauce, sprinkle on cheese.

    Bake 10–15 minutes at 300°.

    Makes 12 enchiladas

    1 enchilada (Note: 3 cups of tomato sauce were used in
the place of the enchilada sauce which had no nutrient information available):

        224 calories
         3g fat
        38g carbohydrates
        12g protein
        7mg cholesterol
         7g fiber
      84mg sodium

Red Enchiladas—Meat

3 cups refried beans
—Replaced by:
   12 ounces cooked ground chicken or turkey (1
     ounce per enchilada)

Makes 12 enchiladas

1 enchilada (Note: 3 cups of tomato sauce were used in the place of the enchilada sauce which had no nutrient information available):

   217 calories
     5g fat
   27g carbohydrates
   16g protein
  32mg cholesterol
    3g fiber
  59mg sodium

37

Desserts and Drinks

Dessert and drink treats tempt us all, but so many out there are just sugar and fat. With a few changes you can train that sweet-tooth to new tastes and still have the treat.

Fruits and juices are included in the recipes to provide "natural" sweetness. More nutrients are included with the whole-grain flour and, of course, fat is reduced by using egg whites, skim milk and non-fat frozen yogurt.

Oatmeal Raisin Cookies*

2 teaspoons butter, softened
2 egg whites
½ cup water
1 teaspoon vanilla
1 ripe medium banana, mashed
3 cups oats
½ cup whole-wheat flour
½ cup unbleached flour
½ teaspoon baking soda
1 cup brown sugar
½ cup raisins
½ teaspoon cinnamon

11% fat

Preheat oven to 350°.

In large bowl beat together butter, egg whites, water, vanilla and banana; set aside.

In medium bowl mix together the remaining ingredients.

Add dry ingredients to wet ingredients and mix until well combined. Drop by heaping teaspoon on nonstick baking sheets. Bake 10–15 minutes. Cool on racks.

*Note: This recipe was adapted from Hoefstra.

Makes 40 small cookies

1 cookie:
    59 calories
    0.7g fat
    12g carbohydrates
    2g protein
    1mg cholesterol
    1g fiber
    4mg sodium

Apple Cobbler

8 large cooking apples, peeled, cored, sliced
1 cup unbleached flour
2 tablespoons sugar
2 teaspoons baking powder
1 tablespoon butter or margarine
$^1/_2$ cup cold water

Topping:
   $^1/_2$ cup sugar
   1 tablespoon unbleached flour
1$^1/_2$ teaspoons cinnamon
   1 cup boiling water

Place sliced apples in 2- or 3-quart casserole.

In medium bowl mix flour, sugar, baking powder and butter. Add water and blend; spread over the apples.

In small bowl mix dry topping ingredients together; sprinkle on top of the batter.

Pour boiling water over top of all and bake 1 hour at 350°. Serve warm.

* Note: Also works well with other fruit such as rhubarb, peaches, cherries, etc.

* Note: Good with a scoop of non-fat frozen yogurt.

Makes 6 servings

1 serving:
   267 calories
   3g fat
   61g carbohydrates
   3g protein
   6mg cholesterol
   4g fiber
143mg sodium

Strawberry Orange Meringues

Meringues:
   3 egg whites
   3/4 cup sugar
   1/2 teaspoon white vinegar
   1/2 teaspoon vanilla
Orange sauce:
   2 cups orange juice
   6 tablespoons sugar
   2 tablespoons cornstarch
   1/2 teaspoon ginger
   1/4 teaspoon nutmeg

   1–2 quarts fresh strawberries
   1 quart vanilla non-fat frozen yogurt

Meringues:
With electric mixer beat egg whites to form stiff peaks. Gradually add sugar while continuing to beat. Add vinegar and vanilla.

On 2 lightly oiled baking sheets drop egg mixture by spoonful to form 12 meringues. With back of spoon form a dip in center of meringue.

Bake 1 hour at 270°. Cool; remove from baking sheet.

Orange sauce:
Combine all in saucepan. Heat and stir until thickened. Remove from heat; set aside.

Strawberries:
Stem, clean, slice, leave smaller ones whole. Refrigerate until ready to serve.

Assemble:

Place 1 meringue in dessert dish. Place 1 scoop (¹/₃ cup) non-fat frozen yogurt in shell. Top with ¹/₂ cup fresh strawberry slices and ¹/₃ cup warm orange sauce. Serve at once.

Makes 12

1 meringue with yogurt, sauce and berries:
    222 calories
    0.4g fat
    54g carbohydrates
    5g protein
    0mg cholesterol
    2g fiber
    54mg sodium

Cherry Cobbler

4 cups fresh tart red cherries, pitted, save
  juice (or 2 cans, drained, save juice)
2 tablespoons cornstarch
⅛ teaspoon nutmeg
⅔ cup sugar
½ cup cherry juice
½ cup whole-wheat pastry flour
½ cup unbleached white flour
2 teaspoons baking powder
¼ teaspoon baking soda
1 tablespoon butter or margarine
⅔ cup buttermilk, ½% low-fat (non-fat, if available)

Place cherries in 8" square baking dish.

In medium bowl mix together cornstarch, nutmeg and ½ cup of the sugar. Stir in juice. Pour over the cherries.

In medium bowl mix flour, remaining sugar, baking powder and baking soda. Cut in butter. Stir in buttermilk just until dry ingredients are moistened. Spread batter on top of cherries.

Bake about 25 minutes at 400°. Serve warm.

Makes 6 servings

1 serving:
    258 calories
      3g fat
    57g carbohydrates
      5g protein
    0mg cholesterol
      2g fiber
  184mg sodium

Sweet and Tart Dessert

3 cups fresh rhubarb, sliced ½" pieces
2 cups fresh strawberries, sliced
1 cup canned pineapple tidbits, save juice
¼ cup pineapple juice
¼ cup sugar
2 tablespoons quick-cooking tapioca
4 egg whites, room temperature
   dash cream of tartar
2 tablespoons sugar

Combine first 5 ingredients in 1- or 2-quart baking dish. Sprinkle with tapioca, mix gently; let stand 15 minutes. Bake 35 minutes at 325°.

Beat egg whites and cream of tartar until soft peaks form. Add the 2 tablespoons of sugar, a tablespoon at a time. Continue to beat until stiff peaks form.

Spread egg white mixture over baked fruit mixture. Bake 8 minutes at 375° or until the meringue is light brown.

Makes 6 servings

1 serving:
   110 calories
   0.4g fat
   25g carbohydrates
   3g protein
   0mg cholesterol
   1g fiber
   38mg sodium

Peach and Raspberry Custard

2 cups peaches, peeled and thinly sliced
2 cups raspberries, fresh or frozen
6 tablespoons sugar
1⅓ cups skim milk
3 eggs (using 3 whites and 1 yolk)
⅓ cup unbleached flour
⅓ cup whole-wheat pastry flour
2 teaspoons vanilla

8%
fat

Preheat oven to 350°.

Lightly spray 8" x 8" glass baking dish with nonstick cooking spray. Place peaches and raspberries in dish. Sprinkle on 1 tablespoon of the sugar.

In blender combine remaining 5 tablespoons sugar, milk, egg whites and yolk, flour and vanilla; process about 30 seconds until smooth; pour over fruit.

Bake about 1 hour or until custard feels set. If top is browning too quickly, turn heat down to 300°.

*Note: 1½ cups of fresh or frozen blueberries may be substituted for the raspberries.

Serves 4

1 serving:
250 calories
2g fat
51g carbohydrates
9g protein
70mg cholesterol
5g fiber
85mg sodium

Carrot Raisin Cake

4 cups grated carrots
1 cup raisins
1½ cups sugar
2⅔ cups water
1 teaspoon cinnamon
½ teaspoon cloves
½ teaspoon nutmeg
2 cups unbleached flour
2 cups whole-wheat pastry flour
2 teaspoons baking powder
2 teaspoons baking soda

In large saucepan combine carrots, raisins, sugar, water and spices; bring to boil, cook on low heat for 10 minutes, cool.

Preheat oven to 350°.

In large bowl combine flour, baking powder and baking soda.

Mix together the wet and dry ingredients; pour into lightly-oiled 9" x 13" baking pan.

Bake 45 minutes or until toothpick comes out clean.

*Note: We enjoy a scoop of non-fat frozen yogurt on the side.

Makes 12 servings

1 serving:

290 calories
1g fat
68g carbohydrates
6g protein
0mg cholesterol
5g fiber
91mg sodium

Banana Split

1 medium banana
1 cup non-fat vanilla frozen yogurt
½ cup fresh or frozen strawberries
1 tablespoon non-fat hot fudge topping,
   warmed
1 tablespoon non-fat caramel topping

Split banana in half lengthwise, place in oblong dish. Scoop on frozen yogurt in 3 lumps. Top 1 lump with strawberries (mashed if desired), 1 with fudge and 1 with caramel.

Serves 1

1 banana split:
   425 calories
     1g fat
   103g carbohydrates
    12g protein
    0mg cholesterol
     6g fiber
  185mg sodium

Drinks

Root Beer Float

1 12-ounce can diet root beer
1 cup non-fat vanilla frozen yogurt

Scoop frozen yogurt into tall, 16-ounce glass.
Pour in root beer. Serve with a spoon and straw.

Serves 1

1 float:

160 calories   0g fat   37g carbohydrates   8g protein
  0mg cholesterol   0g fiber   120mg sodium

Chocolate Malt

1 tablespoon malted milk powder
1 tablespoon chocolate flavor syrup
½ cup skim milk
1 cup non-fat vanilla frozen yogurt

Combine all ingredients in blender, process until smooth and
thick, about 30 seconds. Serve in a tall glass with a spoon.

Serves 1

1 malt:

334 calories   2g fat   70g carbohydrates   16g protein
  2mg cholesterol   0g fiber   301mg sodium

Grape Shake

1 cup grape juice
1 cup non-fat vanilla frozen yogurt

Combine in blender, process about 30 seconds.
Pour into a frosted glass.

Serves 1

1 shake:
288 calories   0.2g fat   69g carbohydrates   9g protein
    0mg cholesterol   0g fiber   125mg sodium

Orange-Pineapple Smoothie

½ cup water
6 ice cubes
1 12-ounce can diet white soda
½ cup instant non-fat dry milk
½ cup frozen pineapple juice concentrate
½ cup frozen orange juice concentrate

In blender combine water, ice cubes and ½ can soda; process until cubes are crushed. Add rest of soda and remaining ingredients; blend until smooth.

Makes about 5 cups

1 cup:
140 calories   0.2g fat   30g carbohydrates   5g protein
    2mg cholesterol   0g fiber   66mg sodium

Strawberry Pineapple Cooler

5 ounces fresh or frozen strawberries, thawed
1 cup crushed pineapple (1/2 of a 20-oz can)
1 cup strawberry sherbet
1 cup non-fat vanilla frozen yogurt
1 12-ounce can diet white soda

Combine strawberries, pineapple, sherbet and frozen yogurt in blender. Process until blended, about 30 seconds. Pour 2/3 cup mixture into a glass, add 1/3 cup soda, stir and serve.

Makes 5 drinks

1 drink:
114 calories   0.6g fat   27g carbohydrates   2g protein
        2mg cholesterol   0g fiber   35mg sodium

38

Toppings and Spreads

Fruit topping choices make pancakes and waffles extra special. Be sure to try them on regular and frozen non-fat yogurt, too. We think hot Orangeberry Sauce over frozen yogurt makes a rather elegant dessert.

Non-fat commercial spreads and sauces are becoming more available, but try the homemade versions. They let you keep additives and preservatives out. They give *you* the choice of ingredients (e.g., salt). They let you benefit from the fresh taste and economy of buying in-season and stocking up (e.g., freezing fruit toppings). The low-fat legume spreads are excellent luncheon meat substitutes in sandwiches or pita stuffers.

Sauces for Stir-fried Vegetables

General Directions: Combine ingredients. Use portion desired on stir-fried vegetables (see Chapter 32 introduction). Refrigerate or freeze remaining sauce.

Sweet and Sour Light

1 cup chicken broth
½ cup pineapple juice
½ cup apple cider vinegar
½ cup brown sugar
1 tablespoon low-sodium soy sauce
2 tablespoons cornstarch in ¼ cup water

3% fat

Makes 2²/₃ cups

Total:

463 calories   2g fat   111g carbohydrates   6g protein
     1mg cholesterol   0g fiber   1282mg sodium

Pineapple

1 cup pineapple juice
¼ cup apple cider vinegar
¼ cup low-sodium soy sauce
1 clove garlic, minced
1 tablespoon cornstarch in 1 tablespoon water

1% fat

Makes 1½ cups

Total:

211 calories   0.3g fat   51g carbohydrates   4g protein
     0mg cholesterol   0g fiber   1935mg sodium

Basic

1 cup chicken broth
2 tablespoons low-sodium soy sauce
1 tablespoon cornstarch in 1 tablespoon water

Makes 1¹/₄ cups, total:
   84 calories   2g fat   11g carbohydrates   6g protein
   1mg cholesterol   0g fiber   1742mg sodium

5-Spice

¹/₂ cup chicken broth
3 tablespoons apple cider vinegar
3 tablespoons low-sodium soy sauce
3 tablespoons brown sugar
1 tablespoon dry sherry
1 clove garlic, minced
¹/₈ teaspoon 5-Spices powder

Makes 1 cup, total:
   172 calories   0.8g fat   35g carbohydrates   5g protein
      1mg cholesterol   0g fiber   1847mg sodium

Sweet and Sour

¹/₃ cup catsup
¹/₃ cup sugar
¹/₃ cup apple cider vinegar
¹/₂ cup pineapple juice
1 clove garlic, minced
2 teaspoons cornstarch in a little water

Makes 1 cup, total:
   404 calories   0.1g fat   105g carbohydrates   2g protein
      0mg cholesterol   0g fiber   589mg sodium

Hot Szechuan

¼ cup catsup
2 tablespoons low-sodium soy sauce
1 tablespoon dry sherry
½ teaspoon sugar
½ teaspoon ground ginger
¼ teaspoon crushed red pepper
1 clove garlic, finely chopped

Makes ⅓ cup
Total:
  81 calories   0.1g fat   15g carbohydrates   3g protein
    0mg cholesterol   0g fiber   1408mg sodium

Ginger

2 cups chicken broth
½ cup dry sherry
½ cup low-sodium soy sauce
⅓ cup water
¼ cup apple cider vinegar
⅓ cup cornstarch
¼ cup brown sugar
2 cloves garlic, minced
1 tablespoon gingerroot, grated
½ teaspoon crushed red pepper

Makes 4 cups
1 cup:
151 calories   0.8g fat   24g carbohydrates   4g protein
  1mg cholesterol   0g fiber   1360mg sodium

Strawberry Freezer Jam

2 quarts fresh strawberries
1 package Sure-Jell Light
3¼ cups sugar
    plastic freezer containers and lids

Remove stems from berries, crush or mash.

In large bowl measure out 4 cups crushed berries.

In separate bowl measure out 3 cups of the sugar.

In small bowl mix ¼ cup of the sugar and 1 box Sure-Jell.

Gradually add the Sure-Jell mixture to the berries, stirring vigorously. Let stand 30 minutes; stir occasionally. Gradually stir in remaining sugar until dissolved.

Fill plastic freezer containers to within ½-inch of tops. Cover with lids. Let stand at room temperature for 24 hours; place in freezer.

After opening, store in refrigerator.

Makes 6 cups

1 tablespoon:
    31 calories
    0.1g fat
    8g carbohydrates
    0g protein
    0mg cholesterol
    0g fiber
    1mg sodium

Orangeberry Sauce

3 tablespoons sugar
1 tablespoon cornstarch
1/4 teaspoon nutmeg
1/4 teaspoon ground ginger
1 cup orange juice
1 cup raspberries, fresh or frozen

3% fat

In small saucepan combine sugar, cornstarch, nutmeg, ginger and orange juice. Cook, stirring constantly, until thickens. Add raspberries and heat through. Serve warm over pancakes, waffles or french toast.

*Note: We often add 1 cup peaches or strawberries (fresh or frozen) in place of the raspberries.

Makes 1²/₃ cups

1/3 cup:

69 calories
0.2g fat
17g carbohydrates
1g protein
0mg cholesterol
1g fiber
1mg sodium

Spiced Apple Topping

2 cups apple juice, unsweetened
1 teaspoon cinnamon
   dash cloves and nutmeg
2 tablespoons cornstarch with 4 teaspoons
   water
3 cups apples, peeled and diced small

4% fat

In medium saucepan bring apple juice and spices to a boil, reduce to low heat. Thicken with cornstarch mixture. Add apple pieces. Heat through. Serve warm over pancakes, waffles or french toast.

Makes 3 cups

1/4 cup:

   52 calories
  0.2g fat
   13g carbohydrates
    0g protein
  0mg cholesterol
    1g fiber
  1mg sodium

Blueberry Sauce

1 cup blueberries, fresh or frozen
½ cup apple juice frozen concentrate
⅓ cup water
½ teaspoon cinnamon
  dash cloves
1 tablespoon cornstarch with 3 teaspoons water

Combine blueberries, concentrate, water, cinnamon and cloves in small saucepan. Bring to a boil, turn down heat, simmer a few minutes. Add the cornstarch and water mixture. Continue to simmer until thickened, stirring constantly. Serve warm over pancakes, waffles or french toast.

Makes 1¼ cups

¼ cup:

    67 calories
  0.3g fat
    17g carbohydrates
    0g protein
  0mg cholesterol
    1g fiber
  9mg sodium

Tartar Sauce

½ cup non-fat mayonnaise
2 tablespoons dill pickle, minced
1 teaspoon onion, minced
1 teaspoon lemon juice

Combine all ingredients in small bowl, refrigerate.

Makes ½ cup

1 tablespoon:

    15 calories
    0g fat
    4g carbohydrates
    0g protein
    0mg cholesterol
    0g fiber
    208mg sodium

Vegetable Dip

1 cup non-fat yogurt
1 cup salsa, homemade (see next page), or
  purchased
¼ cup non-fat bottled French dressing
¼ cup non-fat bottled Italian dressing
2 cloves garlic, minced

Combine all in small bowl, refrigerate. Serve with cut-up raw vegetables.

Makes 2½ cups

1 tablespoon:
     7 calories
 0.02g fat
    1g carbohydrates
    0g protein
  0mg cholesterol
    0g fiber
 38mg sodium

Salsa

1 fresh jalapeño or other hot pepper
½ cup onions, diced
1 clove garlic, minced
1 cup fresh ripe tomatoes, skinned and
  chopped
½ cup tomato puree
½ cup canned green chilies
½ teaspoon cumin
¼ teaspoon oregano

Wear gloves (plastic bags work) when handling hot pepper. Cut in half, discard membrane and seeds, chop finely.

In small pan cook onion, hot pepper and garlic, using non-stick cooking spray as needed. Add tomatoes, puree, green chilies, cumin and oregano; stir well, simmer 15 minutes. Cool and refrigerate until ready to serve.

Makes 2 cups

1 tablespoon:
    4 calories
 0.03g fat
    1g carbohydrates
    0g protein
  0mg cholesterol
    0g fiber
  1mg sodium

Sour Cream Substitute

1 cup non-fat cottage cheese
2 tablespoons skim milk
1 tablespoon fresh lemon juice

Combine all ingredients in blender and process
on high speed until smooth in consistency. Keeps in refrigerator 1–2 weeks.

Makes 1 cup

1 tablespoon:
- 11 calories
- 0.1g fat
- 1g carbohydrates
- 2g protein
- 1mg cholesterol
- 0g fiber
- 64mg sodium

Mayonnaise Substitute

1 cup non-fat cottage cheese
1 tablespoon fresh lemon juice
1 teaspoon sugar
1/2 teaspoon prepared mustard
1/2 teaspoon cider vinegar
1/4 teaspoon salt
1/4 teaspoon garlic powder
1/4 teaspoon onion powder

Combine ingredients in blender and process on high speed until smooth in consistency. Keeps in refrigerator 1–2 weeks.

Makes 1 cup

1 tablespoon:
    12 calories
   0.1g fat
    1g carbohydrates
    2g protein
   1mg cholesterol
    0g fiber
101mg sodium

Dill Sauce

¾ cup non-fat cottage cheese
¼ cup non-fat yogurt
1 tablespoon fresh lemon juice
1 teaspoon prepared mustard
4 teaspoons dill weed
2 teaspoons dried parsley
1 teaspoon onion powder

Combine all ingredients in blender and process on high speed until smooth in consistency. Keeps in refrigerator 1–2 weeks.

Makes 1 cup

1 tablespoon:
    12 calories
    0.1g fat
    1g carbohydrates
    2g protein
    1mg cholesterol
    0g fiber
    54mg sodium

Barbeque Sauce

½ cup catsup, low sodium, lite
¼ cup brown sugar
¼ cup orange juice
½ cup onion, chopped small
1 clove garlic, minced
1 tablespoon cider vinegar
1 tablespoon liquid smoke
½ teaspoon prepared mustard
½ teaspoon worcestershire
¼ teaspoon black pepper

Combine all ingredients in small saucepan. Bring to boil, reduce heat to low, simmer 5 minutes. Cool and refrigerate.

Makes ½ cup

½ cup:
    266 calories
    0.4g fat
    66g carbohydrates
    3g protein
    0mg cholesterol
    1g fiber
    966mg sodium

Bean Loaf Sandwich Spread

3 cups cooked beans, pintos or navys
1 cup onion, diced
1 cup carrots, grated
1/2 cup mushrooms, diced
1/4 cup green pepper, diced
1/4 cup wheat germ
2 egg whites
3 tablespoons catsup
3 tablespoons tomato juice or vegetable broth
1 clove garlic, minced
   salt and pepper

Mash cooked beans with fork. Add rest of ingredients and mix well. Spoon into 9" x 5" loaf pan. Bake 1 hour at 300°. Cool, refrigerate.

Slice off pieces and spread on bread, stuff in pita or wrap in tortilla.

Makes eighteen 1/2" slices (one 1 1/2-pound loaf)

One 1/2" slice (1 1/2 ounces):
   56 calories
   0.4g fat
   10g carbohydrates
   4g protein
   0mg cholesterol
   3g fiber
   28mg sodium

Egg Salad Spread

6 eggs, hard-boiled
2 tablespoons non-fat mayonnaise
   dash salt and pepper

Take shell off eggs, cut in half, dispose of all but
1 yolk. With a fork mash egg whites and yolk. Add mayonnaise and seasonings; mix. Refrigerate.

*Note: Top egg salad sandwich with tomato slice, lettuce
and/or sprouts.

Makes 1 cup

¼ cup with 1 slice light wheat bread:

   128 calories
     3g fat
   18g carbohydrates
    8g protein
 69mg cholesterol
    2g fiber
144mg sodium

Tuna Spread

1 6⅛-ounce can solid white tuna, packed in
   water, drained
2 tablespoons non-fat mayonnaise
1 tablespoon onion, finely chopped
1 tablespoon green pepper, finely chopped
1 tablespoon celery, finely chopped

Rinse tuna under cold running water to wash away salt; drain well.

In small bowl break up tuna into small pieces. Add mayonnaise, onion, green pepper and celery; mix. Refrigerate.

Makes ¾ cup

¼ cup serving:

    90 calories
    2g fat
    3g carbohydrates
    16g protein
    24mg cholesterol
    0g fiber
    305mg sodium

Garbanzo Spread

1 cup cooked garbanzo beans (or canned)
¼ cup bean cooking liquid or juice from can
1 tablespoon lemon juice
1 clove garlic, minced
1 teaspoon onion, minced
¼ teaspoon salt, optional
¼ teaspoon ground cumin
⅛ teaspoon pepper
1 tablespoon fresh parsley, finely chopped

In food processor or blender combine first 8 ingredients; process until smooth. Stir in parsley. Refrigerate.

*Note: Double or triple the recipe and freeze in small containers. Thaw in refrigerator and add fresh parsley.

Makes ³/₄ cup

1 tablespoon:

    24 calories
  0.4g fat
    4g carbohydrates
    1g protein
  0mg cholesterol
    1g fiber
  1mg sodium

Kidney Spread

1 cup cooked kidney beans (or canned, drained)
1 tablespoon catsup, low sodium, lite
1 clove garlic, minced
1 teaspoon onion, minced
¼ teaspoon salt, optional
¼ teaspoon chili powder
   dash cayenne pepper

Combine all in food processor or blender and process until smooth. Refrigerate.

*Note: Double or triple recipe, freeze in small containers, thaw in refrigerator as needed.

Makes 10 tablespoons

1 tablespoon:

    24 calories
  0.1g fat
    4g carbohydrates
    2g protein
  0mg cholesterol
    1g fiber
 70mg sodium

Sloppy Joe

1 pound ground chicken breast
¼ cup onion, diced
¼ cup green pepper, diced
¼ cup celery, finely diced
1 can tomato soup, diluted with 1 can water
   salt and pepper, optional

In nonstick fry pan brown meat, drain off fat. Add onion, green pepper and celery; continue to cook. Add soup-water mixture. Bring to boil, turn to low heat, simmer until most of liquid has dissolved, about 45 minutes. Serve on buns.

Serves 4

1 serving:
   255 calories
   6g fat
   13g carbohydrates
   37g protein
   97mg cholesterol
   0g fiber
   364mg sodium

Mike's Hot Sauce

1 cup tomato sauce
2 tablespoons apple cider vinegar
1½ tablespoons light corn syrup
2 teaspoons paprika
2 teaspoons hot chili pepper, dried and
  ground
1 teaspoon chili powder
1 teaspoon sugar
½ teaspoon garlic powder

Combine all in 1-quart saucepan, simmer 15 minutes. Pour in blender, blend on high speed until smooth, about 15 seconds. Refrigerate.

Makes 1 cup

1 tablespoon:
  14 calories
  0.1g fat
  3g carbohydrates
  0g protein
  0mg cholesterol
  0g fiber
  9mg sodium

Tortilla Chips

1 package (12) corn tortillas
   nonstick cooking spray
   salt, garlic if desired

Preheat oven to 350°.

Stack several tortillas, cut into quarters. Arrange in single layer on nonstick baking sheet that has been coated with nonstick cooking spray. Spray tops of chips, sprinkle on salt or garlic if desired. Bake 10 minutes or until crisp; watch carefully. Serve warm out of oven with salsa, hot sauce or bean dip.

Makes 48

6 chips:

    101 calories
      2g fat
     19g carbohydrates
      3g protein
     0mg cholesterol
      2g fiber
    80mg sodium

Appendix A
Food Values

Abbreviations used in Appendix A:

bkd = baked	dk = dark	pcs = pieces
bld = boiled	enr = enriched	proc = processed
brd = broiled	fl oz = fluid ounce	reg = regular
c = cup	frzn = frozen	rstd = roasted
cltd = cultured	jce = juice	swtd = sweetened
ckd = cooked	lt = light	t = teaspoon
cnd = canned	med = medium	T = tablespoon
conc = concentrate	oz = ounce	unbl = unbleached

	Fat %	Calories	Fat g
CHEESE			
american, proc, 1 oz	75.6	106	8.9
brick, 1 oz	72.0	105	8.4
cheddar, 1 oz	74.2	114	9.4
colby, 1 oz	73.1	112	9.1
cottage, non-fat, 1 c	0.0	160	0.0
cottage, 1% fat, 1 c	12.6	164	2.3
cream, non-fat, 1 oz	0.0	25	0.0
monterey, 1 oz	73.0	106	8.6
monterey, low-fat, 1 oz	45.0	80	4.0
mozzarella, 1 oz	67.8	80	6.1
non-fat cheese, 1 oz	0.0	40	0.0
parmesan, grated, 1 T	58.7	23	1.5
ricotta, low-fat, 1 oz	0.0	20	0.0
swiss, 1 oz	65.6	107	7.8
EGGS			
white, fresh, 1 large	0	16	0
whole, fresh, 1 large	63.8	79	5.6
yolk, fresh, 1 large	80.0	63	5.6
FISH, SEAFOOD			
abalone, raw, 3 oz	6.0	89	0.6
bass, black, raw, 3.5 oz	11.6	93	1.2
bass, freshwater, 3 oz	28.8	97	3.1
bluefish, raw, 3 oz	30.8	105	3.6
clams, canned, 3 oz	12.1	126	1.7
cod, atlantic, 3 oz	7.7	70	0.6
crab, Alaska king, 3 oz	6.3	71	0.5
crayfish, raw, 3 oz	10.7	76	0.9
flounder, raw, 3.5 oz	6.6	68	0.5
haddock, 3 oz	7.3	74	0.6
halibut, raw, 3 oz	19.4	93	2.0
herring, atlantic, raw, 3 oz	51.7	134	7.7
lobster, Northern, 3 oz	9.4	77	0.8
mackerel, atlantic, raw, 3 oz	61.0	174	11.8

Carb. g	Prot. g	Chol. mg	Fib. g	Sod. mg
0.5	6.3	27.0	0.0	406.0
0.8	6.6	27.0	0.0	159.0
0.4	7.1	30.0	0.0	176.0
0.7	6.7	27.0	0.0	36.0
8.0	28.0		0.0	900.0
6.2	28.0	10.0	0.0	918.0
1.0	4.0	5.0		170.0
0.2	6.9		0.0	152.0
1.0	7.0	14.0	0.0	50.0
0.6	5.5	22.0	0.0	106.0
1.0	9.0	5.0	0.0	200.0
0.2	2.1	4.0	0.0	93.0
2.0	4.0	3.0		20.0
1.0	8.1	26.0	0.0	74.0

Carb. g	Prot. g	Chol. mg	Fib. g	Sod. mg
0.4	3.4	0.0	0.0	50.0
0.6	6.1	274.0	0.0	69.0
0.0	2.8	272.0	0.0	8.0

Carb. g	Prot. g	Chol. mg	Fib. g	Sod. mg
5.1	14.5	72.0		255.0
0.0	19.2		0.0	68.0
0.0	16.0	58.0	0.0	59.0
0.0	17.0	50.0	0.0	51.0
4.4	21.7	57.0	0.0	95.0
0.0	15.1	37.0	0.0	46.0
0.0	15.6	35.0	0.0	711.0
0.0	15.9	118.0	0.0	45.0
0.0	14.9		0.0	56.0
0.0	16.1	49.0	0.0	58.0
0.0	17.7	27.0	0.0	46.0
0.0	15.3	51.0	0.0	76.0
0.4	16.0	81.0	0.0	
0.0	15.8	60.0	0.0	76.0

	Fat %	Calories	Fat g
FISH, SEAFOOD, cont'			
mussels, blue, raw, 3 oz	23.4	73	1.9
ocean perch, raw, 3 oz	15.8	80	1.4
oysters, raw, 6 med	32.6	58	2.1
perch, 3 oz	9.4	77	0.8
pike, northern, raw, 3 oz	7.2	75	0.6
pike, walleye, raw, 3 oz	11.4	79	1.0
pollock, atlantic, raw, 3 oz	9.2	78	0.8
roughy, orange, 3 oz	50.5	107	6.0
salmon, atlantic, raw, 3 oz	40.2	121	5.4
salmon, pink, raw, 3 oz	26.4	99	2.9
scallops, raw, 3 oz	7.2	75	0.6
shrimp, raw, 3 oz	15.0	90	1.5
smelt, rainbow, raw, 3 oz	22.8	83	2.1
sole, raw, 3.5 oz	6.6	68	0.5
sunfish, raw, 3 oz	7.1	76	0.6
swordfish, raw, 3 oz	29.7	103	3.4
trout, rainbow, raw, 3 oz	26.1	100	2.9
tuna, white, 3 oz	16.3	116	2.1
whitefish, raw, 3 oz	39.5	114	5.0
FRUIT			
apple, raw, w/ skin, med	5.5	81	0.5
apple, dried, 10 rings	1.2	155	0.2
apricots, raw, 3 med	7.1	51	0.4
apricots, dried, 10 halves	2.2	83	0.2
banana, raw, 1 med	5.1	105	0.6
blackberries, raw, 1/2 c	7.3	37	0.3
blueberries, raw, 1 c	6.6	82	0.6
boysenberries, frzn, 1 c	5.5	66	0.4
cantaloupe, raw, 1 c	6.3	57	0.4
cherries, sweet, raw, 10	12.9	49	0.7
cranberries, raw, 1 c	3.9	46	0.2
currants, raw, 1/2 c	2.9	31	0.1
dates, dried, 10	1.6	228	0.4
figs, raw, 1 med	4.9	37	0.2
grapefruit, pink/red, 1/2 med	2.4	37	0.1
grapes, American, 1 c	4.7	58	0.3

Carb. g	Prot. g	Chol. mg	Fib. g	Sod. mg
3.1	10.1	24.0	0.0	243.0
0.0	15.8	36.0	0.0	64.0
3.3	5.9	46.0	0.0	94.0
0.0	16.5	76.0	0.0	52.0
0.0	16.4	33.0	0.0	33.0
0.0	16.3	73.0	0.0	43.0
0.0	16.5	60.0	0.0	73.0
0.0	12.5	17.0	0.0	54.0
0.0	16.9	47.0	0.0	37.0
0.0	17.0	44.0	0.0	57.0
2.0	14.3	28.0	0.0	137.0
0.8	17.3	130.0	0.0	126.0
0.0	15.0	60.0	0.0	51.0
0.0	14.9		0.0	56.0
0.0	16.5	57.0	0.0	68.0
0.0	16.8	33.0	0.0	76.0
0.0	17.5	48.0	0.0	23.0
0.0	22.7	35.0	0.0	43.0
0.0	16.2	51.0	0.0	43.0

Carb. g	Prot. g	Chol. mg	Fib. g	Sod. mg
21.1	0.3	0.0	2.8	1.0
42.4	0.6	0.0	0.0	56.0
11.8	1.5	0.0	1.4	1.0
21.6	1.3	0.0	0.0	3.0
26.7	1.2	0.0	1.6	1.0
9.2	0.5	0.0	3.3	0.0
20.5	1.0	0.0	4.4	9.0
16.1	1.5	0.0		2.0
13.4	1.4	0.0	0.5	14.0
11.3	0.8	0.0	1.1	0.0
12.1	0.4	0.0		1.0
7.7	0.8	0.0		1.0
61.0	1.6	0.0	4.2	2.0
9.6	0.4	0.0		1.0
9.5	0.7	0.0	0.0	0.0
15.8	0.6	0.0	0.0	2.0

FRUIT, cont'	Fat %	Calories	Fat g
guava, raw, 1 med	10.0	45	0.5
honeydew melon, raw, 1/4 c	8.2	33	0.3
kiwifruit, raw, 1 med	5.9	46	0.3
lemon, raw, 1 med	10.6	17	0.2
lime, raw, 1 med	4.5	20	0.1
mandarin orange, cnd, 1/2 c	0.0	46	0.0
mango, raw, 1 med	4.0	135	0.6
nectarine, raw, 1 med	8.0	67	0.6
orange, naval, 1 med	1.4	65	0.1
papaya, raw, 1 med	3.2	117	0.4
peach, dried, 10 halves	2.9	311	1.0
peach, raw, 1 med	2.4	37	0.1
pear, dried, 10 halves	2.2	459	1.1
pear, raw, 1 med	6.4	98	0.7
pineapple, cnd w/ jce, 1 c	1.2	150	0.2
plum, raw, 1 med	10.0	36	0.4
prunes, dried, 10	1.8	201	0.4
raisins, seedless, 1 c	1.6	450	0.8
raspberries, raw, 1 c	10.3	61	0.7
strawberries, raw, 1 c	12.0	45	0.6
strawberries, frzn, 1 c	3.5	52	0.6
tangerine, raw, 1 med	4.9	37	0.2
watermelon, raw, 1 c	12.6	50	0.7
FRUIT JUICE			
apple, 8 oz	2.5	111	0.3
grape, swtd, 8 oz	1.4	128	0.2
grapefruit, 8 oz	2.6	102	0.3
lemon, 8 oz	0.0	60	0.0
lime, 8 oz	0.0	66	0.3
orange, 8 oz	0.8	112	0.1
pineapple, 8oz	0.7	129	0.1
prune, cnd, 8 oz	0.4	181	0.1
tomato, 6 oz	2.8	32	0.1

Carb. g	Prot. g	Chol. mg	Fib. g	Sod. mg
10.7	0.7	0.0		2.0
7.7	0.8	0.0		12.0
11.3	0.8	0.0		4.0
5.4	0.6	0.0		1.0
7.1	0.5	0.0		1.0
11.9	0.8	0.0		7.0
35.2	1.1	0.0	2.2	4.0
16.0	1.3	0.0		0.0
16.3	1.4	0.0	0.0	1.0
29.8	1.9	0.0	2.8	8.0
79.7	4.7	0.0		9.0
9.7	0.6	0.0	0.5	0.0
122.0	3.3	0.0		10.0
25.1	0.7	0.0	4.1	1.0
39.2	1.0	0.0	1.9	1.0
8.6	0.5	0.0	0.0	0.0
52.7	2.2	0.0		3.0
118.7	4.8	0.0	0.0	
14.2	1.1	0.0	5.8	0.0
10.5	0.9	0.0	2.8	2.0
13.6	0.6	0.0	0.0	3.0
9.4	0.5	0.0		1.0
11.5	1.0	0.0	0.3	3.0
27.6	0.3	0.0	0.0	17.0
31.9	0.5	0.0	0.0	5.0
24.0	1.4	0.0	0.0	2.0
21.1	0.9	0.0		2.0
22.2	1.1	0.0		2.0
26.8	1.7	0.0	0.0	2.0
31.9	1.0	0.0	0.0	3.0
44.7	1.6	0.0		11.0
7.7	1.4	0.0		18.0

	Fat %	Calories	Fat g
GRAIN, GRAIN PRODUCTS			
amaranth, boiled, 1/2 c	1.4	14	0.1
barley, pearled, light 1 c	2.6	698	2.0
buckwheat groats, 1 c	6.4	335	2.4
bulgar, cnd, 1 c	3.5	227	0.9
corn grits, reg, 1 c	3.1	146	0.5
corn meal, yellow, 1 c	10.0	433	4.8
farina, ckd, 3/4 c	1.0	87	0.1
flour, buckwheat, dark, 1 c	6.9	326	2.5
flour, enr, unbl, 1 c	4.9	401	2.2
flour, rye, light, 1 c	2.5	364	1.0
flour, soybean, defatted, 1 c	3.3	327	1.2
flour, soybean, full fat, 1 c	43	368	17.6
flour, whole wheat, 1 c	5.4	400	2.4
macaroni, enr, ckd, 1 c	4.0	159	0.7
macaroni, vegetable, dry 1 c	2.6	308	0.9
macaroni, w. wheat, ckd 1 c	3.9	174	0.8
millet, proso, whole, 3.5 oz	7.9	327	2.9
oat bran, Quaker, 1/3 c	20.5	110	2.5
oatmeal, dry, 1/3 c	15.6	109	1.9
rice, brown, ckd, 1 c	4.7	232	1.2
rice, white, ckd, 1 c	0.8	223	0.2
rice, wild, raw, 1 c	1.8	565	1.1
somen noodle, cooked, 1c	1.0	230	0.3
soy grits, dry, 1 c	15.0	480	8.0
spaghetti, enr, ckd, 1 c	4.0	159	0.7
spaghetti, w. wheat, ckd 1 c	3.9	174	0.8
wheat, whole grain, 1 c	5.3	631	3.7
wheat bran, 2 T	8.6	21	0.2
wheat germ, toasted, 1/4 c	25.0	108	3.0
LEGUMES (boiled, 1 c)			
adzuki beans	0.6	294	0.2
black beans	3.6	227	0.9
broad beans	3.4	186	0.7
butter beans, cnd,1/2 c	3.6	100	0.4

Carb. g	Prot. g	Chol. mg	Fib. g	Sod. mg
2.7	1.4	0.0	0.0	14.0
157.6	16.4	0.0		6.0
72.9	11.7	0.0		
47.3	8.4	0.0		809.0
31.4	3.5	0.0	0.6	0.0
89.9	11.2	0.0	0.0	1.0
18.5	2.5	0.0		1.0
70.6	11.5	0.0		
82.8	12.3	0.0		3.0
79.5	9.6	0.0	0.0	1.0
33.9	51.5	0.0		20.0
27.1	32.1	0.0		11.0
85.2	16.0	0.0		4.0
33.7	5.2	0.0	0.6	1.0
62.9	11.0	0.0		36.0
37.6	7.5	0.0		4.0
72.9	9.9	0.0		
16.2	5.7	0.0	0.0	1.0
18.4	4.6	0.0		1.0
49.7	4.9	0.0		
49.6	4.1	0.0		
120.5	22.6	0.0		11.0
48.5	7.0	0.0		284.0
48.0	76.0	0.0		
33.7	5.2	0.0	0.6	1.0
37.2	7.5	0.0		4.0
130.6	29.6	0.0		4.0
3.6	1.1	0.0		0.0
14.1	8.3	0.0	3.0	1.0

Carb. g	Prot. g	Chol. mg	Fib. g	Sod. mg
57.0	17.3	0.0		18.0
40.8	15.2	0.0	7.2	1.0
33.4	12.9	0.0	8.7	8.0
18.3	5.7			434.0

	Fat %	Calories	Fat g
LEGUMES, cont'			
chickpeas (garbanzo)	14.4	269	4.3
cowpeas (black eye)	4.1	198	0.9
cranberry beans	3.0	240	0.8
french beans	5.1	228	1.3
great northern beans	3.4	210	0.8
kidney beans	3.6	225	0.9
lentils	2.7	231	0.7
lima beans	2.9	217	0.7
mung beans	3.4	213	0.8
navy beans	3.5	259	1.0
peas, green, raw, 1/2 c	4.3	63	0.3
peas, split	3.1	231	0.8
pigeonpeas	2.6	204	0.6
pinto beans	3.4	235	0.9
soybeans	46.5	298	15.4
white beans	2.2	249	0.6
yellow beans	6.7	254	1.9
MEAT and POULTRY (3.5 oz)			
beef round, top, lean, brd	29.2	191	6.2
beef, ground, extra lean, brd	53.7	265	15.8
beef, flank, brd	57.8	254	16.3
chicken breast, no skin, rstd	19.6	165	3.6
chick lt meat, no skin, rstd	23.4	173	4.5
chick lt and dk, no skin, rstd	35.1	190	7.4
ham, cured, regular	57.2	203	12.9
rabbit, domestic, raw	36.7	136	5.6
rabbit, wild, raw	15.8	114	2.0
turkey lt meat, no skin, rstd	18.3	157	3.2
turkey lt and dk, no skin, rst	26.5	170	5.0
Venison, raw	15.1	119	2.0
MILK PRODUCTS			
buttermilk, cltd, 8 fl oz	20.0	99	2.2
condensed swtd, cnd 1 fl oz	24.1	123	3.3
evaporated skim, cnd 1 fl oz	3.6	25	0.1
lowfat 1% milk, 8 fl oz	22.9	102	2.6

Carb. g	Prot. g	Chol. mg	Fib. g	Sod. mg
45.0	14.5	0.0	5.7	11.0
35.5	13.2	0.0	4.4	6.0
43.3	16.5	0.0	6.0	1.0
42.5	12.5	0.0		11.0
37.3	14.8	0.0	6.0	4.0
40.4	15.4	0.0	6.4	4.0
39.9	17.9	0.0	7.9	4.0
39.3	14.7	0.0	6.2	4.0
38.7	14.2	0.0	5.1	4.0
47.9	15.8	0.0	6.6	2.0
11.3	4.2	0.0	2.7	4.0
41.4	16.4	0.0		4.0
39.1	11.4	0.0	7.9	9.0
43.9	14.0	0.0	6.8	3.0
17.1	28.6	0.0		1.0
44.9	17.4	0.0		11.0
44.7	16.2	0.0		8.0

0.0	31.7	84.0	0.0	61.0
0.0	28.6	99.0	0.0	82.0
0.0	25.1	71.0	0.0	82.0
0.0	31.0		0.0	
0.0	30.9	85.0	0.0	77.0
0.0	28.9	89.0	0.0	86.0
0.1	20.2	54.0	0.0	1386.0
0.0	20.0	57.0	0.0	41.0
0.0	22.3		0.0	
0.0	29.9	69.0	0.0	64.0
0.0	29.3	76.0	0.0	70.0
0.0	23.5		0.0	

11.7	8.1	9.0	0.0	257.0
20.8	3.0	13.0	0.0	49.0
3.6	2.4	1.0	0.0	37.0
11.7	8.0	10.0	0.0	123.0

	Fat %	Calories	Fat g
MILK PRODUCTS, cont'			
lowfat 2% milk, 8 fl oz	35.0	121	4.7
skim milk, 8 fl oz	4.1	86	0.4
sour cream, non-fat, 2 T	0.0	30	0.0
whole milk, 3.7%, 8 fl oz	51.0	157	8.9
yogurt, frzn, non-fat, 3 fl oz	0.0	60	0.0
yogurt, skim, 8 fl oz	2.8	127	0.4
MISCELLANEOUS			
baking powder, 1 t	0.0	3	0.0
corn starch, 1 T	0.0	30	0.0
olives, green, 10 large	98.0	45	4.9
vinegar, cider, 1 T	0.0	2.0	0.0
yeast, active, dry, 1 packet	0.0	20.0	0.0
NUTS and SEEDS (unsalted)			
almonds, dry rstd, 1 oz	79.2	167	14.7
cashews, dry rstd, 1 oz	72.9	163	13.2
coconut, dried, flaked, 1 c	61.0	351	23.8
macadamia, dried, 1 oz	94.5	199	20.9
peanuts, dry rstd, 1 oz	76.3	164	13.9
pecons, dry rstd, 1 oz	88.6	187	18.4
pistachio, dry rstd, 1 oz	78.5	172	15.0
pumpkin seeds, dried, 1 oz	76.0	154	13.0
sesame , whole dried 1 T	77.9	52	4.5
sunflower, dried, 1 oz	78.3	162	14.1
walnuts, black, dried, 1 oz	84.2	172	16.1
OILS and FATS			
butter, 1 T	100.0	108	12.2
corn oil, 1 T	100.0	120	13.6
margarine, 1 T	100.0	100	11.3
margarine, non-fat, 1 T	0.0	5	0.0
olive oil, 1 T	100.0	119	13.5
peanut oil, 1 T	100.0	119	13.5

Carb. g	Prot. g	Chol. mg	Fib. g	Sod. mg
11.7	8.1	18.0	0.0	122.0
11.9	8.4	4.0	0.0	126.0
5.0	2.0	0.0	0.0	40.0
11.4	8.0	35.0	0.0	119.0
14.0	3.0	0.0	0.0	45.0
17.4	13.0	4.0	0.0	174.0

0.7	0.0	0.0		426.0
7.2	0.0			0.0
0.5	0.5			926.0
0.9	0.0			0.0
3.0	3.0			10.0

6.9	4.6	0.0		3.0
9.3	4.4	0.0		4.0
35.2	2.4	0.0		189.0
3.9	2.4	0.0		1.0
6.0	6.6	0.0		2.0
6.3	2.3	0.0		0.0
7.8	4.2	0.0		2.0
5.1	7.0	0.0		5.0
2.1	1.6	0.0		1.0
5.3	6.5	0.0		1.0
3.4	6.9	0.0		0.0

0.0	0.1	33.0	0.0	123.0
0.0	0.0	0.0	0.0	
0.2	0.0	0.0	0.0	100.0
0.0	0.0	0.0	0.0	90.0
0.0	0.0	0.0	0.0	0.0
0.0	0.0	0.0	0.0	0.0

	Fat %	Calories	Fat g
SAUCES and CONDIMENTS			
barbeque sauce, 1 T	22.5	12	0.3
catsup, 1 T	5.6	16	0.1
mayonnaise, non-fat, 1 T	0.0	14	0.0
mustard, yellow, 1 t	45.0	4	0.2
soy sauce, 1/4 c	30.0	30	0.1
tomato sauce, cnd, 1/2 c	4.8	37	0.2

SWEETENERS			
corn syrup, 1 T	0.0	59	0.0
honey, 1 T	0.0	64	0.0
maple syrup	0.0	50	0.0
molasses, light, 1 T	0.0	50	0.0
sugar, brown, 1 c	0.0	541	0.0
sugar, powdered, 1 c	0.0	462	0.0
sugar, white, granulated, 1 t	0.0	15	0.0
sugar, white, granulated, 1 c	0.0	770	0.0

VEGETABLES			
alfalfa sprouts, 1 c	18.0	10	0.2
artichoke, bld, 1 med.	3.4	53	0.2
asparagus, bld, 1/2 c	12.3	22	0.3
avocado, raw, calif., 1 med	88.2	306	30.0
bamboo shoots, raw, 1/2 c	8.6	21	0.2
beets, bld, 1/2 c slices	0.0	26	0.0
broccoli, raw, 1/2 c chopped	15.0	12	0.2
brussels sprouts, bld 1/2 c	12.0	30	0.4
cabbage, chinese, raw, 1/2 c	18.0	5	0.1
cabbage, green, raw, 1/2 c	11.3	8	0.1
carrots, raw, 1 med (2.5 oz)	3.0	31	0.1
cauliflower, raw, 1/2 c pcs	7.5	12	0.1
celery, raw, 1 stalk, 7.5 in.	15.0	6	0.1
corn, yellow, bld 1/2 c	11.1	89	1.1
cucumber, raw, 1/2 c slices	12.8	7	0.1
eggplant, raw, 1/2 c pieces	0.0	11	0.0
garlic, raw, 3 cloves	6.9	13	0.1
green beans, bld, 1/2 c	8.2	22	0.2

Carb. g	Prot. g	Chol. mg	Fib. g	Sod. mg
2.0	0.3	0.0		127.0
3.8	0.3			156.0
4.0	0.0	0.0		115.0
0.3	0.2			63.0
4.9	3.0	0.0		3314.0
8.8	1.6	0.0		738.0

Carb. g	Prot. g	Chol. mg	Fib. g	Sod. mg
15.4	0.0			14.0
17.3	0.1			1.0
12.8	0.0			2.0
13.0	0.0	0.0	0.0	3.0
139.8	0.0	0.0	0.0	44.0
119.4	0.0	0.0	0.0	1.0
4.0	0.0	0.0	0.0	0.0
199.0	0.0	0.0	0.0	2.0

Carb. g	Prot. g	Chol. mg	Fib. g	Sod. mg
1.3	1.3	0.0	0.7	2.0
12.4	2.8	0.0		79.0
4.0	2.3	0.0		4.0
12.0	3.6	0.0	4.7	21.0
4.0	2.0	0.0	2.0	3.0
5.7	0.9	0.0		42.0
2.3	1.3	0.0	0.6	12.0
6.8	2.0	0.0	1.1	17.0
0.8	0.5	0.0		23.0
1.9	0.4	0.0	0.4	6.0
7.3	0.7	0.0	1.1	25.0
2.5	1.0	0.0		7.0
1.5	0.3	0.0	0.4	35.0
20.6	2.7	0.0		14.0
1.5	0.3	0.0	0.3	1.0
2.6	0.5	0.0	0.6	1.0
3.0	0.6	0.0		2.0
4.9	1.2	0.0	1.1	2.0

VEGETABLES, cont'	Fat %	Calories	Fat g
jerus. artichoke, raw 1/2 c	0.0	57	0.0
leeks, raw, 1/4 c chopped	6.0	16	0.1
lettuce, loose leaf, raw, 1/2 c	18.0	5	0.1
mushrooms, raw, 1/2 c pcs	20.0	9	0.2
onions, raw, 1/2 c chopped	6.6	27	0.2
parsley, raw, 1/2 c chopped	9.0	10	0.1
peas, green, raw, 1/2 c	4.3	63	0.3
peppers, hot chili, raw, 1	5.0	18	0.1
peppers, sweet, raw, 1/2 c	15.0	12	0.2
potato, bkd w/ skin 1 (7.1oz)	0.8	220	0.2
pumpkin, bld, 1/2 c mashed	3.8	24	0.1
radish, raw, 10	25.7	7	0.2
rhubarb, frzn, raw, 1 c	6.2	29	0.2
spinach, raw, 1/2 c	15.0	6	0.1
squash, summer, raw, 1/2 c	6.9	13	0.1
squash, winter, bkd, 1/2 c	13.8	39	0.6
sweet potato, bkd, 4 oz	0.8	118	0.1
tomato, red, raw, 1	11.3	24	0.3
tomato, stewed, 1/2 c	5.3	34	0.2
tomato, puree, 1 c	2.6	102	0.3
turnip, bld, 1/2 c	12.8	14	0.1
water chestnuts, raw, 1/2 c	1.4	66	0.1
zucchini, raw, 1/2 c slices	10.0	9	0.1

Sources:

Human Information Service. *Composition of Foods, Raw, Processed, Prepared.* Agriculture Handbook No. 8, 8-1, 8-4, 8-5, 8-9 to 8-13, 8-15 to 8-20. Washington, D.C.: U.S. Department of Agriculture.

Product labels.

Carb. g	Prot. g	Chol. mg	Fib. g	Sod. mg
13.1	1.5	0.0		
3.7	0.4	0.0	0.3	5.0
1.0	0.4	0.0		3.0
1.6	0.7	0.0		1.0
5.9	0.9	0.0	0.6	2.0
2.1	0.7	0.0		12.0
11.3	4.2	0.0	2.7	4.0
4.3	0.9	0.0		3.0
2.7	0.4	0.0	0.6	2.0
51.0	4.7	0.0		16.0
6.0	0.9	0.0		2.0
1.6	0.3	0.0		11.0
7.0	0.8	0.0		2.0
1.0	0.8	0.0	0.9	22.0
2.8	0.8	0.0	0.7	1.0
8.9	0.9	0.0	1.2	1.0
27.7	2.0	0.0	2.1	12.0
5.3	1.1	0.0	1.0	10.0
8.3	1.2	0.0		325.0
25.1	4.2	0.0		49.0
3.8	0.6	0.0		39.0
14.8	0.9	0.0		9.0
1.9	0.8	0.0	0.3	2.0

Appendix B
Week-at-a-Glance Schedule

This example schedule incorporates the eating, exercise and meditation routines into a daily/weekly pattern of healthy, low-fat living. Use it and the blank chart we've included to adapt to your own daily routine.

	Sun	**Mon**	**Tue**
6:00–6:30 am	Day off	Meditate	Meditate
6:30–7:30 am	Day off	Walk 40–60 min Strength train 20 min	Walk
7:30–8:30 am	Breakfast— Banana Pancakes	Breakfast— Fiber 20 oatmeal (350 cals)	Breakfast— Granola, juice, toast (350 cals)
10:00 am	Snack— Fruit salad	Snack— Apple muffin (125 cals)	Snack— Bagel, nonfat cream cheese (200 cals)
Noon	Lunch— Leftover pizza	Lunch— Bean soup, egg salad sandwich (375 cals)	Lunch— Nonfat yogurt, fruit (325 cals)
3:00 pm	Make bread, muffins, soup for week	Snack— Apple (75 cals)	Snack— Orange (50 cals)
6:00 pm	Supper— Spaghetti	Supper— Grilled chicken, oven fries, salad (500 cals)	Supper— Bean stew, wheat rolls (450 cals)
8:30 pm	Snack— Skim milk, oatmeal cookies	Snack— Popcorn (75 cals)	Snack— Oat bran muffin, freezer jam (125)
Before bed	Day off	Meditate	Meditate

Wed	Thu	Fri	Sat
Meditate	Meditate	Meditate	Sleep in
Walk 40–60 min Strength train 20 min	Walk	Walk 40–60 min Strength train 20 min	Meditate
Breakfast— Fiber 20 oatmeal (350 cals)	Breakfast— Granola, juice, toast (350 cals)	Breakfast— Fiber 20 oatmeal (350 cals)	Breakfast— Waffles
Snack— Apple muffin (125 cals)	Snack— Oat bran muffin (100 cals)	Snack— Bagel, nonfat cream cheese (200 cals)	Walk 40 min
Lunch— Veg chowder, jelly sandwich (400 cals)	Lunch— Nonfat yogurt, fruit (325 cals)	Lunch— Bean soup, egg salad sandwich (300 cals)	Lunch— Veg chowder, fruit salad
Snack— Banana (100 cals)	Snack— Apple (75 cals)	Snack— Orange (50 cals)	Prepare chicken and beans for week
Supper— Delib. leftover: chick. enchilada (450 cals)	Supper— Beef and broccoli stir-fry (500 cals)	Supper— Meatless pizza (525 cals)	Supper— Chick. enchilada (make 2 batches for leftovers)
Snack— Popcorn (75 cals)	Snack— Wheat toast, nonfat margarine (150 cals)	Snack— Popcorn (75 cals)	Walk 20 min
Meditate	Meditate	Meditate	Snack— Low-fat chocolate sundae

	Sun	**Mon**	**Tue**
6:00–6:30 am			
6:30–7:30 am			
7:30–8:30 am			
10:00 am			
Noon			
3:00 pm			
6:00 pm			
8:30 pm			
Before bed			

Wed	Thu	Fri	Sat

Appendix C
Conversion Tables

Volume

$$1 t = \tfrac{1}{3} T = \tfrac{1}{6} \text{ fl oz} = 4.9 \text{ ml}$$
$$3 t = 1 T = \tfrac{1}{2} \text{ fl oz} = 14.8 \text{ ml}$$
$$2 T = \tfrac{1}{8} \text{ cup} = 1 \text{ fl oz} = 29.6 \text{ ml}$$
$$4 T = \tfrac{1}{4} \text{ cup} = 2 \text{ fl oz} = 59.1 \text{ ml}$$
$$5\tfrac{1}{3} T = \tfrac{1}{3} \text{ cup} = 2\tfrac{2}{3} \text{ fl oz} = 78.9 \text{ ml}$$
$$16 T = 1 \text{ cup} = 8 \text{ fl oz} = 236.6 \text{ ml}$$
$$2 \text{ cups} = 1 \text{ pint} = 16 \text{ fl oz} = 473 \text{ ml}$$
$$4 \text{ cups} = 2 \text{ pints} = 1 \text{ quart} = .946 \text{ liter}$$
$$4 \text{ quarts} = 1 \text{ gallon} = 3785 \text{ ml} = 3.785 \text{ liters}$$

Weight

$$1 \text{ mg} = .001 \text{ g}$$
$$1 g = .035 \text{ oz}$$
$$1 \text{ oz} = 28.35 \text{ g}$$
$$16 \text{ oz} = 1 \text{ lb}$$
$$1 \text{ lb} = .454 \text{ kg}$$
$$1 \text{ kg} = 2.21 \text{ lb}$$

Fruits

apples, 6 small (1¹/₂ lbs)	= 4 c sliced, 4¹/₂ c chopped
apricots, 6–8 med (1 lb)	= 2 c chopped
bananas, 4 small (1 lb)	= 2 c mashed
cantaloupe, 1 med (2 lb)	= 3 c cubed
cherries, 2 c	= 1 c pitted
cranberries, 1 lb	= 4¹/₂ c raw
grapefruit, 1 small (1 lb)	= 1 c sectioned
grapes, seedless, 40 (¹/₄ lb)	= 2 c halved
oranges, 3 med (1 lb)	= 3 c sectioned
papaya, 1 lb	= 2 c cubed
peaches, 3 med (1 lb)	= 2 c chopped
pears, 3 med (1 lb)	= 2 c chopped
pineapple, 1 med (3 lb)	= 2¹/₂ c chopped
strawberries, whole, 4 c	= 4 c sliced
tangerines, 4 med (1 lb)	= 2 c sectioned

Vegetables

beans, green, 1 lb	= 5 c 1-inch pieces raw
beets, 1 lb	= 6 c sliced raw
broccoli, 3 oz	= 1 c pieces raw
cabbage, 1 med head	= 10 c shredded raw
cabbage, 3 oz	= 1 c chopped raw
carrots, 2 med (5 oz)	= 1 c sliced
cauliflower, 4 oz	= 1 c chopped raw
celery, 2 stalks, 8" (5 oz)	= 1 c chopped
corn, 6 ears	= 2¹/₂ c cut raw
cucumber, 1 med (¹/₂ lb)	= 1¹/₂ c sliced raw

eggplant, 1 med (1 lb)	=	6 c cubed raw
garlic, 1 clove	=	1 tsp chopped raw
pepper, green, 1 (5 oz)	=	1 c chopped raw
mushrooms, fresh, 4 oz	=	1 c sliced raw
onion, 1 med (3 oz)	=	½ c chopped raw
onions, green, 6 med	=	1 c chopped raw
potatoes, 6 oz	=	1 c diced raw
potatoes, 1 lb	=	3 c sliced raw
snow pea pods, fresh, 3 oz	=	1 c raw
spinach, frz chopped, 10 oz	=	1½ c cooked
spinach, fresh, 2 oz	=	1½ c cut in thin strips
squash, summer, 5 oz	=	1 c sliced raw
squash, winter, 3½ oz	=	½ c cubes, cooked
tomatoes, canned, drained, 16 oz	=	1¼ c
28 oz	=	2 c
35 oz	=	2½ c
zucchini, 1 med (5 oz)	=	1 c sliced raw

Grains

amaranth, 1 c dry	=	2 c cooked
barley, pearled, 1 c dry	=	3½ c cooked
buckwheat groats, 1 c dry	=	2 c cooked
bulgur, 1 c dry	=	3 c cooked
couscous, 1 c dry	=	3 c cooked
millet, 1 c dry	=	3½ c cooked
oats, whole grain, 1 c dry	=	2½ c cooked
quinoa, 1 c dry	=	3 c cooked
rice, brown, 1 c dry	=	3½ c cooked

rice, wild, 1 c dry = 2½ c cooked
triticale, 1 c dry = 2 c cooked
wheat berries, 1 c dry = 2 c cooked

Legumes

adzuki beans, 1 c dry = 2 c cooked
black beans, 1 c dry = 2 c cooked
black-eyed peas, 1 c dry = 2 c cooked
chickpeas (garbanzo), 1 c dry = 2½ c cooked
cranberry beans, 1 c dry = 2½ c cooked
fava beans, 1 c dry = 2 c cooked
great north. beans, 1 c dry = 2 c cooked
kidney beans, 1 c dry = 2 c cooked
lentils, 1 c dry = 2¼ c cooked
lima beans, 1 c dry = 1¼ c cooked
lima beans, baby, 1 c dry = 1¾ c cooked
mung beans, 1 c dry = 2 c cooked
navy beans, 1 c dry = 2 c cooked
pigeon peas, 1 c dry = 2¼ c cooked
pinto beans, 1 c dry = 2 c cooked
red beans, 1 c dry = 2 c cooked
split peas, 1 c dry = 2¼ c cooked

Pasta

Chinese noodles, ¾ lb = 5 c cooked
linguine, 1 lb = 5 c cooked
macaroni, 1 lb = 3 c dry, 12 c cooked
spaghetti, 1 lb = 8 c cooked

Glossary

Adrenalin - a hormone produced by the adrenal gland during stress situations. It stimulates the cardiovascular and nervous system. Heart beat and blood pressure increase and muscles contract to prepare the body for action.

Angioplasty - the surgical use of a "balloon" to clear clogged arteries. It is inserted into the clogged area and inflated, forcing the blood vessel open.

Antioxidants - micronutrients (vitamin E, vitamin C, beta-carotene, selenium) found in many fruits and vegetables that de-activate free radicals. See also Nutrient.

Artery - a tube-like vessel that carries blood from the heart to the rest of the body.

Atherectomy - a medical procedure where clogged arteries are reamed out with rotary drills and lasers.

Atherosclerosis - the build-up of deposits and clogging of our blood vessels. From the Greek words athera (meaning gruel) and sklerosis (meaning hardening). Fat and cholesterol material called **plaque** is the "hardening gruel" that plugs our arteries and leads to heart attacks, strokes and hypertension.

Body Defense System - our immune and enzyme systems that protect us from the many pathogens and toxic chemicals that invade our bodies. Both are biochemical systems that depend upon the nutrients (chemicals) that come in our foods. Food nutrients, then, are the weapons and ammunition of our resistance forces.

Body fat - see Fat (Dietary).

Bypass Surgery - surgery for clogged arteries. The chest is cut open and sections of healthier arteries (e.g., taken from the patient's leg) are grafted to get around plugged arteries.

Calorie - a measure of the energy in foods that fuels our activity. High-fat, refined and processed foods give us too many calories and too few nutrients. They are **calorie dense**. We get the same calories in three pounds of food that our hunting and gathering ancestors got in five. Vegetables have ample calories but are also **nutrient dense**.

Cancer - uncontrollable growth and spread of abnormal body cells. Our most common kinds are: lung, colon, breast and prostate cancers.

Carbohydrate - a macronutrient that becomes the "fast-burn" fuel, **glucose**. It may also be put in short-term storage in the liver and muscles as **glycogen**. Carbohydrates are found in legumes, grains, dairy products, fruit and vegetables and should comprise 65–75% of daily calories. **Simple Carbohydrates** are sugars found in refined or processed foods (cakes, candies) that provide calories but no vitamins, minerals and fiber. **Complex Carbohydrates** are starches found in fruits, vegetables, legumes and whole grains that provide calories, vitamins, minerals and fiber.

Carcinogen - a cancer-causing substance.

Catecholamines - chemicals produced by the adrenal gland in reaction to stress as part of the fight-or-flight response. They are believed to also raise the levels of fat and cholesterol in our blood. Catecholamine levels can be lowered with meditation.

Cholesterol, "Bad" and "Good"- see Lipoprotein

Cholesterol, Dietary - a fat-like substance found in animal fats and oils. Public health authorities recommend not eating more than 300 mg. of cholesterol a day in our foods.

Cholesterol, Serum - a fat-like substance in the blood that deposits and builds up on the inner walls of the blood vessels. Public health authorities tells us to keep our blood cholesterol level below 200 mg per deciliter.

Complex Carbohydrates - see Carbohydrate.

Diabetes Mellitus - a disease in which the body is unable to convert carbohydrates into energy due to a lack of the hormone insulin or to the body's inability to use insulin. Excess fat and sedentary living play major roles in this disease.

Endorphins - brain chemicals released during exercise that elevate our mood, make us feel happy and self-satisfied. Often referred to as the "runner's high."

Endurance Training - see Exercise (Aerobic).

Evolutionary Design - all forms of life are very gradually designed and redesigned over the long periods of evolutionary history. Our physiology, psychology, biology and chemistry as humans developed over the millions of years we lived as hunters and gatherers. Our bodies are designed for the food and activity of that hunting and gathering lifestyle. We cannot change this design by eating differently for several hundred or even thousands of years. No matter how different our lives have become, our biology hasn't changed one bit for the past 40,000 years. Human biology simply can't cope with the high-fat eating and sedentary living of the 20th century.

Exercise (Aerobic) - meaning "with oxygen," this is a longer-lasting, continuous, moderate-exertion activity such as walking, jogging, swimming, or bicycling. It is fat-burning exercise that builds endurance in the muscles and cardiovascular system and is often referred to as **endurance training**.

Exercise (Anaerobic) - meaning "without oxygen," this is a start and stop activity with short bursts of intense effort. It is a glucose-burning (as opposed to fat-burning) exercise that develops muscle strength and size and is often referred to as **strength training**. With training, strength can be increased throughout life. The training is called **Progressive Resistance**, the gradual increase of resistance for muscular adaption and growth (e.g., adding weight in weight training).

Exercise Response - an increased metabolic rate and appetite for high-carbohydrate foods. The body, experiencing ample supplies of food and regular exercise, "wants" the "high octane" fuel of complex carbohydrates and increases the appetite accordingly.

Fat (Dietary) - a macronutrient and major factor in heart disease, stroke, numerous cancers, obesity, diabetes and other illnesses. Fat should only comprise 20% or less of a person's total daily calories. **Saturated Fat** is found in meat, dairy products and coconut and palm oils and raises "bad" cholesterol levels. **Unsaturated (Polyunsaturated and Monounsaturated) Fat** is found in the oils of certain vegetables and seeds. It doesn't raise "bad" cholesterol as much, but is believed to promote cancer. **Body fat** is the storage form of dietary fat. It is the "slow-burn" fuel of endurance training as well as padding for our internal organs.

Fiber - the undigested bulk and roughage part of plant foods (cellulose, pectin, gar gum). The National Cancer Institute recommends 25–35 grams of fiber a day. The two kinds of fiber offer different benefits. **Insoluble Fiber** (doesn't dissolve in water) such as wheat bran is believed to lower the risk of digestive cancers. **Soluble Fiber** (dissolves in water) such as oat bran is believed to help control diabetics' blood sugar levels and lower blood cholesterol levels.

Fight-Or-Flight Response - see Stress.

Free Radical - a harmful, unstable molecule formed during the oxidation process of the body. Free radicals create conditions that eat away at membranes of body cells and change their program of genetic "instructions." They are believed to play a major role in aging, heart disease, various cancers and cataracts. See also Nutrients.

Glucose - see Carbohydrate.

Glycogen - see Carbohydrate.

Heart Attack - technically known as a myocardial infarction, a heart attack is the death of heart muscle cells when blood (i.e., oxygen) is blocked from reaching the heart (atherosclerosis).

Hypertension - high blood pressure pushing blood against artery walls.

Ideal Weight - our healthiest weight in terms of height, age, sex and body build. Being **overweight** is having excess body fat and more weight than our ideal. When we are 20% or more over our ideal weight we are considered **obese**. Our **target weight** is our estimated ideal weight for a fat-loss program.

Indoles - see Nutrient.

Insoluble Fiber - see Fiber.

Lipoprotein - a fatty protein that transports fat and cholesterol through the bloodstream. **Low-Density Lipoproteins (LDL)** are the "bad" cholesterol that is shipped as a "loose blob" and sticks to artery walls. LDL's are increased with a high-fat diet. **High-Density Lipoproteins (HDL)** are the "good" cholesterol that is shipped in a small, compact package of lipoprotein (fat and protein). HDL's circulate the bloodstream rather than clog arteries, and pick up LDL's on their way out to the liver. Exercise increases your HDL levels.

Macronutrients - see Nutrient.

Metabolic "Afterburn" - the increased rate of fat-burning that continues (often for hours) after an aerobic activity is completed.

Metabolism - the fat- or glucose-burning processes by which the body furnishes energy for the activities of life.

Micronutrients - see Nutrient.

Mitochondria - a microscopic structure found in the cells of the body that converts glucose to usable energy. Mitochondria increase with exercise.

Nutrient - a life-supporting chemical substance. The six types of nutrients are: water, the **macronutrients** (fats, proteins, carbohydrates), and **micronutrients** (vitamins, minerals). Macronutrients are the major nutrients that make up 98% of what we eat each day. They are the fuel and building materials for our bodies. Micronutrients are the small nutrients that act as important catalysts for the many chemical reactions that take place in our bodies. For example, **free radicals**, which play a major role in heart disease and various cancers, are deactivated by **antioxidants** found in many fruits and vegetables. **Indoles** are also found in a variety of vegetables and are believed to protect against various digestive cancers and to lower the risk of breast cancer.

Nutrient Dense - see Calorie.

Obese - see Ideal Weight.

Omega-3 Fatty Acids - a type of fat found in fish thought to lower the risk of coronary heart disease.

Organic - in food labeling, most organic certification programs require farmers not to use chemicals or pesticides for three full years before approval.

Osteoporosis - a common and serious bone disease associated with aging, especially with women after menopause. Bones lose their strength, become more porous and brittle and break more easily. Diet, calcium supplementation and exercise help prevent osteoporosis.

Overweight - see Ideal Body Weight.

Pathogens - microorganisms that produce disease.

Plaque - see Atherosclerosis.

Progressive Resistance - see Exercise (Anaerobic).

Protein - a macronutrient for the building and repair of cells and tissues in the body. Protein is found in meat, dairy products, legumes, grains, fruit, vegetables, nuts and seeds and should make up 15% of a person's daily calories.

Relaxation Response - see Stress Management.

RDA's (Recommended Dietary Allowances) - vitamin and mineral dosage levels recommended by the Food and Drug Administration for preventing deficiency diseases in healthy individuals.

Saturated Fat - see Fat (Dietary).

Sedentary - inactive; accustomed to sit much or take little exercise (couch potato).

Simple Carbohydrates - see Carbohydrate.

Soluble Fiber - see Fiber.

Starvation Response - the effect of a slowed metabolism and an increased appetite for high-fat foods due to low-calorie dieting. It is a survival response of the human body that evolved to protect the lives of our ancestors in seasonal food shortages and famines.

Strength Training - see Exercise (Anaerobic).

Stress - the body's arousal to situational demands and challenges. For thousands of years such challenges would have been life-threatening dangers. Now they are more likely work pressures or family tensions. Our bodies can't tell the difference and react as they always have to danger—they instantly prepare for action in the **fight-or-flight response** (increasing heart rate, breathing, metabolism, adrenaline and catecholamine levels and contracting muscles). Our bodies thus prepare us to either confront the danger or run from it. With the many pressures of modern life our bodies are repeatedly aroused but seldom get to release the tension in action. More often we "grin and bear it." The tension remains, builds up and becomes a chronic stress condition leading to illness and disease.

Stress Management - stress can be managed with tension-reduction methods. Biofeedback training, autogenic training and meditation practice teach us to elicit a **relaxation response** that deactivates the fight-or-flight response (lowering heart and breathing rates, blood pressure, levels of lactate, adrenaline and catecholamines and shifting brain waves from active "beta" to relaxed "alpha").

Stroke - the blockage of blood (i.e., oxygen) to the brain causes the death of brain cells and the functions they controlled (speech, memory, body movement).

Synergy - the mutually stimulating effects of components in an interactive system (the whole is more than the sum of its parts). In the Low-fat for Life Program each area of activity (eating, exercise, and meditation) stimulates and increases the beneficial effects of the others.

Target Weight - see Ideal Weight.

Thromboxane - a hormone that constricts arteries and clots blood. It is believed a high-fat meal stimulates the body to produce it.

Triglyceride - another type of fat or "lipid" found in the bloodstream.

Unsaturated Fat - see Fat (Dietary).

Notes

Chapter 2

1. Ballentine, R. *Diet and Nutrition*. Honesdale, Pennsylvania: Himalayan International Institute, 1978, page 115.

2. Ballentine, R. *Transition to Vegetarianism: An Evolutionary Step*. Honesdale, Pennsylvania: Himalayan International Institute, 1987, page 4.

3. U.S. Department of Health and Human Services. *Surgeon General's Report on Nutrition and Health*. 1988, page 4.

4. Ibid, page 2.

5. National Research Council. *Diet and Health: Implications for Reducing Chronic Disease Risk*. Washington, D.C.: National Academy Press, 1989, pages 12-17.

6. Ornish, D. *Dr. Dean Ornish's Program For Reversing Heart Disease*. New York: Random House, 1990, page 25.

7. Barnard, N. *Food for Life*. New York: Harmony books, 1993, pages 63–64.

8. Barone, J., Herbert, J., Reddy, M. Dietary fat and natural-killer-cell activity. *American Journal of Clinical Nutrition*. 1989, Vol. 50, pages 861–867.

   Barone, J. Less fat, less illness. *American Health*. April 1992, page 112.

9. Are you eating right? *Consumer Reports.* October 1992.

10. Barnard, N. *Food for Life.* New York: Harmony books, 1993.

Ornish, D. *Dr. Dean Ornish's Program For Reversing Heart Disease.* New York: Random House, 1990.

McDougall, J. *The McDougall Program: Twelve Days to Dynamic Health.* New York: NAL Books, 1990.

Campbell, T.C. in Chen, J. et al. *Diet, Lifestyle, and Mortality in China: A Study of the Characteristics of Sixty-Five Chinese Counties.* Oxford: Oxford University Press, 1990.

11. National Academy of Sciences. *Recommended Dietary Allowances.* National Academy Press, 1989.

12. Remington, D., Fisher, A., Parent, E. *How to Lower Your Fat Thermostat.* Provo, Utah: Vitality House International, Inc., 1983, pages 20, 124-125.

Ornish, D. *Dr. Dean Ornish's Program For Reversing Heart Disease.* New York: Random House, 1990.

Hendler, S. *The Doctor's Vitamin and Mineral Encyclopedia.* New York: Simon and Schuster, 1990, page 413.

Kowalski, R. *The Eight-Week Cholesterol Cure.* New York: Harper and Row, 1987.

Stamford, B. *Fitness Without Exercise.* New York: Warner, 1990.

Prewitt, T., Schmeisser, D., Bowen, P., Aye, P., Dolecek, T., Langenberg, P., Cole, T., Brace, L. Changes in bodyweight, body composition, and energy intake in women fed high- and low-fat diets. *American Journal of Clinical Nutrition.* 1991, Vol. 54, pages 304-310.

Connor, S. and W. Connor. *The New American Diet.* New York: Simon and Schuster, 1986, page 13.

Eaton, S., Shostak, M., Konner, M. *The Paleolithic Prescription.* New York: Harper and Row, 1988.

Boston Women's Health Book Collective. *The New Our Bodies, Ourselves.* New York: Simon and Schuster, 1992, page 32.

Chapter 3

1. Robbins, J. *Diet for a New America.* Walpole, NH: Stillpoint Publishing, 1987, page 328.

2. Tufts University, *Diet and Nutrition Newsletter.* October 1989, Vol. 7, No. 8.

3. Kowalski, R. More on antioxidants and atherosclerosis. *The Diet-Heart Newsletter.* Winter 1991, page 2.

4. Ibid, page 3.

5. Lothman, R. Counter attack! keeping arteries clear. *American Health.* December 1991, page 44.

6. Tufts University. Can taking supplements help you ward off disease? *Diet and Nutrition Newsletter.* April 1991, Vol. 9, No. 2, page 4.

7. University of California, Berkeley. Eat five...and make one cruciferous. *Wellness Letter.* December, 1990, Vol. 6, pages 6–7.

8. Are you eating right? *Consumer Reports.* October 1992, page 648.

Chapter 4

1. Eaton, S., Shostak, M., Konner, M. *The Paleolithic Prescription.* New York: Harper and Row, 1988, page 80.

Eaton, S. and Konner, M. Paleolithic nutrition: a consideration of its nature and current implications. *New England Journal of Medicine.* January 1985, Vol. 312, pages 283-289.

2. Leaf, A., and P.C. Weber. A new era for science in nutrition. *The American Journal of Clinical Nutrition*. May 1987, Supplement Vol. 45, No. 5, pages 1048-1053.

    Glazer, S. How america eats. *Editorial Research Reports*. April 29, 1988, page 221.

3. Eaton, S., et. al., *The Paleolithic Prescription*, page 45.

4. Tufts University. Should americans be eating more chinese food? *Diet and Nutrition Newsletter*. September 1990, Vol. 8, No. 7, page 3.

5. Connor, S. and W. Connor. *The New American Diet*. New York: Simon and Schuster, 1986, page 21.

6. Sagan, L. *The Health of Nations*. New York: Basic Books Inc., 1987, page 52.

7. Mayes, K. *Fighting Fat! How to Beat Heart Disease and Cancer, and Lose Weight*. Santa Barbara, California: Pennant Books, 1989, page 81.

Chapter 5

1. Levick, K. Solving the puzzle of childhood obesity. *Fitness Management*. April 1992, page 34.

2. Goldfinch, C. Low-fat to grow on. *Health*. February, 1991, page 18.

3. Newman, W., Freedman, D., Voors, A., et al. Relation of serum lipoprotein levels and systolic blood pressure to early atherosclerosis. *New England Journal of Medicine*. 1986, Vol. 314, pages 138-144.

4. Enos, W., Beyer, J., Holmes, R. Pathogenesis of coronary disease in american soldiers killed in korea. *Journal of the American Medical Association*. July 1955, Vol.158, pages 912-914.

5. Ballentine, R. *Transition to Vegetarianism: An Evolutionary Step*. Honesdale, Pennsylvania: Himalayan International Institute, 1987, page 50.

Chapter 6

1. Byrne, K. *Understanding and Managing Cholesterol: A Guide for Wellness Professionals.* Illinois: Human Kinetics Books, 1991, page 17.

2. Eaton, S., Shostak, M., Konner, M. *The Paleolithic Prescription.* New York: Harper and Row, 1988, page 115.

   Gotto, A., Wittels, E. Diet, serum cholesterol, lipoproteins, and coronary heart disease. in *Prevention of Coronary Heart Disease: Practical Management of the Risk Factors,* ed. N. Kaplan and J. Stamler. Philadelphia: W.B. Saunders Company, 1983, page 37.

3. University of California, Berkeley. A chinese lesson. *Wellness Letter.* May 1991, Vol. 7, No. 8, page 2.

4. Ballentine, R. *Transition to Vegetarianism: An Evolutionary Step.* Honesdale, Pennsylvania: Himalayan International Institute, 1987, page 50.

5. Connor, S. and W.Connor. *The New American Diet.* New York: Simon and Schuster, 1986, page 26.

Chapter 7

1. Conner, S. and W.Connor. *The New American Diet.* New York: Simon and Schuster, 1986, page 28.

2. Coghlan, A. Europe's search for the winning diet. *New Scientist.* November 1991, page 30.

3. Ibid., page 30.

4. Glazer, S. How america eats. *Editorial Research Reports.* April 29, 1988, page 224.

5. Ballentine, R. *Transition to Vegetarianism: An Evolutionary Step.* Honesdale, Pennsylvania: Himalayan International Institute, 1987, page 46.

6. Diamond, H. and M. Diamond. *Fit For Life.* New York: Warner Books Inc., 1985, page 97.

7. Ballentine, R. *Transition to Vegetarianism: An Evolutionary Step*. Page 47.

8. Hill, P. Environmental factors of breast and prostatic cancer. *Cancer Research*. 1981, Vol. 41, page 3817.

   Hill, P. Diet, lifestyle, and menstrual activity. *American Journal of Clinical Nutrition*. 1980, Vol. 33, page 1192.

9. National Research Council. *Diet and Health: Implications for Reducing Chronic Disease Risk*. Washington, D.C.: National Academy Press, 1989, page 14.

   Phillips, R. Role of lifestyle and dietary habits in risk of cancer... *Cancer Research*. 1975, Vol. 35, page 3513.

10. Liebman, B. The best laid trans. *Nutrition Action Healthletter*. December 1992, page 5.

    Mensink, R., Katan, M. Effect of dietary trans-fatty acids on high-density and low-density lipoprotein cholesterol levels in healthy subjects. *New England Journal of Medicine*. August 1990, Vol. 323, pages 3439 -3445.

    Willet, W., Stampfer, M., Manson, J., Colditz, G., Speizer, F., Rosner, B., Sampson, L., Hennekens, C. Intake of trans fatty acids and risk of coronary heart disease among women. *Lancet*. March 6, 1993, Vol. 341, pages 581-585.

11. McDougall, J. *The McDougall Program: Twelve Days to Dynamic Health*. New York: NAL Books, 1990, page 42.

    Carroll, K. Role of lipids in tumorigenesis. *Journal of the American Oil Chemists' Society*. December 1984, Vol. 61, pages 1888-1891.

    Erikson, K., Hubbard, N. Dietary fat and tumor metastasis. *Nutrition Reviews*. January 1990, Vol. 48, pages 6-14.

National Research Council. *Diet and Health: Implications for Reducing Chronic Disease Risk.* Washington D.C.: National Academy Press, 1989, pages 213-214.

12. Department of Health and Human Services. Publication No.(FDA) 92-1188.

13. Natow, A. and J. Heslin. *The Fat Attack Plan.* New York: Pocket Books, 1990.

Chapter 8

1. Politzer, B. Counter attack! winning ways to protect your heart. *American Health.* December 1991, page 43.

2. Ornish, D. *Dr. Dean Ornish's Program For Reversing Heart Disease.* New York: Random House, 1990, page 53.

3. Ibid., page 53.

4. Fisher, L. and W. Brown. *Low Cholesterol Gourmet.* New York: Avon Books, 1989, page 43.

5. Moquette-Magee, E. *Fight Fat and Win!* Minneapolis, Minnesota: DCI Publishing, Inc., 1990, page 28.

6. Boffetta, P., Garfinkel, L. Alcohol drinking and mortality among men enrolled in an american cancer society perspective study. *Epidemiology.* 1990, Vol. 1, No. 5, pages 342-348.

7. Willet, W., Stampfer, M., Colditz, G., Rosner, B., Hennekens, C., Speizer, F. Moderate alcohol consumption and the risk of breast cancer. *New England Journal of Medicine.* May 1987, Vol. 316, pages 1174-1180.

8. Center For Science in the Public Interest. Folicking Around. *Nutrition Action Health Letter.* September, 1993, page 4.

9. Coghlan, A. Europe's search for the winning diet. *New Scientist.* November 1991, page 31.

10. Politzer, Counter attack!, page 41.

Chapter 9

1. Beasley, J. *The Betrayal of Health.* New York: Times Books/Random House, 1991, page 63.

2. Steinman, D. Organic foods—more nutritious? *Veggie Life.* November, 1993, page 10.

3. Beasley, J. *The Betrayal of Health,* page 45.

4. Ibid, page 47.

5. Begley, S., Hager, M. Better watch those fresh fruits: how much risk do pesticides pose to children? *Newsweek.* July 5, 1993, page 53.

6. Lefferts, L. A commonsense approach to pesticides. *Nutrition Action Health Letter.* September, 1993, page 6.

7. Ibid, page 6.

8. Paulsen, M. The politics of cancer: why the medical establishment blames victims instead of carcinogens. *Utne Reader.* November/December 1993, page 84.

9. Ballentine, R. *Transition to Vegetarianism: An Evolutionary Step.* Honesdale, Pennsylvania: Himalayan International Institute, 1987, page 14.

10. Null, G. *The Egg Project: Gary Null's Complete Guide to Good Eating.* New York: Four Walls Eight Windows, 1987, page xix.

11. Ballentine, R. *Transition to Vegetarianism,* page 40.

12. Tufts University. Toxic chemicals in our meat supply? *Diet and Nutrition Newsletter.* 1983, Vol. 3, No. 1.

13. Ibid.

Chapter 10

1. Chandra, R. Effect of vitamin and trace-element supplementation on immune responses and infection in elderly subjects. *Lancet.* November 7, 1992, Vol. 340, pages 1124-1127.

2. Beasley, J. *The Betrayal of Health.* New York: Times Books/Random House, 1991, page 70.

3. Eaton, S., Shostak, M., Konner, M. *The Paleolithic Prescription.* New York: Harper and Row, 1988, pages 81-83.

4. Cowley, G. Vitamin revolution. *Newsweek.* June 7, 1993, page 47.

5. Kanter, N., Nolte, L., Holloszy, J. Effects of an antioxidant vitamin mixture on lipid peroxidation at rest and postexercise. *Journal of Applied Physiology.* 1993, Vol. 74, pages 965-969.

6. Stampfer, M., Hennekens, C., Manson, J., Colditz, G., Rosner, B., Willett, W. Vitamin E consumption and the risk of coronary disease in women. *New England Journal of Medicine.* 1993, Vol. 328, pages 1444-1449.

   Rimm, E., Stampfer, M., Ascherio, A., Giovannucci, E., Colditz, G., Willett, W. Vitamin E consumption and the risk of coronary heart disease in men. *New England Journal of Medicine.* 1993, Vol. 328, pages 1450-1456.

7. Cowley, G. Vitamin revolution. *Newsweek.* June 7, 1993, page 49.

8. Ibid, page 49

9. Ibid, pages 47-48.

10. Napier, K. Should all women take calcium supplements? a qualified "yes." *American Health.* June 1993, page 100.

Chapter 11

1. Riley, V. Psychoneuroendocrine influences on immuno-competence and neoplasia. *Science*. June 1981, Vol. 292, pages 1100–1109.

2. Benson, H. *The Relaxation Response*. Boston: G. K. Hall, 1975, page 15.

3. Cooper, M. and Aygen, M. Effect of meditation on blood cholesterol and blood pressure. *Journal of the Israel Medical Association*. July 2, 1978, Vol. 95, No. 1.

Chapter 12

1. Manson, J., Tosteson, H., Satterfield, S., Hebert, P., O'Connor, G., Buring, J., Hennekens, C. The primary prevention of myocardial infarction. *New England Journal of Medicine*. May 21, 1991, Vol. 326, pages 1406-1416.

2. Goldfine, H., Ward, A., Taylor, P., Carlucci, D., Rippe, J. Exercising to health. *The Physician and Sportsmedicine*. June 1991, Vol. 19, No. 6, page 82.

3. Blair, S., Kohl, H., Paffenbarger, R., Clark, D., Cooper, K., Gibbons, L. Physical fitness and all-cause mortality: a prospective study of healthy men and women. *Journal of the American Medical Association*. November 3, 1989, Vol. 262, pages 2395-2401.

4. Greissinger, L. One more reason to fit in a walk. *Health*. February 1991, page 22.

   Wood, P. and Haskell, W. The effect of exercise on plasma high density lipoproteins. *Lipids*. 1979, Vol.14, pages 417-427.

5. Froelicher, V. Exercise, fitness, and coronary heart disease. in *Exercise, Fitness and Health: A Consensus of Current Knowledge*. ed. Bouchard, C., Shepard, R., Stephans, T., Sutton, J., McPherson, B. Champaign, IL: Human Kinetics Books, 1990, page 430.

6. Ornish, D. *Dr. Dean Ornish's Program for Reversing Heart Disease.* New York: Random House, 1990, page 19.

   Ornish, D., Brown, S., Scherwitz, L., Billings, J., Armstrong, W., Ports, T., McLanahan, S., Kirkeeide, R., Brand, R., Gould, K. Can life-style changes reverse coronary heart disease? *Lancet.* July 1990, Vol. 336, pages 129-133.

7. Dustman, R. et al. Aerobic exercise training and improved neurological function of older individuals. *Neurobiology of Aging.* 1984, Vol. 5, pages 35-42.

   Dustman, R. et al. Age and fitness effects on eeg, erp's, visual sensitivity, and cognition. *Neurobiology of Aging.* 1990, Vol. 11, pages 193-200.

   Elsayed, M., Ismail, A., Young, R. Intellectual differences of adult men related to age and physical fitness before and after an exercise program. *Journal of Gerontology.* 1980, Vol. 35, pages 383-387.

8. Bloch, G. So long, girth control. *Health.* February 1991, page 72.

9. Taylor, F. Building bones with bodybuilding. *The Physician and Sports Medicine.* April 1989, Vol. 19, No. 3, page 51.

10. Menkes, A., Sidney, M., Redmond, R., Koffler, K., Libanati, C., Gundberg, C., Zizic, T., Hagberg, J., Pratley, R., Hurley, B. Strength training increases regional bone mineral density and bone remodeling in middle-aged and older men. *Journal of Applied Physiology.* 1993, Vol. 74, No. 5, pages 2478-2484.

11. Fiatarone, M., Marks, E., Ryan, N., Meredith, C., Lipsitz, L., Evans, W. High-intensity strength training in nonagenarians: effect on skeletal muscle. *Journal of the American Medical Association.* 1990, Vol. 263, pages 3029-3034.

Chapter 13

1. Swinburn, B. and Ravussin, E. Energy balance or fat balance? *American Journal of Clinical Nutrition*. 1993, Vol. 57(suppl), page 768S.

2. Ibid, pages 768S–769S.

3. Ibid, pages 766S–771S.

   Prewitt, T., Schmeisser, D., Bowen, P., Aye, P., Dolecek, T., Langenberg, P., Cole, T., Brace, L. Changes in body weight, body composition, and energy intake in women fed high- and low-fat diets. *American Journal of Clinical Nutrition*. 1991, Vol. 54, pages 304-310.

   Dreon, D., Frey-Hewitt, B., Ellsworth, N., Williams, P., Terry, R., Wood, P. Dietary fat: carbohydrate ratio and obesity in middle-aged men. *American Journal of Clinical Nutrition*. 1988, Vol.47, pages 995-1000.

   Romieu, I., Willett, W., Stampfer, M., Colditz, G., Sampson, L., Rosner, B., Hennekens, C., Speizer, F. Energy intake and other determinants of relative weight. *American Journal of Clinical Nutrition*. 1988, Vol. 47, pages 406-412.

   Lissner, L., Levitsky, D., Strupp, B., Kalkwarf, H., Roe, D. Dietary fat and the relation of energy intake in human subjects. *American Journal of Clinical Nutrition*. 1987, Vol. 46, pages 886-892.

Chapter 14

For a more thorough discussion, see the following books:

1. Roberts, H. *Aspartame (NutraSweet) IS IT SAFE?: A Concerned Doctor's Views*. Charles: 1990.

2. Natow, A. and J. Heslin. *The Fat Attack Plan*. New York: Pocket Books, 1990.

3. Dansforth, E. Diet and obesity. *American Journal of Clinical Nutrition*. May 1985, Vol. 41, page 1136.

National Research Council. *Diet and Health: Implications for Reducing Chronic Disease Risk.* Washington, D.C.: National Academy Press, 1989, page 14.

Chapter 15

1. Khaw, K. and Barrett-Connor, E. Dietary potassium and stroke-associated mortality. *The New England Journal of Medicine.* January 29, 1987, Vol. 316, No. 5, pages 235-240.

Chapter 16

1. Robertson, D. and C. Robertson. *Snowbird Diet: Twelve Days to a Slender Future and a Lifetime of Gourmet Dieting.* New York: Warner Books, 1986.

Chapter 17

1. Tufts University. Exercise burns calories in more than one way. *Diet and Nutrition Newsletter.* December 1989, Vol. 7, No. 10, page 2.

2. University of Victoria. Cycling fat. *Canadian Journal of Sports Science.* Vol. 13, No. 4, pages 204–207.

Chapter 18

1. Cohen, L. Diet and cancer. *Scientific American.* November, 1987, pages 42–48.

2. Eaton, S., Shostak, M., Konner, M. *The Paleolithic Prescription.* New York: Harper & Row, 1988, page 72.

Chapter 19

1. Center for Science in the Public Interest. Eating green. *Nutrition Action Healthletter.* January/February 1992, page 7.

2. Nash, J. The beef against...beef. *Time.* April 20, 1992, page 77.

3. Center for Science in the Public Interest. Eating green. *Nutrition Action Healthletter.* January/February 1992, page 7.

4. Berman, L., Syme, S. Social networks, host resistance and mortality: a nine-year follow-up of alameda county residents. *American Journal of Epidemiology.* 1979, Vol. 109, pages 186-204.

5. Nerem, R., Levesque, M., Cornhill, J. Social environment as a factor in diet-induced atherosclerosis. *Science.* 1980, Vol. 208, pages 1475-1476.

6. Sagan, L. *The Health of Nations.* New York: Basic Books Inc., 1987, page 145.

7. Tufts University. The breakdown of the family meal. *Diet and Nutrition Letter.* July 1991, Vol. 9, No. 5, page 4.

8. Levick, K. Solving the puzzle of childhood obesity. *Fitness Management.* April 1991, page 34.

Chapter 20

1. Tart, C. *Waking Up.* Boston: Shambala Publications, 1986, page 52.

2. Friedman, M., Byers, S., Rosenman, R. Effect of unsaturated fats upon lipemia and conjuctival circulation. *Journal of the American Medical Association.* September 1965, Vol.193, pages 110-114.

    Williams, A., Higginbotham, A., Knisely, M., Increased blood cell agglutination following ingestion of fat: a factor contributing to cardiac ischemia, coronary insufficiency, and anginal pain. *Angiology.* 1957, Vol. 8, pages 29-39.

    Swank, J., Nakamura, H. Oxygen availability in brain tissues after lipid meals. *American Journal of Physiology.* 1960, Vol.198, pages 217-220.

3. Piscatella, J. *Controlling Your Fat Tooth*. New York:
    Workman Publishing, 1991, page 25.

4. Flatt, J. Dietary fat, carbohydrate balance, and weight
    maintenance: effects of exercise. *American Journal of
    Clinical Nutrition*. 1987, Vol. 45, page 304.

5. Barnett, R. The pursuit of health. *U.S. News and World
    Report*. October 7, 1991, page A12.

6. Dustman, R. et al. Aerobic exercise training and im-
    proved neurological function of older individuals. *Neu-
    robiology of Aging*. 1984, Vol. 5, pages 35-42.

    Dustman, R. et al. Age and fitness effects on eeg, erp's,
    visual sensitivity, and cognition. *Neurobiology of Aging*.
    1990, Vol. 11, pages 193-200.

7. Elsayed, M., Ismail, A., Young, R. Intellectual differenc-
    es of adult men related to age and physical fitness before
    and after an exercise program. *Journal of Gerontology*.
    1980, Vol. 35, pages 383-387.

8. Samuels, M., Samuels, N. *Heart Disease*. New York:
    Summit Books, 1991, page 108.

9. Janal, M. et al. Pain sensitivity, mood, and plasma endo-
    crine levels in man following long-distance running: ef-
    fects of naloxone. *Pain*. 1984, Vol.19, pages13-25.

    McArdle, W., Katch, F., Katch, V. *Exercise Physiology:
    Energy, Nutrition, and Human Performance*. 2nd ed.
    Philadelphia: Lea and Febiger, 1986, pages 338-339.

10. Pelletier, K. *Mind as Healer, Mind as Slayer*. San Fran-
    cisco: Robert Briggs Associates, 1977, page 206.

Chapter 22

1. Ballentine, R. *Diet and Nutrition*. Honesdale, Pennsylva-
    nia: Himalayan International Institute, 1978, page 345.

Chapter 23

1. Wald, C. Is it really organic? *American Health.* July/August 1990, page 40.

2. McNutt, S. The ten percent solution. *Muscle and Fitness.* December, 1992, page 259.

3. Robbins, J. *Diet for a New America.* Walpole, NH: Stillpoint Publishing, 1987, page 248.

Chapter 24

1. Meyers, C. *Walking: A Complete Guide To The Complete Exercise.* New York: Random House, 1992, page 93.

2. Ibid, page 52.

Chapter 26

1. Swinburn, B. and Ravussin, E. Energy balance or fat balance? *American Journal of Clinical Nutrition.* 1993, Vol. 57 (suppl), page 769S.

2. Tufts University. The dietary guidelines become more user friendly. *Diet and Nutrition Newsletter.* January 1991, Vol. 8, No. 11, page 5.

3. French, K. and Simon, C. Zap! to yesterday's wisdom. *Walking.* January/February, 1992, page 49.

References

Adams, P. *Gesundheit!* Rochester, Vermont: Healing Arts Press, 1993.

American College of Sports Medicine. *Guidelines for Exercise Testing and Prescription.* Philadelphia: Lea and Febiger, 1991.

Applegate, L. *Power Foods.* Emmaus, Pennsylvania: Rodale Press, 1991.

Are you eating right? *Consumer Reports.* October 1992, page 648.

Bailey, C. *Fit or Fat?* Boston: Houghton Mifflin Company, 1978.

Bailey, C. *The Fit or Fat Target Diet.* Boston: Houghton Mifflin Company, 1984.

Ballentine, R. *Diet and Nutrition.* Honesdale, Pennsylvania: Himalayan International Institute, 1978.

Ballentine, R. *Transition to Vegetarianism: An Evolutionary Step.* Honesdale, Pennsylvania: The Himalayan International Institute of Yoga Science and Philosophy of the U.S.A., 1987.

Barnard, N. *Food for Life: How the New Four Food Groups Can Save Your Life.* New York: Harmony Books, 1993.

Barnard, N. *The Power of Your Plate.* Summertown, Tennessee: Book Publishing Company, 1990.

Barnett, R. The pursuit of health. *U.S. News and World Report*. October 7, 1991, page A12.

Barone, J. Less fat, less illness. *American Health*. April 1992, page 112.

Beasley, J. *The Betrayal of Health*. New York: Times Books/Random House, 1991, page 63.

Begley, S., Hager, M. Better watch those fresh fruits: how much risk do pesticides pose to children? *Newsweek*. July 5, 1993, page 53.

Benson, H. *The Relaxation Response*. Boston: G. K. Hall and Co., 1976.

Benson, H. *The Relaxation Response*. Boston: G. K. Hall, 1975, page 15.

Berman, L., Syme, S. Social networks, host resistance and mortality: a nine-year follow-up of alameda county residents. *American Journal of Epidemiology*. 1979, Vol. 109, pages 186-204.

Blair, S., Kohl, H., Paffenbarger, R., Clark, D., Cooper, K., Gibbons, L. Physical fitness and all-cause mortality: a prospective study of healthy men and women. *Journal of the American Medical Association*. November 3, 1989, Vol. 262, pages 2395-24

Bloch, G. So long, girth control. *Health*. February 1991, page 72.

Boffetta, P., Garfinkel, L. Alcohol drinking and mortality among men enrolled in an american cancer society perspective study. *Epidemiology*. 1990, Vol. 1, No. 5, pages 342-348.

Boston Women's Health Book Collective. *The New Our Bodies, Ourselves*. New York: Simon and Schuster, 1992.

Byrne, K. *Understanding and Managing Cholesterol: A Guide for Wellness Professionals*. Illinois: Human Kinetics Books, 1991, page 17.

Campbell, T.C. in Chen, J. et al. *Diet, Lifestyle, and Mortality in China: A Study of the Characteristics of Sixty-Five Chinese Counties.* Oxford: Oxford University Press, 1990.

Carroll, K. Role of lipids in tumorigenesis. *Journal of the American Oil Chemists' Society.* December 1984, Vol. 61, pages 1888-1891.

Center for Science in the Public Interest. Eating green. *Nutrition Action Healthletter.* January/February 1992, page 7.

Center For Science in the Public Interest. Folicking Around. *Nutrition Action Health Letter.* September, 1993, page 4.

Center For Science in the Public Interest. Run, radicals, run. *Nutrition Action Health Letter.* September, 1993, page 4.

Chandra, R. Effect of vitamin and trace-element supplementation on immune responses and infection in elderly subjects. *Lancet.* November 7, 1992, Vol. 340, pages 1124-1127.

Coghlan, A. Europe's search for the winning diet. *New Scientist.* November 1991, page 30.

Cohen, L. Diet and cancer. *Scientific American.* November, 1987, pages 42-48.

Coleman, D. *The Meditative Mind.* Los Angeles: Jeremy P. Tarcher, Inc., 1977.

Conner, S. and Conner, W. *The New American Diet.* New York: Simon and Schuster, 1986.

Cooper, K. *Controlling Cholesterol.* New York: Bantam Books, Inc., 1989.

Cooper, M. and Aygen, M. Effect of meditation on blood cholesterol and blood pressure. *Journal of the Israel Medical Association.* July 2, 1978, Vol. 95, No. 1.

Cowley, G. Vitamin revolution. *Newsweek.* June 7, 1993, page 49.

Dansforth, E. Diet and obesity. *American Journal of Clinical Nutrition.* May 1985, Vol. 41, page 1136.

Department of Health and Human Services. Publication No.(FDA) 92-1188.

Diamond H. and Diamond, M. *Fit For Life*. New York: Warner Books, Inc., 1985.

Donkersloot, M. *The Fast-Food Diet*. New York: Simon and Schuster, 1991.

Dreon, D., Frey-Hewitt, B., Ellsworth, N., Williams, P., Terry, R., Wood, P. Dietary fat: carbohydrate ratio and obesity in middle-aged men. *American Journal of Clinical Nutrition*. 1988, Vol.47, pages 995-1000.

Dustman, R. et al. Aerobic exercise training and improved neurological function of older individuals. *Neurobiology of Aging*. 1984, Vol. 5, pages 35-42.

Dustman, R. et al. Age and fitness effects on eeg, erp's, visual sensitivity, and cognition. *Neurobiology of Aging*. 1990, Vol. 11, pages 193-200.

Eaton, S. and Konner, M. Paleolithic nutrition: a consideration of its nature and current implications. *New England Journal of Medicine*. January 1985, Vol. 312, pages 283-289.

Eaton, S., Shostak, M., Konner, M. *The Paleolithic Prescription*. New York: Harper and Row, 1988.

Elsayed, M., Ismail, A., Young, R. Intellectual differences of adult men related to age and physical fitness before and after an exercise program. *Journal of Gerontology*. 1980, Vol. 35, pages 383-387.

Enos, W., Beyer, J., Holmes, R. Pathogenesis of coronary disease in american soldiers killed in korea. *Journal of the American Medical Association*. July 1955, Vol.158, pages 912-914.

Erikson, K., Hubbard, N. Dietary fat and tumor metastasis. *Nutrition Reviews*. January 1990, Vol. 48, pages 6-14.

Evans, W., Rosenberg, I., Thompson, J. *Biomarkers: The 10 Determinants of Aging You Can Control*. New York: Simon and Schuster, 1991.

Fiatarone, M., Marks, E., Ryan, N., Meredith, C., Lipsitz, L., Evans, W. High-intensity strength training in nonagenarians: effect on skeletal muscle. *Journal of the American Medical Association.* 1990, Vol. 263, pages 3029-3034.

Fisher, L. and W. Brown. *Low Cholesterol Gourmet.* New York: Avon Books, 1989, page 43.

Flatt, J. Dietary fat, carbohydrate balance, and weight maintenance: effects of exercise. *American Journal of Clinical Nutrition.* 1987, Vol. 45, page 304.

Fleck, S. and Kraemer, W. *Designing Resistance Training Programs.* Champaign, Illinois: Human Kinetics Books, 1987.

Freeman, L. *Light Within.* New York: Crossroad Publishing Company, 1987.

French, K. and Simon, C. Zap! to yesterday's wisdom. *Walking.* January/February, 1992, page 49.

Friedman, M., Byers, S., Rosenman, R. Effect of unsaturated fats upon lipemia and conjictival circulation. *Journal of the American Medical Association.* September 1965, Vol.193, pages 110-114.

Froelicher, V. *Exercise, fitness, and coronary heart disease. in Exercise, Fitness and Health: A Consensus of Current Knowledge.* ed. Bouchard, C., Shepard, R., Stephans, T., Sutton, J., McPherson, B. Champaign, IL: Human Kinetics Books, 1990, page

Gaunt, L. *Recipes to Lower Your Fat Thermostat.* Provo, Utah: Vitality House International, Inc., 1984.

Gavin, J. *The Exercise Habit.* Champaign, Illinois: Leisure Press, 1992.

Gershoff, S. *The Tuft's University Guide to Total Nutrition.* New York: Harper and Row, 1990.

Glazer, S. How america eats. *Editorial Research Reports.* April 29, 1988, page 221.

Goldfinch, C. Low-fat to grow on. *Health.* February, 1991, page 18.

Goldfine, H., Ward, A., Taylor, P., Carlucci, D., Rippe, J. Exercising to health. *The Physician and Sportsmedicine.* June 1991, Vol. 19, No. 6, page 82.

Goor, R. and Goor, N. *Eater's Choice.* Boston: Houghton Mifflin, 1989.

Gotto, A., Wittels, E. Diet, serum cholesterol, lipoproteins, and coronary heart disease. in *Prevention of Coronary Heart Disease: Practical Management of the Risk Factors,* ed. N. Kaplan and J. Stamler. Philadelphia: W.B. Saunders Company, 1983, pa

Greissinger, L. One more reason to fit in a walk. *Health.* February 1991, page 22.

Hendler, S. *The Complete Guide to Anti-Aging Nutrients.* New York: Simon and Schuster, 1984

Hendler, S. *The Doctor's Vitamin and Mineral Encyclopedia.* New York: Simon & Schuster, 1990.

Hill, P. Diet, lifestyle, and menstrual activity. *American Journal of Clinical Nutrition.* 1980, Vol. 33, page 1192.

Hill, P. Environmental factors of breast and prostatic cancer. *Cancer Research.* 1981, Vol. 41, page 3817.

Janal, M. et al. Pain sensitivity, mood, and plasma endocrine levels in man following long-distance running: effects of naloxone. *Pain.* 1984, Vol.19, pages 13-25.

Kamen, B. *New Facts About Fiber.* Novato, CA: Nutrition Encounter, Inc., 1991.

Katahn, M. *One Meal At A Time.* New York: W.W. Norton and Company, 1991.

Katahn, M. *The T-Factor Diet.* New York: W.W. Norton and Company, 1989.

Katch, F. and McArdle, W. *Nutrition, Weight Control and Exercise.* Philadelphia: Lea and Febiger, 1988.

Khaw, K. and Barrett-Connor, E. Dietary potassium and stroke-associated mortality. *The New England Journal of Medicine.* January 29, 1987, Vol. 316, No. 5, pages 235-240.

Kowalski, R. *The 8-Week Cholesterol Cure*. New York: Harper and Row, 1987.

Kowalski, R. More on antioxidants and atherosclerosis. *The Diet-Heart Newsletter*. Winter 1991, page 2.

Kurzweil, R. *The 10% Solution for a Healthy Life*. New York: Crown Publishers, 1993.

Lappé, F. M. *Diet for a Small Planet*. New York: Ballentine Books, 1982.

Leaf, A., and P.C. Weber. A new era for science in nutrition. *The American Journal of Clinical Nutrition*. May 1987, Supplement Vol. 45, No. 5, pages 1048-1053.

LeShan, L. *How to Meditate*. Boston: Little, Brown and Company, 1974.

Levick, K. Solving the puzzle of childhood obesity. *Fitness Management*. April 1991, page 34.

Liebman, B. The best laid trans. *Nutrition Action Healthletter*. December 1992, page 5.

Lissner, L., Levitsky, D., Strupp, B., Kalkwarf, H., Roe, D. Dietary fat and the relation of energy intake in human subjects. *American Journal of Clinical Nutrition*. 1987, Vol. 46, pages 886-892.

Lombert-Lagace, L. *The Nutrition Challenge for Women*. Menlo Park, CA: Bull Publishing, 1990.

Lothman, R. Counter attack! keeping arteries clear. *American Health*. December 1991, page 44.

Manahan, W. *Eat for Health*. Tiburon, California: H.J. Kraemer, Inc., 1988.

Manson, J., Tosteson, H., Satterfield, S., Hebert, P., O'Connor, G., Buring, J., Hennekens, C. The primary prevention of myocardial infarction. *New England Journal of Medicine*. May 21, 1991, Vol. 326, pages 1406-1416.

Mayes, K. *Fighting Fat!* How to Beat Heart Disease and Cancer, and Lose Weight. Santa Barbara, California: Pennant Books, 1989, page 81.

McArdle, W., Katch, F., Katch, V. *Exercise Physiology: Energy, Nutrition, and Human Performance*. 2nd ed. Philadelphia: Lea and Febiger, 1986, pages 338-339.

McDougall, J. *The McDougall Program: Twelve Days to Dynamic Health*. New York: NAL Books, 1990.

McDougall, J. *The McDougall Program: Twelve Days to Dynamic Health*. New York: NAL Books, 1990, page 42.

McNutt, S. The ten percent solution. *Muscle and Fitness*. December, 1992, page 259.

Menkes, A., Sidney, M., Redmond, R., Koffler, K., Libanati, C., Gundberg, C., Zizic, T., Hagberg, J., Pratley, R., Hurley, B. Strength training increases regional bone mineral density and bone remodeling in middle-aged and older men. *Journal of Applied Physiology*. 1993, Vol. 74, No. 5, pages 2478–2484.

Mensink, R., Katan, M. Effect of dietary trans-fatty acids on high-density and low-density lipoprotein cholesterol levels in healthy subjects. *New England Journal of Medicine*. August 1990, Vol. 323, pages 3439–3445.

Metzner, R. *Opening to Inner Light*. Los Angeles: Jeremy P. Tarcher, Inc., 1986.

Meyers, C. *Walking: A Complete Guide To The Complete Exercise*. New York: Random House, 1992, page 93.

Moquette-Magee, E. *Fight Fat & Win!* Minneapolis: DCI Publishing, 1990.

Napier, K. Should all women take calcium supplements? a qualified "yes." *American Health*. June 1993, page 100.

Nash, J. The beef against...beef. *Time*. April 20, 1992, page 77.

National Academy of Sciences. *Diet and Health*. Washington, D.C.: National Academy Press, 1989.

National Academy of Sciences. *Recommended Dietary Allowances*. National Academy Press, 1989.

National Research Council. *Diet and Health: Implications for Reducing Chronic Disease Risk.* Washington D.C.: National Academy Press, 1989, pages 213-214.

Natow, A. and Heslin, J. *The Fat Attack Plan.* New York: Pocket Books, 1990.

Nerem, R., Levesque, M., Cornhill, J. Social environment as a factor in diet-induced atherosclerosis. *Science.* 1980, Vol. 208, pages 1475-1476.

Newman, W., Freedman, D., Voors, A., et al. Relation of serum lipoprotein levels and systolic blood pressure to early atherosclerosis. *New England Journal of Medicine.* 1986, Vol. 314, pages 138-144.

Null, G. *The Egg Project: Gary Null's Complete Guide to Good Eating.* New York: Four Walls Eight Windows, 1987, page xix.

Ornish, D. Dr. *Dean Ornish's Program for Reversing Heart Disease.* New York: Random House, 1990.

Ornish, D., Brown, S., Scherwitz, L., Billings, J., Armstrong, W., Ports, T., McLanahan, S., Kirkeeide, R., Brand, R., Gould, K. Can life-style changes reverse coronary heart disease? *Lancet.* July 1990, Vol. 336, pages 129-133.

Paulsen, M. The politics of cancer: why the medical establishment blames victims instead of carcinogens. *Utne Reader.* November/December 1993, page 84.

Peikin, S. *The Feel Full Diet.* New York: Atheneum, 1987.

Pelletier, K. *Mind As Healer, Mind As Slayer.* San Francisco: Robert Briggs Associates, 1977.

Phillips, G. *The Think Light!-Lowfat Living Plan.* Durango, Colorado: Speaking of Fitness, Inc., 1991.

Phillips, R. Role of lifestyle and dietary habits in risk of cancer... *Cancer Research.* 1975, Vol. 35, page 3513.

Piscatella, J. *Choices for a Healthy Heart.* New York: Workman Publishing Co., Inc., 1987.

Piscatella, J. *Controlling Your Fat Tooth.* New York: Workman Publishing Company, Inc., 1991.

Politzer, B. Counter attack! winning ways to protect your heart. *American Health.* December 1991, page 43.

Prewitt, T., Schmeisser, D., Bowen, P., Aye, P., Dolecek, T., Langenberg, P., Cole, T., Brace, L. Changes in body weight, body composition, and energy intake in women fed high- and low-fat diets. *American Journal of Clinical Nutrition.* 1991, Vol. 54, pages 304–310.

Pritikin, N. *The Pritikin Promise.* New York: Simon & Schuster, 1983.

Pritikin, R. *The New Pritikin Program.* New York: Simon & Schuster, 1990.

Remington, D. and Higa, B. *The Bitter Truth About Artificial Sweeteners.* Provo Utah: Vitality House International, Inc., 1987.

Remington, D., Fisher, A., Parent, E. *How to Lower Your Fat Thermostat.* Provo, Utah: Vitality House International, Inc., 1983.

Riley, V. Psychoneuroendocrine influences on immunocompetence and neoplasia. *Science.* June 1981, Vol. 292, pages 1100-1109.

Rimm, E., Stampfer, M., Ascherio, A., Giovannucci, E., Colditz, G., Willett, W. Vitamin E consumption and the risk of coronary heart disease in men. *New England Journal of Medicine.* 1993, Vol. 328, pages 1450–1456.

Robbins, J. *Diet For A New America.* Walpole, NH: Stillpoint Publishing, 1987.

Roberts, H. *Aspartame (NutraSweet) IS IT SAFE?: A Concerned Doctor's Views.* Charles: 1990.

Robertson, D. and C. Robertson. *Snowbird Diet: Twelve Days to a Slender Future and a Lifetime of Gourmet Dieting.* New York: Warner Books, 1986.

Rodale Press Staff, Bricklin, M. and Ferguson, S., editors. *The Natural Healing and Nutrition Annual.* Emmaus, Pennsylvania: Rodale Press, Inc., 1990.

Romieu, I., Willett, W., Stampfer, M., Colditz, G., Sampson, L., Rosner, B., Hennekens, C., Speizer, F. Energy intake and other determinants of relative weight. *American Journal of Clinical Nutrition.* 1988, Vol. 47, pages 406-412.

Sagan, L. *The Health of Nations.* New York: Basic Books Inc., 1987, page 145.

Samuels, M. and Samuels, N. *Heart Disease.* New York: Summit Books, 1991.

Schell, O. *Modern Meat.* New York: Random House, 1984.

Sheets, C. *Lean Bodies.* Fort Worth, Texas: The Summit Group, 1992.

Smith, N. *Food for Sport.* Menlo Park, CA: Bull Publishing, 1989.

Sokol-Green, N. *Poisoning Our Children: Surviving in a Toxic World.* Chicago: Noble Press, 1991.

Stamford, B. *Fitness Without Exercise.* New York: Warner, 1990.

Stampfer, M., Hennekens, C., Manson, J., Colditz, G., Rosner, B., Willett, W. Vitamin E consumption and the risk of coronary disease in women. *New England Journal of Medicine.* 1993, Vol. 328, pages 1444–1449.

Steinman, D. Organic foods—more nutritious? *Veggie Life.* November, 1993, page 10.

Stutman, F. *Walk to Win.* Philadelphia: Medical Manor Books, 1989.

Swank, J., Nakamura, H. Oxygen availability in brain tissues after lipid meals. *American Journal of Physiology.* 1960, Vol.198, pages 217-220.

Swinburn, B. and Ravussin, E. Energy balance or fat balance? *American Journal of Clinical Nutrition.* 1993, Vol. 57(suppl), pages 766S-771S.

Tart, C. *Waking Up*. Boston: Shambala Publications, 1986, page 52.

Taylor, F. Building bones with bodybuilding. *The Physician and Sports Medicine*. April 1989, Vol. 19, No. 3, page 51.

Tufts University, *Diet and Nutrition Newsletter*. October 1989, Vol. 7, No. 8.

Tufts University. Can taking supplements help you ward off disease? *Diet and Nutrition Newsletter*. April 1991, Vol. 9, No. 2, page 4.

Tufts University. Exercise burns calories in more than one way. *Diet and Nutrition Newsletter*. December 1989, Vol. 7, No. 10, page 2.

Tufts University. Should americans be eating more chinese food? *Diet and Nutrition Newsletter*. September 1990, Vol. 8, No. 7, page 3.

Tufts University. The breakdown of the family meal. *Diet and Nutrition Newsletter*. July 1991, Vol. 9, No. 5, page 4.

Tufts University. The dietary guidelines become more user friendly. *Diet and Nutrition Newsletter*. January 1991, Vol. 8, No. 11, page 5.

Tufts University. Toxic chemicals in our meat supply? *Diet and Nutrition Newsletter*. 1983, Vol. 3, No. 1.

U.S. Department of Health and Human Services. *The Surgeon General's Report on Nutrition and Health*. Washington, D.C.: U.S. Government Printing Office, 1988.

University of California, Berkeley. A chinese lesson. *Wellness Letter*. May 1991, Vol. 7, No. 8, page 2.

University of California, Berkeley. Eat five...and make one cruciferous. *Wellness Letter*. December, 1990, Vol. 6, pages 6–7.

University of Victoria. Cycling fat. *Canadian Journal of Sports Science*. Vol. 13, No. 4, pages 204–207.

Wald, C. Is it really organic? *American Health.* July/August 1990, page 40.

Willet, W., Stampfer, M., Colditz, G., Rosner, B., Hennekens, C., Speizer, F. Moderate alcohol consumption and the risk of breast cancer. *New England Journal of Medicine.* May 1987, Vol. 316, pages 1174-1180.

Willet, W., Stampfer, M., Manson, J., Colditz, G., Speizer, F., Rosner, B., Sampson, L., Hennekens, C. Intake of trans fatty acids and risk of coronary heart disease among women. *Lancet.* March 6, 1993, Vol. 341, pages 581-585.

Williams, A., Higginbotham, A., Knisely, M., Increased blood cell agglutination following ingestion of fat: a factor contributing to cardiac ischemia, coronary insufficiency, and anginal pain. *Angiology.* 1957, Vol. 8, pages 29-39.

Wood, P. and Haskell, W. The effect of exercise on plasma high density lipoproteins. *Lipids.* 1979, Vol.14, pages 417-427.

Index

Recipe Index

About the Authors and the Reading Copy Network

Micamar is the research, publishing and training organization the Heus family is developing as a center for healthy living. Through it they wrote and published *Low-fat for Life* for those who want to make the low-fat change just as they did.

The style of their writing is straightforward. It encourages learning and reflects the skill and commitment of a family of teachers and trainers.

Mike is an experienced university and adult educator with a Ph.D. in Adult Education. Marilyn's teaching degree and experience are in Early Childhood Education and preschool. Greg and Jeff both have Master's degrees in Human Performance and are training consultants in the health and fitness field.

Currently the Heuses are busy with *Low-fat for Life* and making it available through what they call a "reading copy network." They place copies of their book in the waiting areas of clinics, dental and chiropractic offices and beauty salons where they may be read by visiting clients and patients.

They ask only that participating organizations keep the reading copies available—that staff not remove them from the waiting areas or let them out on loan.

Through the Reading Copy Network, the Heuses are getting important health information to people who might not come across it elsewhere. At the same time they're letting health-conscious readers know a comprehensive program for making the low-fat change is available.

Their gamble, of course, is that enough people will order their own copies of *Low-fat for Life* to pay for those they are donating to the network.

Traveling from town to town to deliver the reading copies, taking orders on the 800 number, packing and shipping books and keeping up with the many other chores of Micamar can make things a little hectic for the Heus family…but they always find the time to practice the same eating, exercise and meditation routines they promote in *Low-fat for Life*.

Ordering Information

The fastest, easiest way to get your copy of *Low-fat for Life* is to order it directly from the Heuses. Call their toll-free order number **1-800-269-1630** anytime, 24 hours a day. They'll send one right out to you with a bill.

If you prefer, send a check or money order (figure amount below) to: **Micamar, P.O. Box 56, Barneveld, WI 53507**

Low-fat for Life	16.95
shipping*	+2.00
Total	$18.95
Wis. residents add sales tax	+0.93
Total	$19.88

* If ordering more than one book, shipping is $2.00 for the first and $1.00 for each additional book.

Reader Comments

"To the researchers and people that made this book available— thank you. A person making the low-fat change needs an instruction book. <u>Low-fat for Life</u> is the help I need to improve my health...a very good 'how to' explanation for low-fat living."
Lyla Mae, Madison, WI

"I'm so happy I found your book...the price is right too!!"
Patti Coleman, Oregon, WI

"I've been meaning to get to this for years. Your book motivated me and showed me just what to do."
Elena DePaolo, Bloomingdale, IL

"A thank you from someone who thought he was healthy— jogger, outdoorsman, etc.—then colon cancer. This book has been a godsend in bringing together information, reasoning and procedure to correct my major concern—fat intake."
Mike Routhieaux, Janesville, WI

"I'm so impressed with your book. I've made the low-fat lifestyle change and have already begun to reap many benefits. <u>Low-fat for Life</u> has been such a help and it makes so much sense. As a registered nurse with my Masters in counseling, I've read a lot...your

book defies nit-picking and has a sound physiological basis. My two sisters fight over custody of the copy I purchased for them to share. It's the perfect primer for low-fat novices."

Michelle Mader, Sheboygan, WI

"*Low-fat for Life* is a well written book that not only inspires you to set realistic goals toward a healthier lifestyle, but also provides you with excellent recipes that assist you in achieving those goals."

Sue Jarosh, Dubuque, IA

"...this is the best book on low-fat that I've seen: it's simple and direct, yet it doesn't insult my intelligence or become 'preachy'."

Deb Isensee, Madison, WI

"By following *Low-fat for Life*, my friends have seen the difference in me, not only in inches but in a better outlook on life."

Andrea Richmond, La Crosse, WI

"...this book will be an excellent reference for life!"

Beverly Saylor, Dubuque, IA

"I was so happy to find your book. I have other low-fat cookbooks, but my husband and kids won't eat their 'cuisine-type' recipes. Your recipes are perfect for them — 'regular' tasting meals but without the fat."

Pam Wall, Eau Claire, WI

"I've read a lot of books on nutrition but *Low-fat for Life* is certainly the most complete one. I would recommend it to anyone."

Jackie Manahan, Janesville, WI

"I have been waiting for a book like *Low-fat for Life* for a long time. It made a complicated topic much more understandable...my eating habits are improving and I'm consistent with my exercise."

Eloise Johnson, Fairmont, MN

"The Heus Family has devised a plan that creates positive lifestyle changes in a step-by-step process...an excellent guide for my personal training clients!"

Sandy Rusch, Oregon, WI

"Once I started reading, it was hard to put the book down. This is so exciting. We senior citizens really need to know about low-fat living and this is the book to get us started."

Madeline McCall, Madison, WI

"You did an excellent job in bringing all the facts together in one book. It is delightful to find a ready reference all under one cover."

Elizabeth Elbeck, Racine, WI